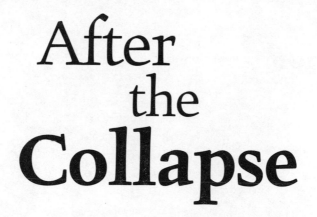

After
the
Collapse

Russia Seeks Its Place
as a Great Power

•

Dimitri K. Simes

Simon & Schuster

SIMON & SCHUSTER
Rockefeller Center
1230 Avenue of the Americas
New York, NY 10020

Designed by *Deirdre C. Amthor*

Manufactured in the United States of America

1 3 5 7 9 10 8 6 4 2

Library of Congress Cataloging-in-Publication Data
Simes, Dimitri K.
After the collapse : Russia seeks its place as a great power / Dimitri K. Simes.
p. cm.
Includes index.
1. Russia (Federation)—Politics and government—1991– . I. Title.
DK510.763.S57 1999
947.086—dc21   98-47287 CIP
ISBN 0-684-82716-6

Acknowledgments

This book could not have been written without Richard Nixon, with whom I traveled to the Soviet Union and Russia four times. Over the years, his wise counsel had a great impact on my evaluation of events in Russia and U.S.–Russian relations. I am also in debt to a number of President Nixon's associates who also took part in his visits to Russia, including particularly Ambassador Robert F. Ellsworth, who contributed his wisdom to the many tough decisions that had to be made during the trips. President Nixon's former chief of staff, John H. Taylor (now executive director of the Richard Nixon Library and Birthplace Foundation), provided order and discipline during the complex trips. Kathy O'Connor, his last chief of staff, and Marin Strmecki, his foreign policy advisor, also played key roles.

At The Nixon Center, Center director Paul Saunders provided indispensable assistance as a sounding board for ideas and as an editor of the manuscript. My executive assistant, Wright Yarborough, was helpful in researching and in coordinating the project. A number of Nixon Center interns also contributed to the research.

Several colleagues, including James Schlesinger, Vladimir Petrov, and Peter Rodman, read all or part of the manuscript and offered many useful comments. John Brockman, my literary agent, provided advice and encouragement throughout the writing and production of the book. My editor at Simon & Schuster, Bob Bender, worked very patiently on the book; his insightful suggestions were essential in refining the manuscript. I am also grateful to a wide variety of Americans and Russians alike who spoke to me both on and off the record.

Finally, I owe a great deal to my wife, Anastasia, for her perceptive comments and her patience during my work on the book—particularly when she had to take the greater share of responsibility in caring for our newborn son.

Needless to say, I alone am responsible for the facts and opinions in the book.

To Anastasia

Contents

Russia and the Former Soviet Union

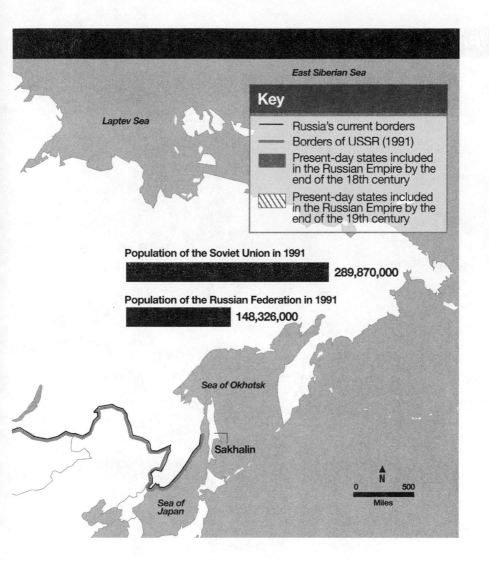

East Siberian Sea

Laptev Sea

Key

—— Russia's current borders
—— Borders of USSR (1991)
Present-day states included in the Russian Empire by the end of the 18th century
Present-day states included in the Russian Empire by the end of the 19th century

Population of the Soviet Union in 1991

289,870,000

Population of the Russian Federation in 1991

148,326,000

Sea of Okhotsk

Sakhalin

Sea of Japan

N

0   500

Miles

Ethnic Russian Populations of the Former Soviet Union

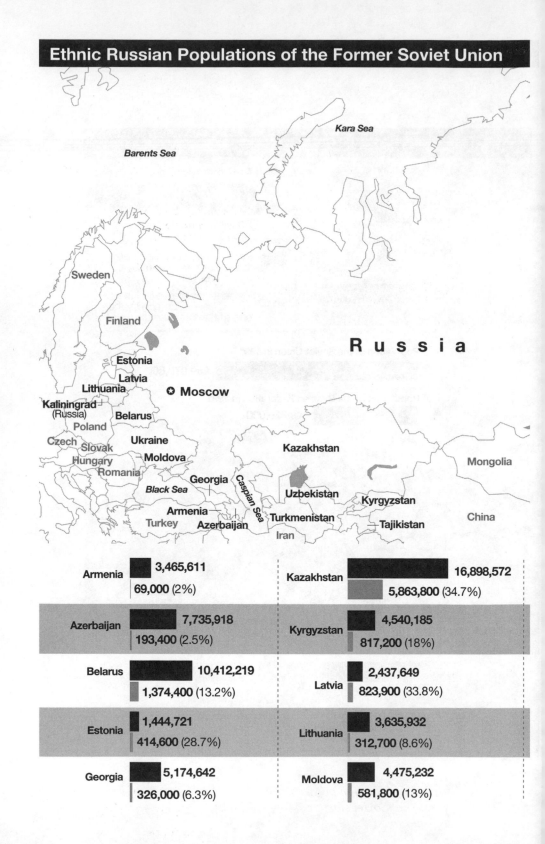

Kara Sea

Barents Sea

Sweden

Finland

Estonia
Latvia
Lithuania
Kaliningrad
(Russia)   Belarus
Poland
Czech   Ukraine
Slovak   Moldova
Hungary
Romania   Georgia
Black Sea   Caspian Sea

R u s s i a

⊕ Moscow

Kazakhstan

Mongolia

China

Uzbekistan
Kyrgyzstan
Turkmenistan   Tajikistan
Armenia
Turkey   Azerbaijan   Iran

Armenia 3,465,611	**Kazakhstan** 16,898,572
69,000 (2%)	5,863,800 (34.7%)
Azerbaijan 7,735,918	**Kyrgyzstan** 4,540,185
193,400 (2.5%)	817,200 (18%)
Belarus 10,412,219	**Latvia** 2,437,649
1,374,400 (13.2%)	823,900 (33.8%)
Estonia 1,444,721	**Lithuania** 3,635,932
414,600 (28.7%)	312,700 (8.6%)
Georgia 5,174,642	**Moldova** 4,475,232
326,000 (6.3%)	581,800 (13%)

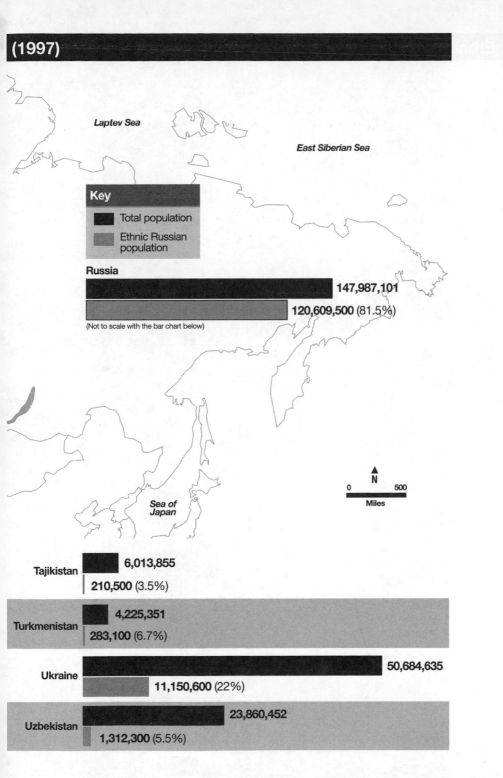

(1997)

Laptev Sea

East Siberian Sea

Key

Total population

Ethnic Russian population

Russia

147,987,101

120,609,500 (81.5%)

(Not to scale with the bar chart below)

Sea of Japan

N

0   500

Miles

Tajikistan

6,013,855

210,500 (3.5%)

Turkmenistan

4,225,351

283,100 (6.7%)

Ukraine

50,684,635

11,150,600 (22%)

Uzbekistan

23,860,452

1,312,300 (5.5%)

Note: Ethnic Russian populations have declined significantly since 1991 in several post-Soviet states, such as Kazakhstan and Tajikistan, as a result of emigration.

Introduction

"Dimitri, it's all over. It's really all over for the Soviet Union. Gorbachev still doesn't get it, he still talks like the clock can be stopped, like he can find a formula to outsmart history. But the poor bastard belongs to the past. The Soviet Union is beyond salvation. It's time for Bush to understand it," said Richard Nixon.

It was late March 1991. The former president had just returned to the plush President Hotel from an hour-long meeting with then Soviet president Mikhail Gorbachev in the Kremlin. Because the hotel was built for the Soviet elite and high-level foreign Communists, who were carefully monitored despite (or perhaps because of) their positions, Nixon took me for a walk along the Moscow River to escape electronic eavesdropping in his room.

The apparent inevitability of the collapse was a startling revelation for the former president, who had become accustomed to managing the Soviet empire when possible and fighting it when necessary throughout his political career. But, always a pragmatist, a "doer," he was already masterminding a strategy to influence American foreign policy in the coming new era.

Being a part of Nixon's design was a great treat for me. This was an hour of destiny for the Soviet Union—the country in which I was born and raised and which I had left eighteen years earlier. It was, however, also a historic moment for my adopted country, the United States, as Richard Nixon instantly understood during his 1991 trip to the USSR.

Confronting the Soviet challenge had been a central precept of American foreign policy for almost half a century—so fundamental that it affected not only U.S. actions abroad but life at home as well. Coping with Moscow often had a profound impact on American domestic politics, and attitudes to the Soviet Union frequently shaped political debates in the United States. The monumental struggle against the Communist superpower became Richard Nixon's life mission. The deep and often bitter divisions brought about by that struggle in American politics and society made a major contribution to the unmaking of his presidency. Both Nixon's own very suspicious and defensive conduct before and during Watergate and the uncompromising hostility of his opponents grew out of old battles over the Communist threat. Now both of us knew this struggle was coming to an end. "It's never going to be the same," Nixon said to me. "But the fact is, Dimitri," he added, "it still can go several different ways. We just cannot afford to screw it up. Russia is a great and proud country. If we don't handle it right, the future may be worse than the past. But the State Department is totally blind to what's going on. They will do everything possible to persuade Bush to stick with Gorbachev and to play it safe. These people would not see the future 'til it hit them like a ton of bricks and then they would blame it on somebody else."

Eight years later, Nixon's gloomy prediction sounds prophetic. The Soviet Union has indeed collapsed. The Cold War has come to an end—almost entirely on Western terms. The United States has become the world's only superpower. No nation in history has enjoyed so much dominance in world affairs and so little opposition from other nations. Russia today has neither the capabilities nor the will to challenge America's global leadership directly.

Yet, the moment that Russia's economy began to turn around—official statistics showed a 0.5 percent increase in gross domestic product in 1997, the first economic growth since Russian independence[1]—its foreign policy became increasingly independent and assertive despite Moscow's continuing dependence on the West and Western-dominated international financial institutions. This trend was interrupted by the 1998 financial crises and the failure of a new multibillion dollar bailout, which made domestic stability (rather than international advances) the utmost priority of Russia's elite. But the basic evolution of Russian foreign policy is clear despite such zigzags. Importantly, this new independence and assertiveness has come not as a result of a Communist comeback or ultranationalist takeover but through the natural evolution of Russian politics. It is rooted in an emerging "patriotic" consensus among the country's elite, including its pro-reform elements, and emerged well before the Communist Party won new influence over government policy in September 1998. Russia's evolution since the disintegration of the Soviet Union demonstrates that history has not come to an end; on the contrary, trends in Russia and many other regions of the world suggest that America's benign hegemony will be no more than a beautiful interlude. Enjoying it is only human, and exploiting it as much as possible to advance U.S. interests and values around the world is entirely appropriate. But assuming that today's easy ride for the United States will last forever, that it amounts to the new normalcy in world affairs, is a profound misreading of history. A combination of wishful thinking, an inability to see beyond tomorrow, and revelry in self-serving congratulations of Russia's democratic "triumphs" explain U.S. policymakers' fundamental misunderstanding of new trends in Russia, which leave little room for complacency.

This is not to say that Russia will once again become a totalitarian state, return to a global ideological crusade against the United States, or even aggressively attempt to reestablish control over portions of the former Soviet Union. It is easy to show why all of these scenarios are nearly impossible today as a result of both the new structure of international politics and Russia's own limited resources and ambitions. Rather, the point is that just seven years after the Soviet Union's demise, Russia is increasingly unrepentant about its history, suspicious of U.S. intentions, and (to the extent its limited capabilities allow) assertive in pursuit of its interests, which it is inclined to define in ways considerably at odds with basic objectives of American foreign policy. And, as in 1991, there is again today a real (even if remote) threat to Russia's social stability and territorial integrity as a result of its continuing economic troubles.

Recognizing that Russia and the United States represent different civilizations is essential in developing a responsible policy toward that important country. Too often, American politicians and opinion-makers talk about Russia as if it were natural for Moscow to try to replicate American society and to defer to Washington in world affairs.

This inability to accept Russia-as-Russia comes at a cost. On one hand, it encourages a tendency to whitewash Russian actions by portraying them in terms familiar to Americans but not truly applicable to the situation in

Russia today. An all too typical illustration of this is President Bill Clinton's description of Boris Yeltsin's victory in Russia's July 1996 presidential elections as a "triumph of democracy." Of course, taking into account the realistically available choices in Russia, it was in the U.S. national interest for Yeltsin to remain in power—from the American standpoint, he was clearly preferable to Communist challenger Gennady Zyuganov. Nevertheless, it is unseemly for the leader of the free world to call those elections "a triumph of democracy" when TV networks were openly fronting for the incumbent, when private banks were laundering government funds into the Yeltsin campaign, when regional governors were told to deliver votes to the president or else, and when the voters were not informed of Yeltsin's heart attack before the second round of the elections.

On the other hand, when Russia has a different perspective from Washington—whether it is on Saddam Hussein's transgressions, nuclear sales to Iran, NATO expansion, Bosnia, or Kosovo—influential voices in the United States often portray these predictable disagreements between major (and quite different) powers, whose needs and aspirations cannot be identical by definition, in the most sinister light. This tendency to think about complex international developments in terms of one-dimensional absolutes is all too frequently shared by both political parties in the executive and particularly the legislative branches. Even a statesman as experienced and generally responsible as Senator Bob Dole sounded appalled by Russia's reluctance to single out the Serbs as the principal culprits in the Bosnian civil war—as if there were not enough ambiguity in Bosnia to entertain the possibility that another nation—with its own history, geography, and political culture—could legitimately dissent from the American view of the conflict.

The apocalyptic rivalry with "the evil empire" is over. But efforts to build a new American century are likely to encounter a determined response from Russia, even before it is firmly on its feet once again. The renewed Russia—and China, an emerging world power—will inevitably become a serious obstacle to the United States if it seeks to remake the world into a democratic and harmonious global village without the expenditure of blood and treasure.

The foreign policy genius of Richard Nixon was his talent to be aggressive, indeed ruthless, in the pursuit of U.S. national interests while remaining remarkably broad-minded and understanding about the circumstances of other nations. He described himself as "the quintessential living

Cold Warrior,"[2] yet he was neither hostile nor condescending to the Russian people. "Even in a struggle as clear-cut as between Communism and freedom there are grey areas," Nixon wrote at the height of the U.S.–Soviet rivalry.[3] Nixon always believed that extremism in the name of freedom was still extremism, and as soon as the Soviet threat to American interests began to fade, he was the first to call for a new approach to Moscow and eventually for offering U.S. assistance to the new Russia and American acceptance of its status as a major power even before it was genuinely deserved. Similarly, Nixon never thought that the United States should try to help Moscow to remake Russia in the American image or to turn Russia into an American dominion.

This came out clearly in a conversation between the former president and then Russian foreign minister Andrei Kozyrev in the spring of 1992. I remember the conversation vividly: Nixon asked Kozyrev how his government was defining Russian national interests. Kozyrev, known for his pro-Western orientation, replied that in the past Russia has suffered greatly from focusing too intently on its own interests at the expense of the rest of the world. Now was the time, he added, for Russia "to think more in terms of universal human values." "Well," Nixon, responded wryly, "that is a very commendable sentiment on the Minister's part. But surely there are some particular interests which Russia considers important as an emerging power?" Kozyrev was not persuaded. Probably there are such uniquely Russian interests, he said, but the Russian government had not yet had a chance to focus on them. "Perhaps, President Nixon, as a friend of Russian democracy you would be willing to help to identify them?" Kozyrev inquired with a shy smile.

The former president somehow kept his poker face. "I would not presume to tell the minister what Russian national interests should be. I am sure that in due time he will find them on his own. But I would like to make one point. Russia cannot and should not attempt to walk in lockstep with the United States on all foreign policy issues. As a great country, Russia has its own destiny. We want Russia as a friend, and we tremendously appreciate your personal friendship, Mr. Minister, but I know that anyone in Russia who tries to follow foreign advice too closely is bound to get into trouble. And we do not want this to happen to our friends."

Once out of the Foreign Ministry building and back in our limousine, Nixon asked me for my evaluation of Kozyrev. I said that he was well meaning but unimpressive, and that unless he were to grow quickly on the job, there was a risk that he would make himself vulnerable to public indignation over a blindly pro-Western policy—and possibly even make the United States guilty by association.

"That is exactly the point. He is a nice man. But you need a real son of a bitch to do this job right, Dimitri," Nixon replied. "You need to be able to see straight, but also to be ruthless to build a new country on the ruins of the empire. I can't see the Russian people respecting wimps like that."

This was vintage Nixon. Here he was, in Moscow, appalled by a Russian foreign minister asking for his guidance and being too deferential to the United States. Surely, being treated with such respect—and, in effect, being offered a role as a senior advisor to the Russian leadership—could not but delight Nixon. He loved confirmations of his influence, and the more public the better. But as much as he wanted to have an impact, Richard Nixon first and foremost wanted to have the right impact, especially on the key foreign policy issues that made him tick. Thus, he was brutally honest in his assessment of Kozyrev's flattering remarks. Subsequent events have demonstrated that he was also absolutely right.

Of course, this is not a book about Richard Nixon; it is a book about U.S. relations with a reborn Russia and, more broadly, American foreign policy choices on the threshold of a new historical era. Nevertheless, my close collaboration with Nixon during his later years was essential in writing this book. My travel with the former president as his foreign policy advisor gave me greater access to Soviet and Russian leaders than a scholar could normally expect. Similarly, acting as Nixon's junior partner in his effort to see America more engaged in Russia gave me an opportunity to interact on a regular basis with senior officials in the United States and to develop firsthand knowledge of their perspectives on both the dramatic changes underway in Russia and U.S. options in responding to the transformation.

•   •   •

I met Nixon for the first time in 1985 in his office in lower Manhattan. My visit to his office followed an exchange of several friendly letters sharing our respective views on world affairs, especially U.S.–Soviet relations, which began with a brief and very gracious note from Nixon to me on August 16, 1984, in response to an op-ed piece I had recently published in the *Christian Science Monitor* on the occasion of the tenth anniversary of his resignation from office. In the article, entitled "Richard Nixon: A Reappraisal," I argued that "Nixon was not only a very impressive President, but also in an important way he was an honorable statesman." I also gave him credit for being basically right on most public policy issues during his era, the guilt of Alger Hiss included. I was particularly positive about Nixon's devotion to American national interests, his courage, insight, and pragmatism, and his success in putting together one of the strongest cabinets in American history. I concluded with the suggestion that Nixon "has, against considerable odds, earned the right to be treated as a legitimate voice in U.S. political discourse."[4]

Still, despite my generally favorable assessment of Nixon, the column was hardly a work of pro-Nixon apology. I acknowledged the fact that Nixon had "a dark side" as "beyond question." I also criticized him for surrounding himself "with a second-rate palace guard whose arrogance, belligerence and inexperience could only reinforce his worst instincts" and added that Watergate "was both illegal and stupid." Having written so bluntly about the former president, I felt it was quite broad-minded of Nixon to say in his note to me that "while you will probably take some heat for your 'reappraisal,' you can understand that I deeply appreciated your generous observations."

Over the years, Richard Nixon became my mentor and my friend. His influence on my life was enormous: I met my future wife at a party in his honor, he literally appointed himself to be the best man at my wedding, and just months before his death he selected me to work as the president of The Nixon Center under the auspices of his own presidential library.

Nixon was a complex and often difficult man. He was extremely good to me, but I have also seen enough to appreciate why others, such as those on the receiving end of his numerous animosities, do not share my admiration and affection for him. Nevertheless, there is one thing about Nixon which any minimally objective observer should be prepared to accept—he was a great foreign policy president.

Well into his late seventies, Nixon followed the momentous changes underway in the Soviet Union. The temptation to evaluate—his favorite term—these changes, to make sure that the United States was able to take the greatest advantage of them, and, ultimately, to have a personal influence on the transition to a new post–Cold War order, was irresistible. I am sure that Nixon was well aware of the benefits of this high-profile private diplomacy for his personal rehabilitation. But I am equally sure that rehabilitation was not his principal motive. For Richard Nixon, the desire to shape history rose above all else.

As a result, I was not surprised in the slightest when, in the fall of 1990, in his suite at the One Washington Circle Hotel in Washington, Nixon expressed deep frustration with the failure of U.S. policy-makers to grasp the likelihood of a Soviet collapse and to stop clinging to Mikhail Gorbachev. "What can be done about it? You can't expect the State Department to help. They didn't come up with a single major initiative during my administration," Nixon said. I suggested that he go to the Soviet Union himself, visit both Moscow and some of the rebellious republics, and, on his return, offer his assessment to President Bush, the congressional leadership, and the media.

The former president was obviously intrigued. Still, before making his decision, he wanted to think over the idea and to consult a few friends. He also wanted me to think carefully about my suggestion and call him in a couple of days with answers to two questions: first, why such a trip would be truly important, and second, why he was the right person to undertake it. Although Nixon did not sound convinced—"The point is, Dimitri, that at my age I just can't go on a long trip like that without good reason," he told me—I saw this as an easy assignment.

Three days later, I phoned Nixon to tell him that he knew as well as I that if we were in a historic moment for not only the Soviet Union but the United States as well, that to move in the right direction and at the right pace history may need a little help, that no academic or journalist could have the kind of access he could in the Soviet Union, that no senior official could take the time or risk diplomatic controversy by talking to key people from all sides, and that he himself would be in a uniquely strong position to have his evaluation of the situation in the USSR make a difference in America.

Nixon asked whether I would be willing to go with him and help to organize the visit. I agreed enthusiastically to do both.

Chapter One

•

The Beginning of the End

Any informed discussion of Russia's future must begin with an analysis of Russia's rebirth from the guttering flame of the Soviet Union. That event—the collapse of the empire from within—was unprecedented.

Throughout history—from Rome to Napoleonic France to modern Britain—the ends of empires have come in the wake of devastating military defeats, protracted struggles of subject peoples for independence, or a combination of both. But neither of these conditions affected the Soviet Union. Although it paid dearly in both financial and moral terms for the war in Afghanistan, the USSR did not suffer a crushing blow similar to those that destroyed two other major continental empires—the German and Austro-Hungarian—after World War I.

Similarly, while nationalist protest sprouted in Central Europe and, to a lesser extent, inside the Soviet Union itself, the USSR did not give in after decades of pressure from often armed popular resistance movements as did the British, French, Spanish, and Portuguese empires. And in any event, the limited disruptions that occurred were not of such scale as to be unmanageable for a brutal regime in Moscow.

In some ways, the collapse of the Ottoman Empire—which became simultaneously militarily overextended and economically and technologically backward—seems most similar. But even the Ottoman Empire lasted for centuries as "the sick man of Europe" and was finally eliminated only after being on the losing side in World War I. The Ottoman model cannot explain the instantaneous, comprehensive scope of the disintegration of the USSR.

By the early 1980s, the Soviet Union was severely overextended geopolitically. The nuclear arms race with the United States and the USSR's simultaneous commitment to build a conventional force capable of defeating any possible coalition of enemies—meaning the rest of the world—was a major strain. President Ronald Reagan's significant military buildup and his assertive support for guerrilla movements fighting pro-Soviet governments only served to increase the pressure on Moscow. Further, Soviet prestige was dealt a significant blow by growing discontent in Central Europe, most visibly manifest in the rise of the independent Polish trade union Solidarity. Significantly, in 1982—the year of Brezhnev's death—the Kremlin finally abandoned its historical claim that the "international correlation of forces" was continuously changing in favor of international communism.

This acknowledgment of the USSR's changing circumstances did not occur automatically. It happened to a large extent as the result of long-term pressure from the West and particularly the United States, which stood up to Soviet expansionist ambitions under several administrations. Ronald Reagan deserves particular credit, of course, for the fact that Moscow's "new thinking" developed on his watch. The combination of American support for anti-Communist insurgents from Afghanistan to Nicaragua, steady increases in the U.S. defense budget, and the successful deployment of American intermediate-range nuclear missiles in Europe—notwithstanding a major Soviet "peace offensive"—demonstrated to the Kremlin that the USSR had to deal with an adversary of renewed determination and power.

The Strategic Defense Initiative, known popularly as "Star Wars," also played an important role in precipitating the new thinking. While the Soviet military command insisted that Moscow would find a reliable and cost-effective response to any U.S. missile defense system, the USSR's top generals also recognized that the SDI project was an umbrella under which America would likely develop a broad range of new and sophisticated technologies that the Soviet Union could not hope to match. Gorbachev's military advisor, Marshal Sergei Akhromeyev—a former chief of the General Staff himself—admitted as much to me in a conversation in New York in 1990. He argued that while SDI was unlikely to achieve its stated goal of serving as an impenetrable barrier against nuclear attack, it was nevertheless a full-scale military-technical offensive planned simultaneously to overcome Moscow militarily and ruin the USSR financially.

The increasing costs of expansionism—and the decreasing chances for success in pursuing it—certainly entered into the USSR's foreign policy calculations. In the absence of Ronald Reagan's policies, Gorbachev's new thinking would certainly have emerged much more slowly, if at all. Nevertheless, it is a gross exaggeration to claim that President Reagan's foreign policy was the sole, or even the principal, reason for the Soviet collapse. Reagan himself would never have said so. In an important revelation, his former National Security Council aide responsible for Soviet matters, Stephen Sestanovich—currently serving as ambassador-at-large to the newly independent states—explained how President Reagan reached the conclusion that the Soviet Union had ceased to be a threat because Mikhail Gorbachev no longer believed in Marxism-Leninism.[1] While this is an oversimplification, Reagan was essentially correct: change was imminent in the USSR once it produced a Communist Party general secretary who questioned fundamental aspects of the Soviet system. Short of war, external challenges were insufficient to force the sudden abandonment of the USSR's global efforts, the liberation of Central Europe, and the disintegration of the Union itself without a profound philosophical change in Moscow. There were many intermediate paths for the Soviet superpower; the empire could have been sustained in a modified form for a number of years, if not decades.

Similarly, internal events within the Soviet Union did not cause its sudden demise. Although the already-inefficient centrally planned Soviet economy was increasingly strained by the absence of strong guidance from the top—as evident in the USSR's growing social problems, especially expanding alcohol abuse and declining life expectancy—the economy did not appear to have reached the breaking point. The Soviet Union was surely experiencing a deep systemic crisis. Nevertheless, as demonstrated by President Franklin D. Roosevelt, a systemic crisis need not lead to revolution or defeat—it could lead to reform and rebirth. The USSR remained a military superpower with enormous natural resources, a well-educated labor force, and a ruling elite that—despite its weakness at the highest levels—incorporated some of the best and brightest in its society.

The USSR would not have collapsed with such ease if the system had not become terribly rotten at its core. Still, the collapse could have taken many different forms and been extended over several years. When it came, the demise of the Soviet Union was as a result of what Lenin would have called a "subjective factor"—the total inability of the ruling class to continue to rule as it had; and, ultimately, "betrayal" by a considerable segment of that ruling class, which turned against both the system and the empire.

When it came, no Russian or foreign analyst had anticipated the Soviet implosion. Some, like the diplomat and scholar George Kennan, predicted early on that if Moscow's expansionist ambitions were properly contained, a domestic transformation would eventually follow.[2] Toward the more hardline end of the political spectrum, analysts like Richard Pipes—a Harvard professor and later a senior NSC staffer for President Ronald Reagan—denied any possibility of significant reform, but argued instead that the Soviet regime could be brought to collapse if the United States could squeeze Moscow hard enough.

In the United States and in the USSR alike, no official or dissident—even among those most persuaded of the urgent need for reform—had a clue what was to happen. No one knew that when Mikhail S. Gorbachev became general secretary of the Communist Party of the Soviet Union in March 1985 the clock was already ticking—and that the USSR had only six years left.

•   •   •

Although I was no different from other American analysts in failing to predict the dramatic death of the Soviet empire, I fully expected meaningful change in the USSR after the Brezhnev succession had run its course. This sense that the system could not last was based in no small part on personal experiences and impressions gathered during my own early life in the Soviet Union. Born and educated in the USSR, I worked for some time at the influential Institute of World Economy and International Relations (IMEMO) in Moscow, where I had firsthand exposure to the Soviet elite. As I traveled widely in the Soviet Union on lecture tours, I was also able to see life outside of Moscow's "beltway." By the time I left the Soviet Union for the United States in January of 1973, I thought the Soviet totalitarian system was ugly, overbearing, and inefficient. I believed that it would continue losing ground to the West, and that the gap between East and West would create real pressure for change.

Since the very same Soviet leadership had already rejected Prime Minister Aleksei Kosygin's proposals for significant economic reform in the
1960s, whatever change did occur would have to be incremental. By the
early 1970s—under simultaneous pressure from economic realities and effective U.S. diplomacy—the first minor shifts could be seen. First, contrary
to their previous pattern, the Soviet leadership was willing to sign strategic
arms control agreements, which at a minimum allowed for more rational
joint management of nuclear competition and in some cases even resulted
in real restrictions. Second—and with a more immediate and personal impact for me—the USSR began to allow substantial emigration by Jews and
others.

While not a major development, this latter change in Soviet behavior
demonstrated one important fact—that, at least at the margins, Brezhnev
and his colleagues were prepared to give in to U.S. efforts to influence Soviet domestic policies. Neither decision was an easy one for the Politburo;
agreement was reached only after intense debate in which Brezhnev eventually became the decisive voice in favor of flexibility.

As a young foreign affairs researcher, I was not close to the very top of
the Soviet establishment, but I had enough access to the second echelon of
the Soviet elite to have a general sense of the thinking in high places on
world matters. For example, late in 1971, I attended a small meeting
chaired by Yevgeny M. Primakov, the current Russian prime minister, and
then a deputy director of IMEMO known for his strong ties to the Communist Party Central Committee. I was able to participate in the meeting because I was the acting secretary of the institute's editorial council. Since the
group was small, Primakov felt comfortable going beyond official clichés.
He spoke with contempt of those who predicted Soviet victory in peaceful
competition with capitalism and added that the West had managed to adjust
to scientific and technological progress and was able to offer enough benefits to the masses to make revolution extremely unlikely in major industrial
nations. Although he did not make the point directly, it was clear that he believed that reform was necessary to avoid facing a serious risk of falling behind the West.

But the fear of falling behind was soon replaced by a new optimism in
foreign policy after the American fiasco in Vietnam, which greatly emboldened the Soviet government. Soon thereafter, President Jimmy Carter's
highly vocal diplomacy on human rights issues—which contrasted sharply

with the quiet diplomacy practiced by Nixon and President Gerald Ford to affect Soviet domestic affairs—reduced the incentives for good behavior. As a result, the Kremlin had the impression that, on one hand, there was no real penalty for fishing in the world's troubled waters and, on the other hand, there was no genuine reward for moderate conduct. Naturally, there were local causes for Moscow's direct and proxy interventions in Angola, Ethiopia, and Afghanistan. But the Soviets were also learning increasingly to disregard U.S. concerns to the point just short of risking outright confrontation.

In addition, the failing health of Brezhnev and other top Politburo members became a barrier to change. With age and sickness, the Soviet leadership gradually lost the sense of reality that had tempered its conservatism in the past. According to his security aide, Vladimir Medvedev, Leonid Brezhnev was in his later years regularly under the influence of sleeping pills, which he took in excess for chronic insomnia. More and more frequently, the Soviet leader was literally unable to comprehend events around him. In Prague in 1981, Brezhnev finished a speech and began reading the prepared text to the audience for a second time. When Czech leader Gustav Husák completed his own presentation by addressing the guest of honor in Russian, Brezhnev loudly complained that his interpreter was not providing any translation. In Baku in 1982, the ailing leader stood at the podium in an obvious state of confusion when he could not find several pages of his remarks.[3]

The deliberate process of policy formulation in Moscow came virtually to a halt. According to Brezhnev's foreign policy advisor, Andrei Aleksandrov-Agentov, weekly Politburo meetings that had lasted several hours now took no longer than forty-five minutes. "Everybody could see that Brezhnev was thinking about only one thing: how he could put an end to the session and leave to rest in [his hunting lodge] in Zavidovo," Aleksandrov-Agentov wrote in his memoirs.[4]

With the tone in the Kremlin being set by a group of aging invalids, younger members were unable to make a case for reforms. Not only could such an attempt get them thrown out of the ruling hierarchy, it would also be an exercise in futility. The principals would have difficulty comprehending what their younger associates were discussing—and would have been completely unable to act on the basis of their recommendations.

•   •   •

Despite its internal problems, the Soviet Union had tens of thousands of nu-clear warheads and a global force-projection capability; it was certainly not a "paper tiger." I could not imagine that the process of reform would, rather than strengthening the Soviet Union, become unstoppable and destroy it al-together. I—and virtually every other Soviet-watcher or insider—was oper-ating under a series of assumptions about how the reform process would occur after Brezhnev left the political scene. Those assumptions led us to believe that reform in the USSR could take place, but that, as in China, it would eventually stop short of fundamental change in the structure of the state. Every assumption in this chain of reasoning was ultimately vindicated by events—except the last one.

The initial assumption was that reform in the Soviet system could only come from the top. There were, of course, distinguished and courageous leaders among Soviet dissidents—most notably Andrei Sakharov—and dis-sidents enjoyed a great deal of sympathy in the West. Inside the Soviet Union, however, they had little popular support. This was largely a function of the pervasive totalitarian apparatus of the Soviet regime, which left little room for anything not sanctioned by the state and effectively stifled any grassroots efforts at change.

However, Soviet dissidents also failed to establish broad public appeal because of their preoccupation with human rights over the bread-and-butter economic issues that most interested ordinary people. Also, in the worst tra-dition of Russia's educated intelligentsia (with the notable exception of the Bolsheviks), dissidents generally had weak organizational skills and little willingness to compromise or build alliances. Thus, despite winning pres-tige as freedom fighters after the collapse of the Soviet Union, most dissi-dents—again, with the exception of Sakharov—failed to transform their stature into a real role in the newly open political process.

In contrast, nationalist movements in the non-Russian Soviet republics often had capable leaders able to strike a chord among their peoples. This potentially explosive force was defused by the combined power of Moscow's totalitarian machinery and local Communist elites, who were given considerable autonomy from the center—including the freedom to engage in a wide range of corrupt practices—in return for helping to keep their ethnic brothers under control.

Thus, in the absence of strong opposition or the pressures of an open society, meaningful change in the Soviet Union could be initiated only by the leadership. The second assumption followed logically: because anyone who came to power in the Soviet Union would be a product of decades of life in the Communist elite, any future leader or group of leaders might want to reform the system but would not be prepared to abolish it.

Despite their possible dissatisfaction with the present state of affairs, Brezhnev's successors were expected to be reformers, not revolutionaries. Everything known about the younger generation of Soviet leaders suggested that they would not be willing to go beyond limited and carefully calibrated reforms designed to enhance rather than destroy the regime. Given the state of the ruling group at the end of the Brezhnev era—when individual leaders looked like walking zombies, large-scale corruption was a way of life, and talent, even in service to the system, was viewed with suspicion—it was easy to imagine how even incremental changes in the system could postpone the Soviet Union's gradual slide into the abyss.

Many argued that reform could develop its own momentum, that a "half-pregnant" partly marketized economy could be unsustainable, and that liberalization of political controls could have far-reaching consequences—particularly among nationalist movements, which could even demand independence from the USSR. It was widely assumed, however, that the regime had both the resources (the Communist Party, the KGB, the media, and a docile population) and the will to retrench if and when reform seemed to go too far.

The flaw in this line of thinking was the underestimation of the "human factor," or more precisely, of the complexity of Gorbachev's personality. No one anticipated that a leader would come to power who knew the rules of the Communist Party apparat and could use them with tactical genius to outmaneuver his opponents while simultaneously not understanding the fundamentals of the system that created him—and which he was expected to defend and strengthen. In the spring of 1992, I visited Mikhail Gorbachev in the offices of the private foundation bearing his name. Gorbachev, who had just been removed from power, was understandably still bitter over his unceremonious exit from the Kremlin—orchestrated by Russian president Boris N. Yeltsin—and charged that the Russian, Ukrainian, and Belorussian presidents had no right to abolish

the USSR. He argued that once peoples of the dissolved Soviet Union realized what had happened, they would find a way to reestablish the
Union. Gorbachev was also clearly implying that once this happened, he
could be offered the opportunity to lead his country once again.

I asked him how he could have expected to preserve the Soviet Union
while systematically undermining its very foundations: pervasive political
controls, the dominance of the highly centralized Party apparatus, the ubiq-
uitous security services with their multimillion-strong army of secret in-
formers, and the state monopoly on the media. "You are describing
everything that went wrong with our system," he replied, adding "we have
admitted to and worked hard to correct the mistakes of the past. But you
cannot reduce the Party to these crimes and errors. And if not for the [Au-
gust 1991] coup attempt, we would have seen the signing of the Union
Treaty and the creation of a new, voluntary federation of sovereign states."
When I related this conversation to Nixon several days later in the United
States, he was not surprised.

"Gorbachev belongs to the past," he said. "And he is still incredibly
naïve about what Soviet communism was all about. It's remarkable that a
statesman can be so smart and so blind at the same time. But one point is
clear—Gorbachev has failed to learn his lesson and continues to live in a
world of illusion. Because of that, he has no future—not as a president, and
not even as a voice in Russian politics," Nixon observed.

In conversations with a range of Gorbachev's former associates, I frequently tried to understand how a man of his background and intellect
could fail to see that what he portrayed as obstacles to the development of
socialism were in fact the essential foundation of the Soviet system. No one
was able to give me a satisfactory answer to this question. And, of course, if
other members of the Politburo had remotely suspected what Gorbachev intended to do to the regime before he came to power, he would have been instantly expelled from the leadership and could never have been elected as
the Party's general secretary.

Two-and-a-half years after Gorbachev became Party leader, his more
conservative colleagues still could not imagine how far he would later be
willing to go in dismantling the political system. "I could not see in my
worst nightmare that what we would have to defend, to fight for, would be
not just the concept of perestroika adopted in 1985 but the most sacred

concepts—socialism, the Soviet government, and the Communist Party," wrote Yegor K. Ligachev, a former close ally who later became Gorbachev's leading conservative opponent in the Politburo.[5] When Ligachev visited Washington as a private citizen in late 1991, I asked him why he and other conservative Party leaders did not stop the general secretary when they still had a comfortable majority in the Politburo. "He never told us what he was really up to," Ligachev explained. "Every time I said to him that he was making too many concessions to the radical forces, he would say, 'Yegor, I am on your side, but as the general secretary I have to have a broader view and have to talk to these people in their own language. Everything will be fine in the end.' How could it occur to me that the general secretary of the Communist Party was secretly an anti-Communist?"[6]

Even at the beginning of the Gorbachev era, the willingness—indeed, the determination—to introduce major change in the Soviet Union was hardly limited to the general secretary and his close advisors. Nor is there any reason to believe that Gorbachev did not take at least the basics of Communist ideology at face value. In addition to Gorbachev's numerous public statements, several authoritative private accounts suggest that he was fully committed to the tenets of Communist theory. In her own book published on the eve of the August 1991 coup attempt—well after Boris Yeltsin's dramatic break with the Party—Raisa Gorbacheva still opted to portray her husband as an ideal Communist. She went so far as to claim that her own father was favorably influenced by his ideologically correct son-in-law, despite long-standing reservations about the regime as a result of his family's suffering during the Stalinist purges. "Faith in the Party came to my father from Mikhail Sergeevich, my husband," she wrote. "Despite the difference in age, [Mikhail Sergeevich] became a model Communist for [my father] symbolizing truth and justice."[7]

Aleksandr N. Yakovlev, a former Soviet ambassador to Canada who served on the Politburo with Gorbachev, confirms this view of Gorbachev. Yakovlev, perhaps Gorbachev's strongest ally in the reform process, or even his alter ego, was lionized to a greater extent than Gorbachev himself by Moscow's liberal intellectuals. He was also more deeply hated by perestroika's conservative critics, some of whom, like then KGB chairman Vladimir Kryuchkov, raised suspicions that he was manipulating the general secretary on behalf of the CIA.[8] I asked Yakovlev what he thought of Ligachev's allegations: "Nonsense," he said. "Initially Gorbachev was the greatest true believer of us all. And even at the end of his days in office, he would sometimes become angry with me for saying something too critical about Marxism-Leninism. Subjectively, he never meant to do anything against the Party."

Gorbachev despised Boris Yeltsin after Yeltsin openly challenged him at the October 1987 Party Central Committee Plenum. Nevertheless, after discharging Yeltsin from the Politburo, the general secretary stopped short of ending his political career altogether—a step easily within his power. Instead, he gave his humiliated critic a cabinet-level appointment and the opportunity to remain in Moscow, which Yeltsin eventually transformed into a spectacular comeback.

When nationalist forces began to gain momentum in the Baltic republics and elsewhere, Gorbachev attempted to persuade them, to outmaneuver them, and to harass them, but never to destroy them with the overwhelming and brutal force that was still very much at his disposal. Even in the bloody interethnic conflicts in the Caucasus region and Central Asia—when he could have easily justified doing whatever was necessary to stop ongoing violence—the Soviet president just could not quite draw the line. Despite pressure from many of his colleagues on the Politburo, Gorbachev could not bring himself to apply the full weight of the Soviet Union's repressive machinery. There could be no better illustration than Gorbachev of the fact that honorable instincts are not always a prescription for effective leadership—particularly in times of great transition.

•   •   •

Until October 1987, I could observe these developments only from the outside. While the authorities had allowed me to leave my native country, even legal emigration was widely seen as the moral equivalent of treason at the time. Thus, those who left the USSR as I did assumed that after our departure Soviet borders would be closed to us permanently. Gorbachev's perestroika brought me an element of hope. His brave talk about democratization—as uncertain as I was about what it really meant—tempted me to test how far the new openness would go. Would the Soviet Union issue me a visa? On my first attempt, the answer was no. In the spring of 1987, Moscow rejected an application from the CBS television network to take me to Moscow as a consultant for a planned documentary about the changes underway in the USSR.

Disappointed but undeterred, I made a second attempt several months later—this time through the State Department—seeking to travel to Moscow with Secretary of State George Shultz as a part of his press entourage (at the time, I wrote a syndicated column distributed by the *Los Angeles Times*). Accordingly, the State Department included my name on the application list for Soviet visas with the rest of the press group. Nevertheless, the visa was denied again.

Fortunately for me, the Reagan administration was not known for easily taking no for an answer from the Soviets. The day before the press plane was scheduled to depart, I received a telephone call from Undersecretary of State Michael Armacost. "On instructions from Shultz, I phoned [Soviet Ambassador Yuri] Dubynin yesterday and explained to him that denying a visa to someone who is supposed to travel with the Secretary of State is of considerable concern to the U.S. government and asked for his help," he said. "Minutes ago Dubynin informed me that your visa has been approved. Congratulations."

I was extremely grateful to Armacost and also very proud of the U.S. government, which was prepared to spend political capital with another superpower to do what was right on behalf of a private individual. Most of all, however, I was excited to have an opportunity to see Moscow once again with my own eyes.

Luck had it that, because of fog in Moscow, the Shultz party had to travel to Moscow by train from Helsinki, which reduced our time in the Soviet capital to just thirty-six hours. Nevertheless, I was able to talk to a variety of old friends, ranging from a Jewish refusenik to a translator of American literature, a police colonel, and even a Central Committee official. All were struck by my sudden appearance in the city; it was almost as if had I returned from the dead. I was similarly struck with the knowledge that none of them was afraid to meet with me—despite the fact that each knew full well that I could be under surveillance by the KGB. Yet more striking, however, was their sense of excitement about perestroika and the new and unprecedented feelings they shared of having the opportunity to become the masters of their own destinies. As I spoke with them well into the night, I saw firsthand what Gorbachev meant in his soon-to-be-infamous statement *"Protsess poshel"*—"The process is under way."

Once I returned to Washington, I called Nixon and gave him a full account of my experiences. "So," the former president said, "Gorbachev is beginning to unleash the real potential of the Russian people. Then there may be more to perestroika than I thought. But I wonder how he's going to keep it under wraps. You know what I mean?" Nixon added that he would call President Ronald Reagan and share my impressions with him.

Meanwhile, I had a long meeting with President Reagan's top aide on the Soviet Union, Fritz Ermarth. A person of great creativity and intuition, Fritz instantly understood the significance of my observations and volunteered to share them with key people in the administration. After I published an article in the *Washington Post* emphasizing that there could be more to Gorbachev's reforms than many of us originally thought, I was asked to brief Senators Bob Dole and George Mitchell. Somewhat later, I had a brief conversation with President Reagan himself, who said that if the Soviet people could indeed be free to have an impact on their government, "things would get just fine" between the two countries.

In December 1987, Gorbachev came to Washington for a summit with Reagan. The two leaders signed the Intermediate Nuclear Forces Treaty (INF), thereby eliminating the entire category of intermediate-range nuclear weapons. There also were reports of movement on other issues, including the Strategic Arms Reduction Treaty (START I). Despite this visible progress, the most remarkable impression for me, as an outsider, was the spirit of the summit. Washington, of course, was overrun with "Gorby-mania"—which probably reflected America's celebrity-oriented culture more than anything else. But there was more to the summit than superficial excitement. For those who were involved in the undertaking in one way or another—government officials, journalists (I was asked by NBC News to serve as a consultant and commentator during the event), and businesspeople—it was hard not to be moved by an inexplicable feeling that history was in the making.

Meanwhile, at the state dinner for Gorbachev at the White House, I was fortunate enough to encounter another perspective on the Soviet reform process. Seated between Barbara Bush and Aleksandr Yakovlev for several hours, I was able to discuss the changes underway in the USSR with Yakovlev, who was viewed as Gorbachev's closest confidant at the time in the Soviet Union. At first, the Politburo member was somewhat uncomfortable at being seated next to one who, until only very recently, could have been viewed as a dangerous outcast. Gradually, however, he warmed up to the discussion and we switched our conversation from English to Russian.

Nothing Yakovlev told me was particularly remarkable—all of his statements about the Soviet Union's need for democratization and new thinking in foreign policy were very much in the public domain. Nevertheless, the way he talked—like a normal human being rather than an arrogant party boss—was refreshing. I was even more impressed when he said, "You should not judge us too severely. We do not mind to be criticized. It actually helps us to hear opinions from afar. But if you want to have an impact, do not talk as if we are enemies, as if our every defeat is a success for you. We have to get out of this cycle of the United States and the Soviet Union acting like two scorpions." This was quite different from the way in which Soviet officials defended Moscow's policies in the past.

After my exposure to ordinary people in Moscow and Aleksandr Yakovlev and his colleagues in Washington, I began to feel strongly that the Soviet reforms were serious and real. I was not certain how far they would go—or exactly in which direction—but there was no doubt that the train had left the station and that there was probably no return.

Shortly after the summit, I hosted a meeting of a small group of leading Soviet specialists—from both inside and outside the administration—at the Carnegie Endowment for International Peace. At the meeting, there was an emerging consensus regarding the far-reaching nature of the Soviet transformation, but there was also real concern that Gorbachev and his allies were encountering increasing opposition from Party conservatives that put the future of perestroika into question. Still, no one in the group seriously entertained the possibility that the death of the Soviet Union was only four years away.

Five thousand miles away, in Moscow, that possibility had also likely not yet occurred to the man who would soon play a key role in the last act of the Soviet drama. When I met that man two years later, during his first trip to Washington, future Russian president Boris Yeltsin spoke only of the need for radical reform in the Soviet Union—something he argued Mikhail Gorbachev could not bring about. He did not yet suggest dissolving the USSR or even replacing the Union with a loose confederation. Nevertheless, while no one in Moscow or Washington realized it, the powerful centrifugal forces released by perestroika would soon dramatically affect the Soviet state.

Chapter Two

•

The Unmaking of the Soviet State

Despite a seventy-year effort by the Soviet propaganda machine, the people of the USSR were never successfully socialized to believe themselves to be citizens of one great multiethnic country. This failure to bring together the peoples of the former USSR—arguably the greatest weakness of the Soviet system—ultimately proved to be its undoing.

Thus, the USSR was able to create *Homo sovieticus* only to the extent that the inhabitants of the territory of the Soviet Union were raised as obedient subjects of a repressive totalitarian state. Communism, the founding revolutionary ideology, was transformed into a convenient state religion—although few took it literally, the numerous obligatory party rituals served as an important force to maintain the unity of diverse national groups. Nevertheless, that unity was neither the unity of the "melting pot" nor, conversely, that created by the genuine acceptance of diversity and real respect for each other's identities and interests. It was instead a product of—and contingent upon the survival of—the Russian-dominated Soviet totalitarian state.

Under Stalin, traditional Marxist-Leninist internationalism was supplemented by a heavy dose of Russian chauvinism. In this manner, the Communist ideology that destroyed tsarist Russia gradually evolved into the official philosophy of its successor state, the Soviet/Russian empire. Thus, no nationalism was tolerated—except Russian nationalism. Similarly, as in the prerevolutionary period, individuals of other nationalities—

especially local elites—were given the opportunity for advancement within the Soviet regime, including enrollment in the ruling *nomenklatura,* as long as they were willing to be Russified, swear allegiance to the new empire, and play by Moscow's rules. Joseph Stalin himself—who gave up his Georgian surname, Dzhugashvili—was the most notable example of this phenomenon. There were a large number of other non-Russians and non-Slavs in the central Party and government structures throughout the Soviet period. Outside of Moscow, republican hierarchies enjoyed considerable autonomy by the end of Brezhnev's tenure, when guidance from the top had dramatically eroded. Local Party and government officials were also increasingly free to engage in massive, blatant corruption so long as they were prepared to compete in sycophancy to Brezhnev and loyalty to Communist doctrine. Accordingly, no one in the republican establishments, to say nothing of the regional party organizations, was willing to risk this cozy arrangement by openly challenging Moscow. Some of today's proud and genuinely impressive post-Soviet leaders, such as Georgian president Eduard Shevardnadze and Azerbaijani president Heidar Aliyev, mastered the art of protecting their local authority and prerogatives while running their respective republics during the Brezhnev era by paying lavish tribute to the aging general secretary.

But there were some notable exceptions. For example, many intellectuals among the Crimean Tatars—exiled to Central Asia by Stalin for their alleged support of the Germans during World War II—were willing to identify themselves publicly with nationalist causes. Nationalism was also always quite strong in western Ukraine, which became a part of the USSR after being occupied by Stalin through a secret pact with Hitler in 1939. A part of the Austro-Hungarian Empire or Poland for centuries, western Ukraine was overwhelmingly Roman Catholic (rather than Orthodox like the rest of Ukraine) and generally identified with Europe rather than with Russia, which was often contemptuously called Muscovy. Finally, anti-Russian sentiment was also very strong in the Baltic republics of Lithuania, Latvia, and Estonia, which were annexed by Stalin in 1940 as a part of another deal with the Nazis.

Nevertheless, these strong nationalist feelings were generally reflected in everyday life, such as attitudes toward Russian neighbors and visitors, and were only extremely rarely manifest in any kind of organized activity. By the mid-seventies, small groups of dissidents emboldened by the

Helsinki Accords won measurably greater public sympathy in the Baltics, Ukraine, Georgia, and elsewhere than in Russia itself. That sympathy, however, remained rather silent—in terms of practical political action, nationalists in the ethnic republics, like dissidents in Russia, were an irritant and no more. It was certainly never a serious threat to the Kremlin's control over the empire.

Of course, a variety of factors contributed to the limitation of political opposition to the Soviet regime to no more than a few individuals. But the most frequently cited factors—fear, indoctrination, and conformity—tell only a part of the story. The paramount barrier to dissent was much more subtle: it was the futility of opposition. The Soviet state was remarkably successful in bringing up several generations of citizens who knew instinctively that any challenge to the system was inherently useless. In fact, so successful was the regime that opposition to it was seen as evidence of extreme irresponsibility—and even madness—rather than a sign of courage and determination. Under such circumstances, in a country with no tradition of seeing freedom of thought as an end in itself, it could hardly be surprising that the vast majority of Moscow's subjects, including people of talent and integrity, chose not to beat their heads against the Kremlin wall, and watched anyone who did with a measure of skepticism. Dissidents were, in fact, often viewed by the general population with a complex mixture of guilt—at lacking the moral courage to oppose the regime openly as well—and resentment of the fact that dissent could provoke the regime to tighten the screws, worsening conditions for the rest of society, particularly intellectuals.

•   •   •

It is easy for me to identify with these sentiments because I shared them myself. After a brief flirtation with dissent in my late teens—including helping to organize a 1966 student meeting to denounce Soviet involvement in Vietnam, for which I was briefly expelled from Moscow State University—I decided quickly that the path of open opposition to the regime was not for me. Under the conditions of the time, outright dissent seemed to me to be heroic but futile.

Thus, the only solution was to try to change the system from within. There was no question that this was also a far safer path than dissent and that it offered many comforts and rewards. However, in my view at the time, it was also the only road that offered the possibility of real results. Fortunately for me, after Khrushchev's reforms the system was sufficiently broad-minded to forgive adolescent mistakes and to offer a second chance to those prepared to mend their ways.

When my then father-in-law, the influential columnist Yuri Timofeyev, offered to get me a job at the Institute of the World Economy and International Relations (IMEMO), I agreed without hesitation. The opportunity to work at the most prestigious Soviet foreign policy think tank was a real break for me.

As with all fundamental choices in a totalitarian state, my decision to become a part of the system came at a price. While perfectly rational, it was also—as I knew only too well—quite self-serving and involved regular moral compromises. The most difficult among those compromises was sacrificing my ability to write honestly about the United States, the country I had chosen to study at IMEMO. It was disgusting to be forced to repeat Marxist-Leninist clichés, which almost no one in my circle of acquaintances took seriously, but I could live with my disgust as one can live with participating in any ridiculous but basically harmless obligatory ceremony. But being unable to be truthful in my professional activity was a different matter. Being forced to adjust my substantive analyses gave me a real sense of being violated.

It was also difficult for the *nomenklatura* to accept me as one of their own. As a Jewish intellectual who had committed youthful political transgressions, I was not fully reliable. This situation was exacerbated by the fact that my mother was frequently mentioned in the Western media, including on Radio Liberty and the Voice of America, as a defense counsel to some of the most celebrated dissidents. Even the more enlightened officials, such as IMEMO deputy director Yevgeny Primakov, understandably felt that I could not be entirely trusted, or at least that I was a potential embarrassment to the institution.

Despite these handicaps, at twenty-four, I was the acting secretary of IMEMO's Komsomol (Young Communist League) organization, where new Russian foreign minister Igor Ivanov was a deputy secretary, and a well-connected consultant to the Committee on Youth Organizations—essentially the Komsomol's foreign office. The articles I wrote for the *In-*

formation Bulletin (for senior officials) were prepared seriously and honestly and, looking back, proved to be basically accurate. My op-ed pieces—with a dose of the expected (and, as I thought then, fairly innocent) demagoguery—were beginning to appear in leading newspapers, and I became the youngest IMEMO staffer authorized to deliver lectures on foreign policy to prestigious party audiences across the Soviet Union. With that honor also came the ability to give so-called public lectures for a nice fee—which tripled my modest income.

My willingness to play along with the regime dwindled very quickly, however, once emigration from the USSR became possible for Soviet Jews in the early seventies. I knew that it would be difficult to win an exit visa; not a single person at IMEMO had yet attempted to emigrate. The institute was too close to the Central Committee for emigration by staffers to be considered "safe." I expected a long period of unemployment and perhaps even time in jail before being allowed to leave the country. Nevertheless, marshaling the courage was easy. Despite all the difficulties and risks, the opportunity to emigrate was real. The chains of hopelessness that kept me from challenging the regime were destroyed.

Thirteen years later, Gorbachev's perestroika broke those chains for the Soviet people as a whole, with tremendous, historic consequences. Standing up for one's beliefs and interests was quixotic no more. The impact of this radical change on the Kremlin's ability to keep the empire together was devastating.

•   •   •

In the late 1980s, ethnic rioting occurred in Kazakhstan and among Armenians and Azeris, while peaceful demonstrations took place in the Baltic republics. By 1989, there were violent demonstrations in Belorussia, Moldavia, Uzbekistan, and Georgia, where 21 people died in a violent clash with Soviet troops in Tblisi. There was a common denominator to the unrest in the republics: just barely released from totalitarian constraints, ethnic groups across the country saw the reestablishment of their national identity and the assertion of nationalist demands as their first priority. Even when these demands were not explicitly directed against Moscow, they could not but lead to estrangement from the imperial center if the Kremlin either

failed to accommodate them or, conversely, used brutal force to demonstrate beyond doubt that, perestroika or not, the Moscow Communist leadership was still very much in charge.

But choosing to make concessions to defuse the crisis or simply to
crush opposition required a clear understanding of the fundamental nature
of the USSR's ethnic divisions and a willingness to take decisive preemptive action, one way or the other. Such realism and decisiveness were, however, alien to Gorbachev, who remained a prisoner of illusions. The general
secretary was convinced that persuasion and "appeals" would be sufficient
to resolve the ethnic crises that signaled the beginning of the end of the Soviet empire. For example, when large-scale violence erupted in Nagorno-
Karabakh, Gorbachev sent top-level delegations to the Azeri and Armenian
capitals. "Their mission was to establish contacts and reassure the people in
these republics," the Soviet leader wrote in his recent memoirs.[1] Gorbachev
does not understand even today that in the case of Nagorno-Karabakh the
demands of the two sides were simply incompatible. Local Armenians were
determined that the province leave Azerbaijan and become an integral part
of Armenia. The Azeris were equally determined that this should not happen. No reassurances from Moscow could bridge this gap.

When the conflict predictably continued unabated, Gorbachev responded by publishing an official analysis of the situation in the press, by
speaking on television, and by discussing the crisis in the newly elected
Congress of People's Deputies. The leadership considered the possibility of
dispatching troops on a mass scale, but in the end not even a curfew was
imposed. Instead, "the Azerbaijan and Armenian leaders were again told to
come to understanding," Gorbachev explains.[2]

When discontent reached the Baltic republics, Gorbachev's response
was similarly *ad hoc* and inconclusive. His first instinct was again to issue
an appeal "for the restoration of the USSR Constitution immediately and in
its entirety."[3] The Soviet leader appears to have been psychologically unable
to accept the notion that some conflicts cannot be resolved to everyone's
satisfaction—that in certain cases, as in the Baltic republics, far-reaching
preemptive concessions could be the best means to avoid a chain reaction
throughout the USSR, and that in others, such as the Caucasus region and
Central Asia (where blood had already been spilled by uncontrollable
mobs), drawing the line and demonstrating that the regime was not a paper
tiger could be the only appropriate solution.

Gorbachev, however, chose neither to give up enough to win goodwill nor to act with ruthlessness sufficient to intimidate increasingly assertive nationalist movements. In the end, he looked increasingly like a noble but hapless leader, much smaller than the great historical transformation he unleashed so courageously and yet so blindly. Some of Gorbachev's advisors, however, such as Eduard Shevardnadze, were better able to understand the graveness of the situation. As Shevardnadze later told me, he first began to entertain the notion that the disintegration of the Soviet Union was possible as early as 1980. By 1989, he had already concluded that the USSR could not be kept together much longer. Fearing retaliation, he did not share his observations with anyone beyond his most trusted aides.[4]

By the summer of 1989, the Soviet empire was in deep trouble. The Kremlin's chances of restoring a modicum of control were, however, far from hopeless. The Party *nomenklatura* was still basically running things in Moscow and in the republics alike. It retained the enormous resources of the so-called power ministries—the Ministry of Defense, the Ministry of the Interior, and the KGB. Moreover, with the exception of the Baltic republics—where local hierarchies were increasingly in tune with popular secessionist sentiments—republican elites were still unprepared to ask for more than greater autonomy. Despite Gorbachev's hesitation, these republican leaders still held a deeply ingrained fear of provoking the central Party leadership and its known hard-liners. They were also uncertain that they personally would outlive their Soviet rulers. After all, republican nationalist opposition movements viewed their local Communist elites as Moscow proxies who would be eliminated as soon as the circumstances allowed. As a matter of fact, in some parts of the Soviet Union (especially in Central Asia), local reformers felt much more affinity for Gorbachev than for their conservative and corrupt local leaders. Conversely, local elites could despise the general secretary but, as in the case of Central Asian leaders, they were forced to rely upon him for their continued survival.

•   •   •

The magnitude of the emerging discontent in the USSR was still not fully appreciated in the United States. Majority opinion inside and outside the new Bush administration held that the Soviet reforms were essentially on track and that the principal challenge to Gorbachev was from Party conservatives.

Initially, President Bush and his national security advisor, Brent Scowcroft, were suspicious that Ronald Reagan—who had a well-known predisposition to think of the world in terms of personalities—had relied too heavily on the still unproven Gorbachev. But soon the Soviet leader's benign attitude toward the peaceful revolutions underway in Central Europe, his major concessions on arms control, and his encouragement of political pluralism at home persuaded Bush and his advisors that Gorbachev was for real and that betting on his success was in the U.S. national interest.

After a number of trips to the USSR during this period, I had also reached the conclusion that there was much more to perestroika than I'd originally suspected. I was also impressed with the Kremlin's reluctance to rely on traditional instruments of coercion to maintain control. But how far would the process be allowed to go? At what point would Gorbachev join the hard-liners in saying enough is enough and tighten the screws? Would the Soviet leader and his colleagues hesitate so long that the disintegration of the Soviet Union would become unstoppable?

These were some of the difficult questions with no definitive answers that I discussed with Richard Nixon during several meetings and telephone conversations in 1988–89. In my capacity as a senior associate at the Carnegie Endowment for International Peace, I organized a study group on U.S.–Soviet relations with a generous grant from the Blum-Kovler Foundation. Ably chaired by James R. Schlesinger—Nixon's CIA director and then secretary of defense, who later became the first energy secretary in the Carter administration—the invitation-only group included some of Washington's most prominent Soviet-watchers from both government and academia. Nixon was not an official member of the group, but it was he who strongly encouraged me to organize it, who approved the selection of Schlesinger as its chairman, and who was a constant invisible presence. Schlesinger and I briefed him on a regular basis about any interesting insights, and he relied on the group to get systematic firsthand information on the best American thinking on Soviet matters.

The arrangement was not a one-way street. With the help of Nixon's chief of staff, John Taylor, we arranged for the former president to address the group on May 12, 1989. In his presentation, Nixon put Soviet developments in an overall geopolitical perspective. His main message was that the Soviet situation was evolving very quickly and seemingly in the right direction, but that many uncertainties remained. Accordingly, in his view, the rapid consolidation of the historic gains of the Soviet Union's "new foreign policy thinking" (to use Gorbachev's own words), particularly in Central Europe, had to be a high priority of American diplomacy. He also argued that the United States should spend less time worrying about the general secretary's personal fortunes. "Nobody is indispensable. I happen to know that first-hand," the former president said with a laugh.

There were no startling revelations in Nixon's speech, but his ability to place Soviet events in a global context and to define the developments that mattered most in terms of U.S. national interests genuinely impressed the group. Strobe Talbott, then a *Time* magazine columnist, told me that he knew no statesman who was capable of such clear thinking.

Less than two months after the Nixon performance, I received a telephone call from a Lithuanian community organization inquiring whether I would be interested in meeting Vytautas Landsbergis, the leader of the Lithuanian reform movement known as Sajudis. I was aware that Landsbergis was considered one of the most impressive pro-independence Baltic leaders, but that some in the Bush administration considered him a dangerous extremist who should be avoided in order to keep from alienating Gorbachev. I was naturally more than eager to form a personal impression.

The impression Landsbergis made on me was strong and positive. While new in politics, he sounded like a serious politician. His steely determination to see Lithuania win independence was coupled with tactical flexibility in fighting for it. For example, he made it clear that if Moscow accepted the principle of Lithuanian independence—on which he would not compromise—everything else, ranging from the nature of Lithuania's new relations with the USSR to the timing of the withdrawal of Soviet troops and even the temporary presence of Soviet military bases, would be negotiable. And since all public opinion polls indicated that he and his Sajudis were bound to win the forthcoming Lithuanian parliamentary elections, I had a feeling that if people of such caliber and determination were to come to power in the Baltics their secession from the Soviet Union was only a question of time. That was particularly true because Estonia, Latvia, and Lithuania were never recognized as a part of the Soviet Union by the West and, accordingly, could count on stronger foreign support in their drive for independence. And I knew that the Baltic republics were also a special case in the Soviet mind—they were not considered to be an integral part of the USSR to the same degree as other constituent republics. Both their

European heritage and their short-lived independence between the two world wars had won them a certain unique status within the Soviet Union.

At the time, my impression was that, outside the Baltics, the Kremlin probably had both the will and the power to arrest the disintegration processes. Landsbergis basically agreed. He preferred to treat Lithuania, Latvia, and Estonia as special cases rather than to talk about the dissolution of the Soviet Union altogether. Later, however, over dinner at my home—after we had become more comfortable with one another—he said, "Analytically, it is hard to envision Ukraine or, for that matter, Georgia being allowed to secede from the Soviet Union. But as you said yourself, Russia is not about analyses. And I want to tell you that we are getting excellent cooperation from Yeltsin and his people. They sound totally sympathetic to our demands. If Yeltsin turns the Russian government against the Soviet regime, other republics will follow his lead."

It was still unclear just how far Boris Yeltsin would be able to go in establishing meaningful control over the largest Soviet republic, the core of the empire. But when I called Nixon to brief him on my conversation with Landsbergis, he immediately seized on the centrality of the Yeltsin factor. "Yeltsin is now the key to the whole goddamned Soviet situation. They still do not understand in the Bush administration that Gorbachev is beginning to lose it. Bush and Brent Scowcroft are such nice orderly gentlemen that they simply cannot believe that somebody as unpredictable and ill-mannered as Yeltsin can come out on top. But let me tell you, Yeltsin is the key. I just know it," the former president said.

Indeed, Gorbachev started the process leading to the Soviet collapse, and Yeltsin finished it. Of course, both leaders reflected great forces of history. But neither was a blind instrument of history either. Their personalities, values, and actions had a profound impact on the dynamics of Soviet politics, the multiple and often contradictory inputs that drove events during the empire's last chapter.

•　　•　　•

A great deal has already been written about Boris Yeltsin, including two volumes of memoirs prepared by the Russian president himself. Nevertheless, for Americans, Yeltsin remains a greater enigma than Mikhail Gorbachev. Despite his "man of the people" facade, Yeltsin—like most major statesmen—is a complex and contradictory man. He is an avowed democrat who launched an armored assault on his own democratically elected parliament. He is also an economic reformer under whom corrupt state capitalism has flourished at the expense of a genuinely free market. He is a pro-Western leader who has made it a foreign policy priority to challenge American global leadership. Finally, he is a Russian patriot who played a pivotal role in the dismemberment of the Russian empire. Boris Yeltsin is all of this. As a result, popular views of the Russian leader inevitably reflect the facets of Yeltsin's character that have had the most immediate impact on the viewer.

I had the opportunity to meet Yeltsin personally during his first trip to the United States in September 1989. I encountered him first at a meeting in his honor at the Council on Foreign Relations in New York and subsequently in a smaller, more private setting in Washington where I was able to converse with the future leader. He impressed me instantly as a politician of great charisma, with a strong sense of himself, natural intelligence, and considerable political shrewdness. It was also apparent, however, that his economic and political views were unsophisticated at best. His understanding of democracy was limited to the notion that free elections offered him his best chance to come to power in Russia and to do whatever he chose. He also lacked intellectual discipline to the point that he almost seemed to have difficulty thinking logically and seeing even the most obvious implications of his actions beyond their effect on him personally. He was thus able to be completely sincere in making improbable and seemingly contradictory statements—such as his insistence that he was determined to work constructively with Gorbachev and his simultaneous, categorical assertion that Gorbachev was a phony and a fake who could not be trusted to keep his promises.

When one adds to this Yeltsin's propensity to have one drink too many—which I have witnessed firsthand and heard described by several others well disposed toward him—it is easy to understand why Bush and Scowcroft were not overly impressed with the aspiring Russian leader. Yeltsin was no match for Gorbachev—not only in terms of manners, but intellectually as well.

Despite these impressions, I drew precisely the opposite conclusion about Yeltsin's future. Yeltsin could never have succeeded as a national politician in a mature democracy like the United States, but he did not have to—he was operating in a new Russian political arena governed by vastly different rules. To voters with no experience making real electoral choices, sounding sincere was much more important than making sense. Further, Yeltsin's apparent coarseness and occasional drunkenness meant that he was just "one of the guys" and, accordingly, easily identified with and trusted by the Russian people.

Making irreconcilable statements with a straight face was also considered normal. As the great Russian poet Fedor Tyutchev wrote, "Not by the mind is Russia understood / Nor is she measured by a common rule / She has a special stature of her own / In Russia one can only put his faith."[5] Yeltsin, in contrast to Gorbachev, appealed to trust and national mysticism rather than to the minds of the Russian people and, by the standards of the time, made that appeal in a very believable manner. Although Russian voters today are already learning to make more responsible electoral choices— with consequences for the Russian president's own popularity—Boris Yeltsin was almost irresistible in the climate surrounding Russia's first-ever democratically organized presidential election.

Accordingly, there was little doubt in my mind that Yeltsin had the potential for a great future. And since the road to that future would clearly be built on the ruins of the totalitarian Soviet empire, there was every reason for the United States to wish him well—at least up to a point.

I soon shared my own assessment of Yeltsin with Nixon, who agreed completely. The former president reminded me of Khrushchev's ill-fitting clothes and poor manners, including one incident in which he fell drunk under the table during an official dinner in London. Nevertheless, as Nixon observed, Khrushchev had formidable political instincts and an extremely quick mind. "If statesmen were judged by their outfits, Alger Hiss would have been everyone's role model," he said, returning to a favorite topic.

•   •   •

To understand Yeltsin's role in the destruction of the Soviet Union, it is important to appreciate both his background and character and the traditional conduct of Russian elites during times of great uncertainty. As far as Yeltsin personally is concerned, he was even more of a typical provincial apparatchik than Gorbachev before being summoned to Moscow in April 1985. Also from a humble background, Yeltsin graduated from Sverdlovsk's Urals

Polytechnic Institute in 1955. Like many other Party functionaries, he began his career in industry—in Yeltsin's case in the construction industry in
Sverdlovsk (now Yekaterinburg), a large city in the Ural Mountains near
which he was born. In 1972, he was asked to move to the Sverdlovsk Communist Party apparatus, where he became the chief of the construction department of the provincial Party committee. As Yeltsin wrote in his
memoirs, "I was not surprised to receive this offer—I had been constantly
engaged in Party work outside of working hours—and I accepted it."[6]

Yeltsin clearly did well in the eyes of his Party superiors as only four
years later, in 1976, he was elected first secretary of the Sverdlovsk provincial Party committee on the orders of Leonid Brezhnev himself. This important post also brought Yeltsin membership on the Central Committee of
the Party, the most prestigious body in the USSR next to the Politburo. As
the Sverdlovsk Party boss, according to his own memoirs, Yeltsin behaved
entirely according to the Soviet-style political correctness of the time. He
even "developed reasonably good relations with the provincial directorate
of the KGB."[7] In fact, by Yeltsin's own account, the local KGB chief was so
pleased with his cooperation that he praised the first secretary to the KGB
leadership in Moscow.

In Sverdlovsk, Yeltsin played completely by the rules and does not
seem to have been willing to stand up to Moscow even with significant local support. For example, Yeltsin argues in his memoirs that it was Moscow,
not Yeltsin himself, which made the decision to destroy Ipatiev House, the
Sverdlovsk building in which Tsar Nicholas II and his family were executed by the Bolsheviks in 1918. However, despite "sharp opposition" from
his Sverdlovsk colleagues, Yeltsin did nothing to challenge what he himself
called the "senseless decision" to destroy what had become almost an unofficial historic site. Instead, Yeltsin sent bulldozers to demolish the building
and cover the site with asphalt.

Not rocking the boat came naturally to Yeltsin, who, unlike Gorbachev,
was thoroughly provincial until his transfer to Moscow in 1985. Called to
Moscow to join the Central Committee staff, Yeltsin was soon invited to
stay as Moscow's Party secretary. Yeltsin's recruitment to run the crucial
Moscow Party organization was the next logical step in a very successful
Party career.

Once in Moscow, Yeltsin soon saw both the limitations and some of
the unintended consequences of Gorbachev's reforms. He realized that

perestroika was beginning to undermine the very foundations of the system—despite the general secretary's continuing illusions. But he believed that perestroika should be accelerated and broadened to the point that the old regime would cease to exist. At that early stage, in the summer and fall of 1987—just two years after perestroika began—there was no other Party politician who was prepared to challenge the Soviet system so directly.

There were three reasons behind Yeltsin's break with Party conservatives, which culminated with his resignation speech at the October 1987 Central Committee plenum. First, given his experimental and impatient nature, Yeltsin was psychologically more comfortable with change than his conservative Politburo associates. Once he understood intuitively that the previous order had been severely undermined, his instinct was to push forward rather than to look back. Also, in this new environment, Yeltsin discovered in himself qualities that no one—including Yeltsin himself—had previously recognized. "After all those years of following strict rules, it was wonderful to be able to act spontaneously, to meet with people informally, and to make unorthodox decisions," Yeltsin said when I saw him in Washington in September 1989. The new Moscow Party boss reveled in the opportunities to engage in previously unheard-of populist politics, to make allies, and to become popular—and he was clearly successful.

Second, notwithstanding the vastly greater scope and excitement of his new job in Moscow, Yeltsin felt trapped as the Party boss of the Soviet capital. In Sverdlovsk, almost one thousand miles from Moscow, the power of the provincial Party secretary was, as Yeltsin himself wrote, "practically unlimited" during Brezhnev's lethargic rule.[8] This was not so in the capital, where Yeltsin operated with dynamic leadership from Gorbachev and stern supervision from Yegor Ligachev, then second secretary of the Central Committee.

Yeltsin's impatience quickly overwhelmed his limited understanding of how to operate in these new circumstances, and he proceeded with endless organizational changes. In eighteen months, he fired two entire groups of city district Party secretaries in rapid succession. This brought absolute panic to the Moscow Party hierarchy, which appealed to the Central Committee—whose offices were next door—for help. Once Ligachev began to constrain Yeltsin's reorganizational zeal, the Moscow Party leader ran to Gorbachev to complain about unwarranted interference with his prerogatives. However, the general secretary did not understand how alienated the

Moscow secretary had become, was not sure that he was right anyway, and—most important—did not want to cross swords with Ligachev, a conservative whom he hoped to keep in the pro-reform camp. At the time, it was much more important to Gorbachev to remain on good terms with his deputy Ligachev than with the erratic Yeltsin. The Soviet leader never imagined the consequences. Instead, in an action totally unprecedented since Stalin's introduction of iron Party discipline in the late 1920s, Yeltsin openly challenged the general secretary of the Communist Party of the Soviet Union, without any prior notification, in public, at a plenary meeting of the Party Central Committee.

Finally, Yeltsin's impulsive nature was a major factor in his revolt. A man of great ego and enormous pride, he seems to be almost physiologically unable to accept personal offense. "I could see that every time we had an argument and he could not have his way, he almost exploded. His temper was matched only by his capriciousness," Ligachev observed in November 1991 in response to a question I asked about the origins of his conflict with Yeltsin.

According to Yeltsin himself, he did not prepare his crucial address at the October 1987 plenum in advance, although he generally rewrote speeches ten to fifteen times. "Perhaps I was not one hundred percent sure I would speak, and I was leaving a tiny crack open in case I decided to retreat," Yeltsin acknowledged in his memoirs.[9] In fact, his remarks at the plenum were so incoherent that some participants thought he was drunk. "At first, I could not quite figure out what he was saying, what he was driving at. He sounded like a man not in total control of his thoughts," Georgian president Eduard Shevardnadze, then a candidate member of the Politburo, observed in a conversation with me years later. Another person present, who now supports Yeltsin, was more graphic: "I could smell the alcohol on his breath. He was probably drinking all night talking himself into beating the hell out of them."

Several days after being overwhelmed by predictably harsh and largely unfair criticism at the plenum, Yeltsin was admitted to the hospital with, as he describes it himself, "a severe headache and chest pains." According to Yeltsin, he "suffered a physical breakdown" and was given a great deal of medication, "mostly tranquilizers." In fact, his doctors at Clinical Hospital No. 1 (for senior officials) revealed confidentially that Yeltsin had experienced a nervous breakdown and showed symptoms of acute psychological withdrawal. This episode was to become only one among several similar withdrawals Yeltsin subsequently experienced after major crises.

During his treatment at the Kremlin hospital, Yeltsin's irritation with Gorbachev evolved into a near hatred for the Soviet leader. His feelings became particularly intense after the general secretary personally telephoned Yeltsin in his hospital bed to order him—still physically very weak and emotionally devastated—to attend the Moscow Party plenum, which followed the national plenum. At the Moscow meeting, Party functionaries hungry for revenge against their much-despised boss—and equally eager to please Gorbachev—attacked Yeltsin in a savage, demagogic style reminiscent of Stalinist show trials. Yeltsin, still medicated, was in no position to fight back. In fact, again in the tradition of the show trials, he was "encouraged" to admit his mistakes. The very proud, even macho Yeltsin has never forgiven Mikhail Gorbachev for forcing him to humiliate himself at the Moscow plenum. "However much Gorbachev may have disliked me, to act like that was inhuman and immoral," Yeltsin wrote.[10]

Thus, the stage was set for a bitter personal struggle between the two men in which Gorbachev had all the advantages of being in charge of the Soviet system and Yeltsin had the advantages of running against it. In 1989, the semifree elections to the new Soviet Congress of People's Deputies gave Yeltsin the opportunity he needed for a spectacular political comeback. Although Gorbachev did not want to see Yeltsin in the parliament, he nevertheless issued instructions to Party organizations not to interfere in the conduct of the election. As Ligachev writes, "Instructions were sent one after another from the Central Committee to local Party organizations: 'don't become involved! Keep your distance.' "[11] Enough was said to make clear that the general secretary opposed Yeltsin's return to politics, but very little was actually done to prevent it. This ineptitude served only to win free publicity for Yeltsin and to bolster his image as a courageous underdog. Campaigning on a wave of disillusionment with Gorbachev, Yeltsin carefully crafted the image of a man of the people who had suffered because of his opposition to the *nomenklatura* and its privileges. Nevertheless, despite his increasing popular appeal, Yeltsin had only a modest institutional role in the legislature's permanent working body, the Supreme Soviet, in which he served as chairman of the Committee on Architecture and Construction. And even that position was his as the result of a decision by Gorbachev.

Yeltsin's real chance came a year later during relatively free elections to the Russian Republic parliament in 1990. Winning the electoral race in his native Sverdlovsk by a huge margin, he secured a seat in the Russian Supreme Soviet. Then, despite the strong opposition of the Party establishment—and vigorous personal lobbying by Gorbachev—Yeltsin was chosen by a small majority to serve as chairman of the parliament.

In the past, parliamentary bodies were essentially irrelevant in the Soviet Union. The Russian parliament in particular had been strictly a pro forma institution used primarily to reward (with membership) those in the *nomenklatura* who were not senior enough to deserve election to its more prestigious Soviet counterpart. While officially subordinate to the Russian parliament, the Russian Council of Ministers actually took its orders directly from the Soviet Council of Ministers and, ultimately, from the Communist Party Central Committee.

However, Gorbachev's democratization changed the rules. The Party was slowly losing power in the republican parliaments, and republics gradually gained autonomy from the Soviet federal government. As the core of the empire in almost every sense, Russia faced a unique problem in striving for autonomy in that any attempt to loosen ties to the federal center could not but bring greater independence for other republics as well. Thus, Russia could not undermine the power of the union without risking the viability of the Soviet/Russian empire as well.

No matter how much Yeltsin wanted to improve his own standing at Gorbachev's expense, he could accomplish little without the support of a significant part of the Russian elite against its own imperial center. Interestingly, in supporting Yeltsin, the Russian elite was following the historical precedent of another great Russian upheaval—the Time of Troubles at the beginning of the seventeenth century. Suddenly released from their totalitarian chains and facing the declining legitimacy of the Communist state, Russian subjects—the rulers and the ruled alike—found themselves disoriented and in desperate need of simple, dramatic solutions. Thus, the observations of renowned historian Vasily Klyuchevsky about the Time of Troubles were almost entirely applicable to the situation in the USSR during its final years. Klyuchevsky wrote:

> For them [the Russian population] the indivisible categories were
> not the state and the people but rather the state and the ruler of a
> particular dynasty. They could more easily imagine the state

without the people than the state without its ruler. . . . Thus, when
a dynasty came to its end and, accordingly, the state belonged to
no one, the people became lost, stopped understanding who and
where they were, and entered a state of turmoil. It was as if they
became anarchists against their own will, out of a sense of unfor-
tunate but inevitable duty: since there was no one from whom
they could take orders, rebellion was the thing to do.[12]

As the reform process undermined and delegitimized the Communist
dynasty established by Lenin and Stalin, the Soviet people—who had been
raised to identify themselves more with the system than with the country itself—lost their sense of identity. If the Party was no longer the ultimate authority and the undisputed voice of truth, who, then, determined that federal
bodies were entitled to have authority over the republics? The Soviet system became a free-for-all, and yesterday's Kremlin subjects were not about
to start treating one another as fellow citizens. There was a growing sense
that the only way to succeed in the untested waters of post-totalitarianism
was for every group, every city, and certainly every republic to give precedence to its own needs for survival and to let the rest of the nation fend for
itself.

Boris Yeltsin and his colleagues in the Russian parliament had no
power outside the enormous borders of the Russian Soviet Federative So-
cialist Republic. But they could sense that the Gorbachev leadership was either unwilling or unable to reassert its authority. The temptation to fill the
vacuum was irresistible, and on June 12, 1990, the Russian Federation Congress of People's Deputies adopted in a 907-to-13 vote a declaration on
Russian state sovereignty. Even the vast majority of hard-line Communists
voted for the declaration, which guaranteed Russia's right to secede from
the Soviet Union and dramatically established the primacy of Russian laws
over Soviet federal legislation. "The observation of the acts of the USSR
which contradict sovereign rights of the R.S.F.S.R. [the Russian Republic]
is suspended by the Republic on its territory," the declaration stated.

There was extensive debate on the floor of the Russian parliament
about the optimal distribution of responsibilities between the Russian and
federal governments. Nevertheless, no one said plainly that this declaration,
if interpreted literally, could not but mean the end of the Soviet Union.

This apparent lack of understanding of the consequences of the sovereignty declaration among members of the Russian parliament may have simply reflected their own uncertainty as to whether the declaration was in fact the verdict of history or merely empty rhetoric. But the declaration drew prompt attention in other republican capitals: by October—only four months later—similar legislation establishing the supremacy of local laws over those of the Soviet Union was passed by the Ukrainian parliament. Neither Yeltsin nor any other senior official of the Russian Republic expressed concern.

Two years later, the then-president of Ukraine, Leonid Kravchuk, told Nixon and me in Kiev that Boris Yeltsin's drive for Russian sovereignty led him to believe for the first time that secession from the USSR was a credible option for Ukraine. More unusual events have occurred in history than Russia's leading Ukraine to independence, but not many.

Chapter Three

•

The Yeltsin Challenge

There is a strong case to be made that hegemony over the Soviet Union was not in Russia's long-term interest. Although Russia (including its Soviet incarnation) presided over one of the largest and most durable empires in history, its people paid an enormous economic, political, and moral price to build and maintain their huge monolithic state over the centuries. As a result, the burden of Russia's imperial greatness precluded it from developing into a normal, free, and prosperous country.

As observed by Vasily Klyuchevsky—perhaps the most perceptive and brutally honest Russian historian—"in our country as the territory expanded, as the nation's external strength increased, its internal freedom was constrained further and further. [Expansionist] activity demanded the suppression of the peoples' strength and growth in the scope of government powers in the conquered space while the uplifting power of the popular spirit declined. The new Russia's external successes resembled the flight of a bird, carried by the wind beyond the strength of its own wings."[1]

The search for new imperial glory abroad was an organic component of Russia's centuries-old despotism, which can be traced back to the country's very emergence as a unified independent state. In a letter to Tsar Basil III shortly after the fall of Constantinople in 1453, the abbot Philotheus (or Filofei) wrote that Muscovy was destined to become the "third Rome": "Be aware and accept O holy Tsar, that all Christian kingdoms have united into yours, that two Romes have fallen, but that the third stands and that there shall never be a fourth," he declared.[2] Russia, which had just liberated itself from two centuries of Mongol domination, found a new and extremely ambitious world mission. As the prominent twentieth-century Russian philosopher Nikolai Berdyayev observed, "The doctrine of Moscow as the third Rome became an ideological foundation of the Muscovy tsardom."[3] This messianic imperial urge became the lasting curse of Russian history and was complicated from the start by Russia's ethnic complexity. While the rest of the original Kievan Russia was under foreign (Polish and Lithuanian) control, Muscovy was quite successful in incorporating the Tatars and other nationalities located to the east and south of its territory.

In the sixteenth century, the financial and political requirements of Ivan the Terrible's endless military campaigns contributed to his despotic tendencies. In the eighteenth century, they added an absolutist dimension to Peter the Great's reforms and, later, slowed Catherine II's liberalizing impulses. In the nineteenth century, suppression of "internal" (as in the case of Poland in 1830 and 1863) and external revolts (as in Hungary in 1848) undermined the regime's inclination to introduce even modest civil liberties. Similarly, during the Soviet period, the need to crush rebellion in Hungary in 1956 and Czechoslovakia in 1968 reminded the regime that experiments with freedom could easily develop their own dangerous momentum.

While I was strongly opposed to the suppression of the Prague Spring at the time, I understood its essential geopolitical logic from the perspective of the Soviet leadership. After all, if global competition with the United States was important enough to risk military escalation in the Middle East, fight a proxy war against America in Vietnam, and send the Soviet navy into the Indian Ocean, how could one justify letting Czechoslovakia go its own way, threatening the Kremlin's domination of Central Europe in the process?

Still, beyond being a tragedy for Czechoslovakia, the intervention also had negative consequences in the Soviet Union. Frightened by the brief liberalization of a Soviet satellite, the regime was ultimately heartened by the relative ease with which brutal force proved effective as well as by the more-or-less complacent response of the outside world. Soviet leaders were thus encouraged to rely increasingly on coercion inside the USSR.

The economic cost of empire-building (and maintenance) was very high for Russia and later the Soviet Union. At the simplest level, constant financial support for a huge standing army brought tremendous hardship to

the Soviet people. But the costs did not stop there. Long before the Bolshe-
vik Revolution, Russian expansionism strained ties to the outside world and
became an obstacle to foreign investment and loans, to access to technology
and information, and to other unquantifiable but real benefits Russia could
have derived from being perceived as a normal member of the international
system.

Relatedly, unlike most other empires also created through the power of
arms rather than persuasion, Russia derived little material benefit from its
imperial possessions. This was a consequence of the fact that Russian empire-building was primarily driven by the needs of an absolutist government seeking to expand its reach, not an outward flow of merchants or
settlers. Its dynamics were precisely opposite to the building of the American nation.

It would be wrong to claim that there were no important economic or
demographic reasons behind what Harvard's distinguished Russian specialist Richard Pipes, who served as President Reagan's Soviet policy advisor,
described as the "relentless movement outward" that brought Russia "to oc-
cupy one-sixth of the earth's land surface."[4] The combination of a shortage
of arable land, population pressures, and a desire for access to open seas
and other international trade routes were important motivating factors behind Russia's territorial drive. Nevertheless, in relative terms, the degree to
which expansion was initiated by the autocratic state rather than society, to
which soldiers preceded traders and colonists, made the Russian experience
unusual in comparison with the United States and European powers, including other continental empires.

Conquests, of course, did not come without loot. The massive Soviet
expropriation of German and other Central European assets at the end of
World War II is a prime example of Russia's ability to extract resources
from its empire. But by the end of the Brezhnev era, faced with the choice
between subsidizing failing Communist regimes in Central Europe and suffering regular rebellions, the Kremlin had to settle for the former. The imperial nation—despised by its dependencies but lacking the will to impose
its preferences by force—was reconciled to bribing them into submission.

Inside the Soviet Union itself, the non-Russian republics were increasingly seen as a burden rather than an asset in analyses by Moscow economists in the late 1980s. Calculations publicized in the Moscow press made
the case that the other republics—notorious in Russia for their incompe-

tence and corruption—were allegedly receiving much more from the federal treasury than they contributed.

The prominent conservative economist A. A. Sergeyev argued that "as a result of the uneven exchange of [goods and commodities] inside the Soviet Union, Russia loses approximately 70 billion rubles each year from the total Soviet national income of 625 billion rubles. . . . The time has come to state loudly that Russia should feed itself first and foremost rather than feeding others at its own expense. . . . If Russia were to secede from the Soviet Union, it would become the richest country in the world in four years—even if oil and natural gas production and export decline."[5] Of course, few Russian economists went quite as far as Sergeyev. Nevertheless, at the time, the Russian Republic did produce over 90 percent of the USSR's total oil and timber output and 76 percent of its natural gas—and generated 80 percent of its hard currency revenues. A significant number of Russians—ordinary citizens and elites alike—began to feel that the Union was becoming a prohibitively expensive form of philanthropy. And facing increasingly apparent economic stagnation, if not decline, they were in a decidedly uncharitable mood.

Before long, not only constituent republics but individual provinces and even cities began to believe that the best answer to shortages and other economic problems was a series of tough protectionist measures against neighboring regions. As the Gorbachev leadership increasingly lacked both moral authority and the means to exercise effective control, the USSR descended into a "war of sovereignties" at every level of government. One Moscow city district even went so far as to attempt to ban aircraft from flying in its "sovereign" airspace without obtaining special permission.

The federal government's response was weak and inconsistent. The leadership opposed demands for meaningful sovereignty from the Union republics; yet, Gorbachev was not above encouraging demands for greater independence from the so-called autonomous republics, nominally self-governing regions within the Union republics, to demonstrate to Yeltsin and other republican leaders that the center could outflank them in the battle for sovereignty.

But by threatening to undermine the republics' cohesion, Gorbachev's maneuvering only further alienated the republican establishments from the federal center—particularly as the center was clearly unable to provide assistance in overcoming growing economic problems. Further, Gorbachev's moves against the republican leaders—as was true of many of his reform efforts—were ultimately executed only halfheartedly, without any overarching strategic plan. In the end, Yeltsin found an effective response to Gorbachev's plan: he tried to portray himself as an even greater champion of regional autonomy. This culminated in the Russian leader's soon-to-be-famous proclamation during a speech in Ufa, the capital of the Bashkir Autonomous Republic, "Take as much sovereignty as you can stomach!"[6]

Setting aside the Yeltsin-Gorbachev struggle for power, there were legitimate reasons for the Russian government to doubt Gorbachev's ability to halt the Soviet economic slide, let alone to introduce meaningful reforms. In the summer of 1990, an effort to implement a far-reaching joint economic program under the auspices of both the Soviet Union and Russia fell victim to the Soviet president's indecisiveness. After indicating tentative support for the 500-Day Plan, developed under the leadership of the young reformist economist Grigory Yavlinsky, then a Russian Republic deputy prime minister, Gorbachev eventually refused to choose between the proposal and a much more conservative alternative put forward by Soviet prime minister Nikolai Ryzhkov. In vintage Gorbachev fashion, the Soviet leader ordered the creation of a commission to formulate a compromise between the two completely irreconcilable approaches. Both Yavlinsky and Ryzhkov were appalled—the former gave up all hope that the federal government could proceed with real reform and the latter resigned from that very government in disgust. It was soon apparent that Ryzhkov's replacement, Soviet finance minister Valentin Pavlov—a mediocre official and an alcoholic as well—was profoundly inadequate to the task that lay before him.

Thus, the personal ambitions of Yeltsin and his associates to lead the Russian Republic were not the only forces behind the Russian drive for sovereignty. For many Russians, there were real reasons to believe that being the "older brother" and the core of the empire was a mixed blessing at best. Yet, as it was hard to imagine a USSR without Russia, it was no less difficult to conceive of the Russian Republic going it alone—and abandoning the rest of the Soviet empire.

Russia and its empire had been inseparable for centuries. Sergei Witte, Russia's first constitutional prime minister and one of the few outstanding statesmen to emerge in the last decades of Tsarism, observed that "examining the maps of Russia's development since Riurik, any high school student would be convinced that during the thousand years of its existence, the great Russian empire was created gradually through the force of arms and other means as the Slavic tribes living in Russia slowly swallowed whole masses of other ethnic groups. That is how the Russian empire came to-gether—as a conglomerate of various nationalities—and as a result there is no 'Russia'; there is, rather, the Russian empire."[7]

The British, French, Spanish, and Portuguese empires were able to surrender their overseas colonial possessions without great damage to their identity. The ends of the multiethnic Ottoman and Austro-Hungarian empires were much more difficult; their disintegration was considerably more painful in the imperial center and also generated significant regional turmoil, which contributed to the origins of World War II. That disinte-gration was, however, imposed by the victors on the defeated—neither Vienna nor Constantinople sought to divest itself of its conquests. The Russian Empire fit in the same general category, but it did not suffer a devastating military defeat, as did the other two continental empires. De-spite its perceived hardships at the hands of the imperial center, the Rus-sian Republic was undisputedly the core of the empire and had far greater freedom of choice in determining the future of the Soviet Union. Further, although powerful forces pushed Russia to break away from the Soviet Union, Russia itself had an important stake in preventing the collapse of the empire—particularly its spontaneous, uncontrollable disintegration.

There was an element of truth to Russian claims that their republic was subsidizing the remainder of the Soviet Union. However, given that the prices of goods and services exchanged between republics were set arbi-trarily by government central planners, it would have been very difficult to make an informed judgment about who had done more for whom. Further, the USSR's other Union republics had their own economists who had done their own calculations, which, predictably, almost universally indicated that it was they—not the Russians—who were the real victims of the empire. Just as Russia's oil and natural gas were provided to the other republics at artificially low prices, so were Ukrainian grain, Uzbek cotton, and Georgian wine. Moreover, the planned economy created interdependence of the worst sort in which enterprises relied on distant suppliers for inputs often unavail-able anywhere else. Although evolving market mechanisms could gradually correct this and other inefficiencies of the Soviet economic system, those mechanisms were still in an embryonic stage in 1990–91. As a result, there

was no responsible alternative to Union-wide government regulation to initiate reform and save the Soviet economy. As Yavlinsky stated to the Russian parliament, his program "to get out of the crisis" required both
"sufficiently strong rule and support from the people." In his view, "not a
single republic could carry out on its own" the "major measures for financial stability" necessary to reverse the USSR's economic downturn.[8]

Borders established in large part under the direction of Josef Stalin and
his successors were also a problem for leaders of the Russian Republic
seeking to withdraw from the USSR. Dictated by the Communist regime
not to reflect demographic or economic realities, but rather to assure easier
governance from Moscow, Union republic borders appeared almost a non-
issue in the sovereignty debates of 1990 and 1991. But because Russia was
by far the largest republic and Russians were considered to be "at home"
throughout the USSR, the leadership frequently attached ethnically Russian
areas to other republics in order to bind those republics more firmly to the
Communist state and to assure a significant Russian presence as a tool of
central control through the machinery of the Communist Party. Thus, while
Union republics had been formally granted the right to secede in the Soviet
Constitution, there were no provisions to explain the mechanics of separation and, more important, the constitution also established the dominance of
the Communist Party. Needless to say, the Party was hostile to even the
slightest signs of nationalism (except, as previously noted, Russian nationalism) or separatism. Former Soviet leader Nikita Khrushchev would probably turn in his grave if he learned that his gift of Crimea—and its
overwhelmingly Russian population—to Ukraine in 1954 (ironically on the
occasion of the three hundredth anniversary of Ukraine's decision to give
its allegiance to the Russian tsardom) would result in Crimea's becoming
part of a new and different sovereign state.

A related problem was the effect of the disintegration of the Soviet
Union on the almost 26 million ethnic Russians and Russian-speakers living outside the borders of the Russian Republic. Many of them migrated to
other Soviet republics involuntarily when, for example, their enterprises
were moved there on the government's orders. In Stalin's time, abandoning
one's enterprise without permission led straight to the gulag; thus, moving
a factory usually meant moving its employees and their families as well.
For most, living as Russians in Tashkent or Riga was perfectly natural. As
all of the republics had been a part of the empire for centuries—with the

exception of the interlude of independence for the Baltic states from 1920 to 1940—Russians living outside the Russian Republic genuinely felt that they were at home anywhere in the USSR. In fact, Kiev and Riga, the capitals of Ukraine and Latvia, respectively, even had majority ethnic Russian populations. Russian was spoken in Kiev much more than Ukrainian, and habit was at least as important as official encouragement in that regard. If the other republics were to obtain genuine sovereignty, these 26 million would at best be forced to make a major adjustment.

Moreover, if Union republics were to gain independence, why should the autonomous republics and regions not be entitled to follow suit? Tatarstan, for example, was merely an autonomous republic, but it had a larger population and a greater tradition of statehood than the Estonian SSR.[9] The distinct population of Muslim Chechnya, which was incorporated into the empire in the nineteenth century after a long and bloody war and whose whole population was exiled by Stalin in retribution for alleged collaboration with the Germans during World War II, had no less reason to seek independence than largely Orthodox and Slavic Ukraine. The fact that the Communist regime gave some republics Union status and others only autonomous status would likely have little meaning to local nationalist movements if the Soviet state were to disintegrate. Thus, for the Russian Republic and its thirty-one autonomous republics and regions—many including large Muslim populations culturally quite different from the Russians—the collapse of the Soviet state could threaten Russia's own dismemberment.

Russian national identity was also a real complication. Few Russians identified themselves as Soviets; if asked about their identity, most would likely answer, "I am a Russian." However, identifying oneself as Russian did not at all mean being a resident of the Russian Republic. For Russians much more than other Soviet ethnic groups, the Soviet Union—the Russian Empire reincarnated—was their home. Thus, to Russians living in the Russian Republic, the republic was just an administrative entity inside the real, greater Russia.

This feeling was not restricted to ethnic Russians. For many millions of other Soviet subjects, particularly among the upwardly mobile, the Russian language, Russian history, Russian civilization, and Russian imperial greatness were their own. Like U.S. citizens of different ethnic and religious backgrounds who are proud to be called Americans, many non-Russians—even non-Slavs—grew to identify with the Russian Empire built in part by their ancestors and in which they themselves played prominent roles. Both before and after the revolution, some Russified ethnic elites had good reasons to consider the Russian Empire their own: the German and, to a lesser extent, Georgian aristocracies had intermarried with the Romanovs to a remarkable degree. Similarly, some of the greatest Russian generals, statesmen, and poets, including such icons as Aleksandr Pushkin and Mikhail Lermontov, were of non-Russian ancestry. Even Stalin himself—despite his promotion of Russian chauvinism—had his roots in the Georgian peasantry.

Finally, as tired as most Russians were of the burdens of empire, few were indifferent to the possible loss of their great-power status. Russia as just another state located between Europe and Asia would be an experience unprecedented since the early eighteenth-century conquests of Peter the Great. It was not simply an issue of Russian imperial pride—there were practical implications as well. As Witte wrote with frankness exceptional for a senior tsarist official: "In reality, what was the Russian Empire based on? It was based not just primarily, but exclusively on its army. Who created the Russian Empire, transforming the semi-Asiatic Muscovite tsardom into the most influential and dominant European power? The army's bayonets. The world did not bow before our culture, our bureaucratized church, or our wealth and prosperity. It bowed before our power. Once it appeared that we were not as strong as everyone thought, that Russia was a colossus on clay legs, the picture immediately changed. All our enemies—both internal and external—raised their heads and the neutrals ceased to give us their attention."[10]

Witte's observations in the aftermath of Russia's defeat by Japan in 1905 was very relevant to the Soviet predicament in the late 1980s. After Khrushchev's revelation of Stalin's crimes, the international Communist movement lost most of its appeal. And where Communist parties maintained significant popular support, such as in Italy and France, they were eager to distance themselves publicly from the Soviet Union. China—another Communist giant—was already by then a bitter foe. Moscow's international status was based almost entirely on raw power. If that power (or the willingness to use it) were to dissipate, especially if this occurred rapidly, Russia could face many old but enduring animosities without adequate means to defend its interests. Thus, to destroy the empire without damaging Russia in the process would be a most challenging task.

Given the complex interrelationship between the Russian Republic and the rest of the empire, Boris Yeltsin and his supporters had three realistic options when faced with growing disarray in the USSR.

First, they could try to change the Soviet Union without breaking it altogether. This would require working to expand their republic's prerogatives while cooperating, to the extent possible, with the Union authorities. Yeltsin would have to control his distaste for Gorbachev as long as the latter remained at the helm in order to protect the Union presidency, which was indispensable if the USSR—even in a considerably modified form—were to survive as a unified state. Whatever happened, the Baltic republics and perhaps Georgia (where, after the bloody suppression of popular demonstrations in April 1989, the mood decisively turned against Moscow) would probably have to be let go. But, with Russian support, the rest of the Union was not beyond salvation. Liberalizing impulses triggered by Gorbachev would eventually force him to call an election in which the much more popular Yeltsin would have an excellent chance to become Soviet president. Then Yeltsin would have an opportunity to reshape the remaining Union in a more democratic fashion.

The second option was to say that the train had left the station and the Soviet Union could and should no longer be preserved. The Russian Republic should then urgently address such issues as how to replace administrative borders between Union republics with stable frontiers between independent states, how to arrange a relatively painless division of the huge Soviet estate, including the armed forces and the still largely centrally planned economy, and what kind of arrangements to make for Russian residents of other Union republics. Deliberate discussions involving the central government, Russia, and the other republics would be required to negotiate an amicable divorce among the components of the empire. The British withdrawal from India and the French departure from Algeria demonstrate how difficult it is to manage a smooth disengagement with even the most careful diplomacy. And neither India nor Algeria was as important to its imperial center as Ukraine was to the Russian Empire.

The final option was to improvise and hope for the best. This option was based on the assumption that whatever was to happen to the Soviet Union, the other republics would realize that going it alone without Russia simply would not work. From this perspective, nationalists in the other Union republics would appreciate the Russian role in the destruction of the

USSR and would view post-Communist Russia as a key ally in a common struggle rather than as the heir-apparent of "the evil empire" with which they had had so many tragic experiences. Then, fairly soon, the other republics would accept Russia as the first among equals—because of its size and power—and would voluntarily form a new union with Russia as its core.

One of the leading proponents of this approach, Sergei Shakhrai, then chairman of the Russian parliament's Legislation Committee and a close Yeltsin advisor, explained in a radio interview that "a strong Union, a strong center is possible as a process, is possible as a unification, a voluntary unification of the efforts of the Union Republics." He made clear, however, that in order for this "more powerful center" to be established, the old Soviet center must first be destroyed.[11]

On the surface, the third scenario—the creation of a revitalized Union—appeared perfectly plausible at the time. Economically, the constraints of interdependence were significantly greater for the other republics than the much larger, wealthier Russia. Politically, in 1990 the vast majority of republican governments were still controlled by Communist Party functionaries whose sole legitimacy was based on the continuing existence of some form of unified state. As regional opposition movements were fairly weak—except in the Baltic republics, western Ukraine, and Georgia—the Russian "democrats" led by Yeltsin appeared to be natural allies for local nationalists against both the Soviet government in Moscow and their own Communist elites.

Similarly, in Russia, many former dissidents and liberal intellectuals who became involved in high politics during perestroika felt more comfortable with nationalist activists than with their own Communist elite. In the Soviet Congress of People's Deputies in Moscow, nationalists from the republics generally worked hand in hand with Yeltsin's supporters as members of the so-called Interregional Group.

Early Russian optimism about an easy understanding with the republics was partly a function of Russians' inexperience with democratic politics. Had the Soviet Union possessed competing political parties, genuine freedom of the press, and independent nongovernmental policy analysts, it is likely that Russian politicians and experts would have questioned whether newly sovereign former Soviet republics would again be prepared to accept Moscow's dominance—only in the name of Great Russia rather than international communism. They would likely also have asked what else—that is, what beyond the economic support Russians did not want to provide—the new Moscow could offer them in return for accepting continued hegemony. Or how the historically brief tactical alliance with Russia's democrats could overcome centuries of abuse under tsarist and Soviet rule. Finally, they would surely have wondered why, on discovering Russia's democratic transition on the one hand, and its selfish disregard of fellow republics' economic interests on the other, the republican Communist establishments would not quickly decide to replace Marxist-Leninist ideology with new nationalist slogans in order to reinvent themselves and remain in power.

In the excitement of the political struggle against the Gorbachev leadership, however, these and other obvious but uncomfortable questions were rarely asked and even more rarely taken seriously. Pro-Union politicians such as Prime Minister Ryzhkov charged that "in essence the Russian leadership is pretending to become the center of power instead of all currently existing state structures," questioned whether the other republics would tolerate such an approach, and argued that it could "lead to the collapse of the state which was created over centuries." But these and other warnings were dismissed as predictable complaints from unreconstructed conservatives.[12] In the absence of a tradition of responsible public decision-making, analytical thinking and common-sense approaches were rare on all sides in the USSR's political battles. Instead of this careful analysis and strategic planning, Yeltsin and his followers preferred to rely on a combination of morality and fatalism typical of the Russian political mind-set for centuries. They were certain that their cause was just and were equally certain that somehow, some way, things were supposed to work out. Failure would only have confirmed that the goal was unachievable—that no one can prevail against the forces of nature. Yeltsin himself displayed this fatalism at the conclusion of his first book of memoirs, writing, "Our huge country is balanced on a razor's edge, and nobody knows what will happen to it tomorrow."[13] Yeltsin did not acknowledge, however, that his own conduct was an essential component in continuing—or destroying—that balance.

Yeltsin cannot be faulted for failing to support Mikhail Gorbachev's efforts to maintain the unity of the USSR. Short of widespread reliance on overwhelming force, those efforts—at least in the Baltics—were probably doomed by 1990 anyway. In any event, such a use of force by Gorbachev would have turned back the clock in Russia, too—the Soviet leader had already formed a tacit alliance with the power ministries (the Ministries of Defense and Interior and the KGB) and, to stay in office, would have been forced into greater dependence on them as well as on the remnants of the Communist Party apparat. This could not but have been a major setback for economic and political reform in the Russian Republic and, of course, the Soviet Union as a whole.

Yeltsin did not, however, simply fail to support Gorbachev. Instead, he consistently backed other Union republics' efforts to establish sovereignty without making the slightest effort to negotiate arrangements to protect Russian interests against the likely consequences. When the Soviet president criticized legislators in the Moldavian SSR for their separatist stand, Yeltsin quickly replied that "this is not the first mistake of the President, especially in questions of relations with the republics, with sovereign states which have already declared their sovereignty."[14] Similarly, Yeltsin denounced the Soviet use of force to quell protests in Lithuania in January 1991 and even went so far as to call on Russian soldiers in the Baltic republics to refuse to participate in moves against pro-independence government bodies.[15] Yeltsin thus greatly emboldened politicians in the republics in their drive for secession. Baltic political leaders in particular saw Yeltsin's election to the Russian presidency as possibly the most significant single development in their push for independence. As one Estonian legislator said after Yeltsin's June 1990 election, "Pressure from the West . . . may have helped, but the decisive factor was the victory of democratic forces [led by Yeltsin] in the Russian republic."[16]

Yeltsin's continuing personal conflict with Mikhail Gorbachev was, of course, also a determinant of the Russian president's course. "But why hide it," Yeltsin later wrote in his memoirs, "the motivations for many of my actions were embedded in our conflict."[17] Despite his personal battle with Gorbachev, Yeltsin may have been on the right side of history in understanding the futility of efforts to preserve the Soviet Union. Nevertheless, the Russian leader did not have the foresight to recognize the likely consequences of disintegration. As he himself later wrote, in reference to a 1991 conference at Novo Ogarevo to create a new Union Treaty, "With the existence of the two centers, two poles, the Soviet Union and Russia, everyone else found it convenient to choose their own position and maneuver between the two centers."[18] But what would happen when one of the centers was destroyed? Yeltsin did not ask himself why, when the Union was no longer there, other republican leaders would continue to accept Russia's role as the self-appointed hegemon.

Perhaps more important, the Russian president did not think carefully about how to overcome republican leaders' inevitable suspicions that once Gorbachev and the USSR were finished, Russia would be tempted to resume its role as "elder brother." In fact, at Novo Ogarevo, Yeltsin unwittingly encouraged those very sentiments. In a revealing discussion of events at and away from the negotiating table, Yeltsin describes how his security staff "defended Russia's interests" after one long day of meetings by driving his limousine around the long line of vehicles belonging to the other republican leaders to ensure that Yeltsin's car would be first in the departure procession (after having been the first on each previous day as well).[19]

Although Yeltsin seemed oblivious to the consequences of his reflexive "Russia first" approach, its implications were surely not unnoticed by other republican leaders, who found it offensive. For example, about a year later in Kiev, another participant in the talks—Ukrainian president Leonid Kravchuk—explained to Nixon and myself that "Yeltsin is probably Ukraine's best hope to develop normal relations with Russia, but even he has a tendency to talk to us as if he were the tsar."

From the American standpoint, Gorbachev and Yeltsin represented two distinctly different political courses: one wanted to give the Soviet Communist empire a last chance, while the other wanted to bury the empire once and for all. Similarly, in foreign policy, Gorbachev—despite his role in ending Soviet domination of Central Europe and his acquiescence in the coalition war against Iraq—clearly believed that the USSR could and should remain a global superpower. Yeltsin, in contrast, implied that he was willing to accept a considerably more modest international role through his support of other republics' aspirations toward independence.

Of course, as in any complex political situation, there were many important nuances to these broad outlines. For example, Gorbachev was subjectively an honest man who simply did not believe that all possible means were justified in preserving the Soviet state. In fact, he sought to replace the USSR with a new and different union in which the old repressive methods would never again be used. Conversely, while Yeltsin was clearly more willing to destroy the empire, his view of democracy seemed disturbingly similar to other "democrats" around the world who believed in "one man, one vote, one time" as a device to attain power. As Sakharov feared, for the

Russian leader, democracy and the end of the Soviet state appeared too often to be no more than tools in his bitter struggle for power.

But regardless of Yeltsin's ambitions for the post-Soviet period, in the
absence of the old imperial center and its coercive machinery, it was unlikely that whoever was in charge in Russia—or if it proved feasible, in a
new post-Soviet confederation—would be able to act on serious great-
power aspirations for quite some time. From this perspective, either an independent Russia or a reconstructed, nonrepressive non-Communist
union—both outcomes promoted by Yeltsin—would have been a favorable
development with respect to U.S. interests.

Nevertheless, speculation about Yeltsin's objectives for Russia could
not be the principal consideration in evaluating the relative benefits for the
United States of alternative Soviet futures. There was simply no way of
knowing how the Russian leader would evolve after gaining real power.
Yeltsin's earlier transformation demonstrated a considerable capacity to
learn and to grow, but it left many questions unanswered, such as his commitment to democracy and his ability to become an architect of the new
Russia.

In the turbulent, transforming Soviet Union, Mikhail Gorbachev was
still viewed by most Western governments as the best hope for political
stability in the USSR—which, despite Gorbachev's apparent good intentions, was still a nation with tens of thousands of nuclear warheads, numerous nuclear power stations, and stockpiles of chemical and biological
weapons possibly at risk in any domestic upheaval. By 1990, however, it
was apparent that Gorbachev's strategy of orderly evolution directed from
above was no longer sufficient and that events had overtaken the Soviet
president. By the fall, after the fiasco of the 500-Day Plan signified the
general failure of economic reform, Gorbachev had become a leader without a clear program or reliable allies. He also seemed to have lost the less
tangible but crucial sense of self-confidence without which no statesman
can truly lead in a time of great uncertainty. And his uncoordinated, reac-
tive attempts to quell nationalist sentiments in the republics went only far
enough to irritate opposition leaders without intimidating them. As a result—despite perceptions in the West—Gorbachev's leadership was
slowly becoming a destabilizing factor. I began increasingly to believe
that the only way to prevent the growing disorder from developing into a
full-scale civil war was to bet on those, like Yeltsin, who were moving

with the flow of history—and against those, like Gorbachev, who wanted to stop it.[20]

Nixon had a similar opinion. He wrote a note to me complimenting an October 1990 *Washington Post* article I had written to present this perspective. Nixon also expressed concern that "we seem to be basing our policy toward the Soviet Union on the assumption that Gorbachev's popularity abroad would shore up his declining support at home. This happens to an extent in the United States and other Western countries, but I doubt if it has any significant impact on the great masses of the long suffering Soviet people."[21] We met shortly thereafter, during one of Nixon's visits to Washington, and agreed that U.S. efforts to help Gorbachev when it was already too late needlessly and dangerously prolonged the agony of the disintegrating USSR. "It's like giving painkillers to a cancer patient as a substitute for radical surgery," Nixon said.

Nixon was also a strong believer, whenever possible, in hardheaded détente, the merits of which he tried to demonstrate to the Reagan administration when it seemed committed to an all-out crusade against the Soviet empire.[22] And Nixon had true respect for Gorbachev as well, whom he considered a different kind of Soviet politician—especially after the benign Soviet response to the collapse of communism in Central Europe.[23] In fact, on a personal level, he was impressed by the Soviet leader's intelligence and vigor after meeting Gorbachev during a short visit to the USSR in 1986.

But on issues of international grand strategy, Nixon had no use for misplaced sentimentality toward policies or people—and there was no grander challenge to the United States on Nixon's mind than how to handle the profound transformation of the USSR. Contrary to his public image, Richard Nixon was a sentimental man who was very proud of and protective of his family and fierce in his support of those of his associates whom he considered to be genuinely loyal to him, particularly his younger protégés. He also believed firmly in the importance of American values in foreign policy—as indicated by his admiration for Woodrow Wilson—and that the United States should stand for more than its narrow trade and economic concerns. Nevertheless, when approaching international issues of seminal importance to U.S. interests, he always asked first how possible outcomes would affect the United States. It was through that prism that Nixon assessed the dramatic competition between Yeltsin and Gorbachev. And in his view, betting on Gorbachev against Yeltsin—as the Bush administration seemed to do—appeared increasingly to be betting on the past against the future.

During the summer of 1990, the idea of a "grand compromise"—offering Gorbachev a multibillion-dollar aid package in exchange for radical reform—was gaining broad acceptance in the U.S. foreign policy community. Promoted by Harvard professor Graham Allison, whom Nixon knew and respected, and the aforementioned Russian economist Grigory Yavlinsky, the concept also had strong supporters inside the Bush administration. Both proponents and opponents of the grand compromise approached Nixon to enlist his support; typically, the former president wanted to hear all of the arguments and think hard before making a decision.

When Nixon talked to me about the idea of a grand compromise, he gave particular attention to the composition of the Soviet leadership. At the time, it included prominent reactionaries such as Defense Minister Dmitri Yazov, Interior Minister Boris Pugo, and KGB chairman Vladimir Kryuchkov, all of whom had been brought in by Gorbachev himself (and all of whom would ultimately attempt to oust the Soviet leader in the failed August 1991 coup attempt). Was this the leadership that the United States was being asked to support? We also noticed that while Gorbachev sent the young Yavlinsky to Washington as his semiofficial emissary to impress the Bush administration with his commitment to radical reform, he also sent Yevgeny Primakov on the same mission as Yavlinsky's superior. Then a member of Gorbachev's Security Council, Primakov was not a reactionary himself, but was linked to the past much more strongly than Yavlinsky. So, we asked, would U.S. acceptance of a grand compromise promote change in the Soviet Union or, on the contrary, would it delay the USSR's tough choices, helping anti-Western Soviet conservatives and risking a greater crisis later?

Nixon and I eventually agreed that on balance the grand compromise would inevitably involve the United States too deeply in the USSR's unstable, unpredictable political process—and probably on the wrong side. "So," Nixon said, "Gorbachev really wants to snooker us with this Yavlinsky fellow, who sounds too good to be true. What we should say is that it is not a grand compromise but a grand robbery and then we should oppose it every way we can." I told Nixon that from what I had heard from Bush administration officials, no decision had yet been made and that Nixon's position could influence the decision, particularly if he were to make clear that he would vigorously exploit the "grand robbery" line if a compromise were announced. "So you think they would be afraid of me," Nixon said with a smile. "You think that Bush and Scowcroft wouldn't want me to blast them for being soft on Gorbachev?"

"Absolutely, Mr. President," I answered, "and I don't think you will have to blast them if you make it clear in private and through important friends on the Hill what the administration would be up against if they adopt this grand compromise nonsense."

"That's exactly right," Nixon responded. "Make clear to our friends in Washington where I stand."

I told the former president that I would call several people right away to inform them of his views, including Ed Hewitt, then the senior Soviet specialist at the National Security Council, and Nixon's long-time confidant Robert Ellsworth, a former Republican congressman from Kansas and key advisor to Senator Robert Dole.

In the end, the "grand compromise" never happened. It was killed by Gorbachev's own political zigzags inside the Soviet Union. And other major voices in American politics, such as influential Democratic senator Bill Bradley, also argued that the United States "should support perestroika, but shouldn't pay for it." But Nixon believed—correctly, in my view—that his strong opposition had also made a difference. He was again in the arena, having an influence on events, and loving every second of it.

It was against this background of Nixon exercising renewed influence in the grand compromise debate that I proposed his trip to the Soviet Union in early 1991. I was convinced that he was the right man to assess the situation in the USSR and that he could have a unique impact on the American policy debate. I also knew, however, that I was accepting an enormous responsibility in suggesting such a trip to a seventy-eight-year-old man who, while superb intellectually, was not in the best physical health and who certainly did not need to suffer further disappointments at that stage of his life.

If Nixon could spend enough time in the USSR to meet with all of the key political players, both in Moscow and in the republics, and share his evaluation with President Bush, the Congress, and the American people, he could perform an important public service in a time of great confusion in the United States about matters Soviet. But precisely because we were discussing such a uniquely comprehensive effort, focusing on not only the central government but the competing Russian government as well—and

including a firsthand look at rebellious republics—the potential for trouble
was a serious concern. Would Gorbachev agree to see Nixon if he knew of
Nixon's plans to meet with Yeltsin and to visit secessionist republics? And
what would happen once Nixon visited the republican capitals? Could he
be viewed as inciting dangerous unrest for personal glorification? Finally,
would the Bush administration give at least tacit approval to the trip, which
could work at cross-purposes to its own policy of treating Gorbachev as the
best hope for the Soviet Union? The more ambitious the trip, the greater
was the potential that somehow, somewhere, Nixon would face embarrassment or worse in the chaotic Soviet Union.

Such thoughts must have occurred to Nixon, too. After all, I had proposed the idea and was expected to play a key role in arranging the trip. A
great deal would depend on my contacts, judgment, and personal commitment to him. But all that Nixon knew about me was that he found me a
good Russia analyst and an interesting intellectual interlocutor, and that I
was one of many people in Washington who liked to have access to, and
particularly to have an impact upon, an influential former president. With so
much at stake for Nixon, I realized that accepting my proposal to go to the
Soviet Union could only be an exercise of faith and his renowned intuition.
Ultimately, his decision was natural and graceful. He never implied the obvious: that the trip was probably more his favor to me than vice versa. This
made me grateful for his confidence in me and, more important, truly impressed that at almost eighty, with all the baggage of his life's experiences,
he had the courage to take such a trip and risk a public failure if he accomplished little or nothing.

Chapter Four

•

Russia Is Reborn

While Nixon planned his March 1991 trip to the Soviet Union, the USSR was reaching its moment of truth. The cumulative impact of the delegitimization of the regime, the decline of the authority of the Communist Party, the rise in assertiveness of the republics, and the growth in momentum of democratization precluded a return to the old system built by Lenin and Stalin across eleven time zones. But while there could be no return to the past, the Soviet future was uncertain—there were still several conceivable outcomes.

The prevailing view in the United States at the time was that the greatest threat to continued reform in the USSR came from Soviet conservatives and their influence over Gorbachev. Thus, the first scenario was that the conservatives would oust Gorbachev and crack down or that the Soviet leader would give up on reform—at least temporarily—to stay in power and form an alliance with the conservatives to try to manage a repressive reversal himself. The second possibility was also obvious: the total disintegration of the USSR with full statehood for each of its Union republics. This was the direction in which events were already moving. The third potential path was much more fearsome both within the Soviet Union and beyond its borders: bloody civil war in a country with large stocks of the most modern and devastating weapons in the world—nuclear, chemical, biological, and conventional—and no less dangerous civilian targets, including nuclear power stations. As a final option, Gorbachev could realize that Yeltsin held most of the cards and cut a deal with the Russian leader in which the two would manage a transition to a new, post-Soviet confederation (perhaps without the particularly recalcitrant Baltic states). Gorbachev may have been able to gain extended tenure in office in exchange for recognizing Russia's (and, of course, his rival Yeltsin's) predominance in a reformed state.

Although the attempted coup in August 1991 quickly failed, the possibility of a successful brutal crackdown with Gorbachev's acquiescence—a variant of the first possible future for the USSR—could not be ruled out earlier in the year. After all, in early 1991 the military and security services were still loyal to the regime and, to that point, there had been no major incidents in which soldiers refused to obey the orders of their commanders. Further, despite the growing disarray in the Soviet Union, army, KGB, and Interior Ministry units were still fairly well trained and supplied. Also, with a few exceptions—such as the Armenian militia in Nagorno-Karabakh—there were simply no military formations under the control of republican leaders that could challenge federal forces.

The path down which the Soviet Union would ultimately move depended upon a series of complex and often intangible factors. One of the biggest unknowns was Gorbachev himself. It was already clear that the Soviet leader had initiated the process of perestroika without a real action plan. Similarly, it was apparent that he was a man of good intentions who, while reluctant to spill blood, still struggled intellectually and emotionally with many doctrines and practices of the past from which he could not break free. By the beginning of 1991, however, Gorbachev could little afford to continue procrastinating in resolving his internal debate: his room for maneuver was shrinking daily and the price of inaction was becoming prohibitive.

There was still a chance that Gorbachev would, despite himself, take decisive action. The Soviet leader even had a contemporary example to follow: the other great Communist reformer of the 1980s, Chinese leader Deng Xiao-ping, had launched the brutal crackdown at Tiananmen Square just two years earlier in 1989—shortly after Gorbachev visited Beijing. Perhaps no less significant, Russian history also provided an example of an autocrat-turned-reformer who opted to restore some traditional repressive methods when his reforms developed uncontrollable momentum—Tsar Alexander II.

In 1861, Alexander II granted freedom to Russia's serfs. Shortly thereafter, he established his country's first independent judiciary, created the
zemstvo system of rudimentary local self-government, and expanded press
freedoms. Remarkably, like Gorbachev, Alexander II was not known as a
reformer prior to his ascension to supreme power; on the contrary, he ap-
plauded the suppression of the Hungarian Rebellion of 1848 by his father
Nicholas I.[1] Prior to his coronation in 1855, Alexander II was, if anything,
considered more reactionary than his notoriously conservative father in his
views on the institution of serfdom.

But Russia's humiliating defeat at the hands of Britain, France, Turkey,
and their allies in the Crimean War (1853–56) changed everything for
Alexander II. As the important prerevolutionary historian A. A. Kornilov
wrote, he understood immediately that "drastic changes were necessary in
the name of saving and strengthening the power of the Russian state without which, as the conduct of the Crimean War demonstrated, the state
would be totally undermined by the course of events."[2]

Gorbachev reacted similarly to the Soviet fiasco in Afghanistan and
what it told him about the overall state of the Soviet system. Commendably,
after witnessing the totalitarian excesses of his predecessors, he made a
great effort to avoid repressive methods—particularly, spilling blood on a
massive scale. Nevertheless, whatever his noble instincts, there was still the
possibility that, when pushed into a corner, the Soviet leader would resort to
a temporary alliance with the reactionaries and strike back. Alexander II,
whom Gorbachev reputedly admired, did precisely that when the Poles exploited his relaxation of controls to arm themselves and demand independence as well as when liberal trends in Russia itself began to threaten the
very foundations of the absolute monarchy. The tsar brutally repressed the
Polish rebellion and restored a series of state controls over Russian political
life. Would history repeat itself?

There is no question that the Soviet president was tempted to flex his
military muscle. By the beginning of 1991, Gorbachev—like Alexander II
over a century earlier—could not fail to recognize that the unintended consequences of his reforms were tearing apart his political system and, indeed, his country. A contemporary play on words summarized the state of
Soviet society with the phrase *Posle perestroiki, budet perestrelka*—"After
perestroika, there will be a shoot-out."

And faced with the apparently imminent collapse of the entire Soviet system, the use of the iron fist—one of the few instruments still under firm central government control—had to have been one of the few available options. Turning to force, however, also meant turning to the power ministers, the only individuals who could deliver the military and security services to the president, to form a tactical alliance.

This happened in late 1990, when Defense Minister Dmitri Yazov, KGB chairman Vladimir Kryuchkov, and Interior Minister Boris Pugo (all future junta members) replaced Soviet foreign minister Eduard Shevardnadze and Aleksandr Yakovlev as Gorbachev's closest associates. Sensing the changing political winds, Shevardnadze resigned dramatically in December, publicly warning that "dictatorship is coming." At about the same time, Yakovlev was ousted from the decision-making Presidential Council after being vilified by the Soviet conservatives.[3] Although Gorbachev soon appointed Yakovlev to head his panel of advisors, the president's former alter ego found himself in a prestigious position with little real power. And Gorbachev's relations with the future coup plotters were not based solely on political expediency: as the Soviet president himself admitted, at the time he also had great trust in each of them—particularly General Yazov, whom he considered a straight shooter.[4]

Gorbachev's reliance on the power ministers had practical implications. This was quickly evident in the beginning of January 1991 when predominantly ethnic Russian pro-Moscow demonstrators surrounded the parliament building in Vilnius, the capital of the increasingly rebellious Lithuania. The protests, which provoked anti-Moscow counterdemonstrations, were used as an excuse by Yazov, Kryuchkov, and Pugo to send additional security forces to Vilnius, including the KGB's notorious Alfa antiterrorist team. The new units, in cooperation with the Vilnius military garrison, seized the city's television broadcasting center in a deadly shootout and surrounded the Lithuanian parliament building on January 13.

The Soviet president immediately denied having any knowledge of or responsibility for the attacks. Nevertheless, not a single individual was punished for the "unauthorized actions" and a similar display of force soon took place in Riga, the capital of neighboring Latvia. It became difficult to believe that Gorbachev had not at a minimum tacitly approved the bloodletting in the Baltics.

The violence in Vilnius and Riga seemed to demonstrate a new willingness to use force against peaceful opponents of the regime. When viewed alongside the increasing power of reactionaries in the Soviet leadership, January's events raised new questions about Gorbachev's intentions. Had the Soviet president finally decided to follow the example of Alexander II? This question, whether there was a new Gorbachev less committed to democracy and more willing to use force—and thus, whether the USSR would move toward the first, and short of civil war the darkest, of its possible futures—was one of the most important questions Nixon hoped to address during his fact-finding mission to the Soviet Union.

•   •   •

The uncertainty regarding Gorbachev's intentions made a meeting with the Soviet president a priority for Nixon. However, Nixon's other, no less important priorities—to meet with the newly powerful Russian leader Boris Yeltsin and to examine firsthand developments in the USSR's independence-minded republics—would make the meeting difficult to arrange. Because Nixon's visit came at such a sensitive time for Gorbachev, the Soviet president and his aides could not avoid seeing the trip first and foremost as a political event. As a result, there was a danger that if Gorbachev and his staff had the impression that Nixon might aid their opponents, they would be reluctant to increase the visibility of his visit by granting a presidential audience. Conversely however, traveling to the USSR to meet only with Gorbachev and other officials of the central government could hardly provide the former president a balanced picture of developments in the Soviet Union which, after all, were less under the control of the Soviet regime each day.

The lukewarm attitude of the Bush administration toward the trip further complicated the matter. Nixon made clear to me that he did not want to go to the Soviet Union if the administration had any objections to his visit. The former president was not only reluctant to appear too obviously at cross-purposes with official U.S. policy, he was also very practical—he realized that even the appearance of disapproval from the administration could drastically reduce his chances of seeing Gorbachev and undermine the status of the trip before it even began.

After some carefully calculated maneuverings, Nixon phoned me in March to say that he had just received a call from Bush's national security advisor, Brent Scowcroft, who said that since the former president planned to travel as a private citizen, the White House had no objection to his trip to the USSR and would be interested in his findings. The administration had not given a ringing endorsement or an offer of help—merely the minimum necessary to proceed.

After some initial hesitation that I managed to overcome, U.S. ambassador Jack Matlock agreed to greet Nixon at the Moscow airport and briefed Nixon as well. Nevertheless, while Matlock's highly visible presence at the airport was certainly good news, we quickly discovered that Nixon's meeting with Gorbachev could not be taken for granted. Viktor Kuvaldin, a former IMEMO colleague of mine then serving as an aide to Gorbachev, said that the Soviet president considered Nixon's visit "unhelpful" because of his intention to see Yeltsin and visit the republics.

As it stood, no one had said directly that Gorbachev would not see Nixon, but the implications were not good. We decided on a series of steps to increase the pressure on the Soviet leader. First, I distributed to our contacts in Moscow a photocopy of a *U.S. News & World Report* article describing the importance of Nixon's advice to Bush. The article, entitled "Nixon's the One for Bush," emphasized Nixon's frequent contact with Bush and Bush's trust in the former president.[5] I then explained privately to everyone I could reach who had access to Gorbachev that if the Soviet leader did not see Nixon, the former president would have no choice but to rely on the assessments of Gorbachev's conduct provided by others when he shared his views of the Soviet situation with President Bush, the Congress, and the American media. I added, in graphic terms, that these assessments—including that of the Russian president—could hardly be helpful to Gorbachev's image in the United States. Finally, with Nixon's permission, I told several reporters covering Nixon's arrival that we had received "not so subtle signals" from Gorbachev's staff that Nixon might not get a meeting with the Soviet leader if he saw Yeltsin and other republican leaders pushing for independence. I also told them that Nixon would not sacrifice any of his meetings "just to curry favor" with Gorbachev.[6] In addition to creating public pressure on Gorbachev, this helped to prepare our fallback position if no meeting took place—that Nixon was standing tall in Moscow even at the expense of an appointment with the Soviet president. Remarkably, although he was anxious about the meeting, Nixon never seriously contemplated appeasing Gorbachev by canceling the trips to the republics and giving up on the session with Yeltsin.

With important assistance and wise counsel from advisor Robert Ellsworth, a former deputy secretary of defense and ambassador to NATO, and chief of staff John Taylor, Nixon eventually accomplished everything he had hoped to do and more in his two weeks in the Soviet Union. He had lengthy meetings with Gorbachev and Yeltsin, he went beyond Moscow to visit Ukraine, Lithuania, and Georgia, and he had a series of conversations with both the conservatives and the reformers in the Soviet leadership. Nixon also saw how real people were affected by the Soviet Union's growing turmoil during visits to shops, farmers' markets, and—for the first time since he began traveling to the USSR as Eisenhower's vice president—private citizens' apartments.

These discussions were often among the most interesting for the former president. While proud of his ability to be brutal when important American interests were at stake—and even bragging in private conversations about his willingness to do whatever was necessary to get foreign policy results—Nixon was broad-minded about and interested in other cultures. China and Russia were his principal interests outside Western civilization; I was very impressed by Nixon's familiarity with Russian history and literature. He was able to engage in sophisticated conversations about issues as far-ranging as the rule of Tsar Peter the Great and the merits of Alexander Pushkin's poetry.

I was particularly intrigued to notice during several meetings with Russian officials that Nixon seemed to understand at least the main thrust of what was said to him before hearing the English translation. Nixon did not speak Russian, but he admitted to me after I mentioned my observation that he had had Russian language training before his first trip to the Soviet Union, in 1959, and that he took Russian lessons for a time thereafter. "You know, Dimitri," he said, "I like to hear what people are saying firsthand. I can't get the nuances in Russian, but I can get the message, and I like to hear it in their own voices with all of the intonation. When I dealt with Brezhnev and had to evaluate his sincerity, his intonation was sometimes more important than what he actually said. But we're not going to tell this to anyone, right?"

The meetings were generally "good news"; the answer to the question of whether the USSR was led by a new, less humane and more conservative Gorbachev seemed to be in the negative. Soviet officials were predictably reassuring. "You are dealing with the same Gorbachev who initiated perestroika and wants to continue it," said Vice President Gennady Yanayev, who only five months later became the nominal leader of the anti-Gorbachev junta. Yevgeny Primakov was even more explicit: "We have the same Gorbachev. If I thought he was abandoning reform, I would not stay here another day."

The fairly optimistic appraisals of two of the Soviet president's closest pro-reform associates—Aleksandr Yakovlev and Eduard Shevardnadze—were particularly reassuring to Nixon. Although neither of the two remained in Gorbachev's inner circle, each expressed the view that the Soviet leader's conservative policies were primarily a tactical move to cope with the USSR's growing political and economic crises, which Gorbachev had no adequate strategy to address.

Ironically, conversations with conservatives in the leadership, including Yazov, Kryuchkov, and Pugo, confirmed the assessments of Yakovlev and Shevardnadze. Although they avoided open criticism of Gorbachev, the future junta members—particularly KGB head Kryuchkov—made clear that they were not happy with many of the Soviet president's policies. They were definitely not people who thought that they had Gorbachev in their collective pocket.

Finally, Nixon's one-on-one meeting with the Soviet president reinforced the conclusion that the same Mikhail Gorbachev was still in the Kremlin.[7] Their conversation lasted longer than expected—over an hour—and was both substantive and friendly. The Soviet president assured Nixon that he was still "dealing with the old Gorbachev. The course toward changing all forms of society's life remains." However, Gorbachev explained, "Firm authority supported by laws is necessary for democracy to function" and those republics determined to leave the Union should do so in accordance with the Soviet Constitution (of course, since the Soviet Constitution did not specify procedures for secession, this meant that the process would occur on Gorbachev's terms).[8] This sounded logical in the abstract but was totally unrealistic at the time when such clean, orderly solutions were no longer possible—particularly without Yeltsin's support, which the Soviet president seemed either unprepared or unable to secure.

The discussion essentially confirmed Nixon's instinctive impression of Gorbachev: that the Soviet president was a highly intelligent and basically decent person who simply did not have what was required to complete the historic process of the Soviet transformation. "It's really sad. History is so unfair to leaders," he said, thinking perhaps of himself as well. "You start the process, but you're not given an opportunity to finish it."

But the fact that it was basically the "old Gorbachev" who was still Soviet president had important consequences. It led first to the inescapable conclusion that, regardless of his constant tactical zigzags, Gorbachev would not ultimately join the conservatives in a massive, violent crackdown. And since nothing short of truly ruthless, full-scale suppression of nationalist and populist movements could stop the powerful centrifugal forces Gorbachev had unwittingly unleashed, a nationwide Soviet Tiananmen scenario was, for all practical purposes, impossible. The hard-liners may have been riding high, but they were not high enough to be safe from the tidal wave of Soviet change.

I saw the power of the wave in Moscow on March 28, when hundreds of thousands of demonstrators (100,000 according to official estimates, 500,000 according to the organizers) converged on central Moscow to protest Gorbachev's attempt—in cooperation with conservative Russian parliamentarians—to oust Boris Yeltsin from his chairmanship of the Russian Supreme Soviet. As in Vilnius, the government claimed that the demonstrators planned violence; in fact, official sources alleged that the protest's organizers intended to storm the Kremlin. Again as in Vilnius, the government called in the troops. Future coup leaders Prime Minister Valentin Pavlov and Interior Minister Boris Pugo threatened the demonstrators with a tough response.

However, despite strong words from Pavlov and Pugo, the organizers of the demonstration were not intimidated, in part because the marchers were joined by dozens of pro-reform deputies from both the Russian and Soviet parliaments. The deputies' presence—and that of numerous Western camera crews—doubtless restrained the government's hand, particularly as the demonstration was peaceful.

Ultimately, both sides claimed victory: the demonstrators because they were allowed to proceed, and the government because it prevented the rather unlikely sacking of the Kremlin. Nevertheless, the Russian public knew who had won—Gorbachev had tried again to cut Yeltsin down to size but had failed.

In the other Union republics, the Soviet federal government had even less influence over events. This loss of control by the center illustrated how far the Soviet Union had already moved down the second possible path—

the one that led to its complete disintegration. As Nixon discovered in Vilnius and Tblisi, the Georgian capital, the USSR was perilously close to reaching the point of no return along that path—in the republics, Moscow seemed to have no power at all beyond its continuing ability to harass and intimidate.

Nixon's visit to Vilnius came only two months after the last attempt at intimidation—the allegedly unauthorized assault on the Lithuanian capital's television broadcasting center and siege of its parliament building. The former president's visit had great political significance to the Lithuanian government, which dispatched a special aircraft to carry Nixon from Moscow and sent a delegation of senior officials, led by the vice chairman of the State Council, to meet him on his arrival. The potential political importance of the trip was not lost on Lithuania's citizens either: over 5,000 braved a late winter blizzard to see Nixon step off the airplane, and additional crowds lined the route along which his limousine traveled into the city. Of course, the Lithuanians did in fact have reasons to be genuinely delighted with Nixon's visit: he was surely the most distinguished American to visit Lithuania, and his arrival so soon after January's bloody events could easily be interpreted as a show of support—particularly as individual clashes still continued almost daily between elite police units (the so-called "Black Berets") and the regular police force, which was allied with the pro-independence republican government.

Nixon met with a wide range of Lithuanian political leaders, including parliament chairman Vytautas Landsbergis, Communist leader Algirdas Brazauskas, government ministers, and a number of ethnic Poles and Russians serving in the parliament. All of those whom he met shared a commitment to independence from Moscow and to resolving their differences through dialogue. He saw the Communist leader Brazauskas as a genuine "loyal opposition" to the Landsbergis government, and was greatly encouraged by the unity of purpose of the government, the Communist opposition, and Lithuania's ethnic minorities. After we left Lithuania, Nixon commented to me that anywhere that both Communists and anti-Communists talked about political pluralism and tolerance, democracy seemed to have a bright future.

Although Georgia was no less determined to win independence from Moscow than was Lithuania, the contrast between Nixon's experiences in Vilnius and those in Tblisi was great. One of the most significant differences was that between Vytautas Landsbergis and the Georgian president, Zviad Gamsakhurdia. Landsbergis was determined but sophisticated and judicious, while Gamsakhurdia appeared disturbingly simplistic and excessively excitable. The son of a classic Georgian author, Gamsakhurdia made a name for himself as a dissident in the 1970s. Although he was arrested and forced to confess publicly to his "anti-Soviet crimes," he managed to reemerge as a leading opposition figure in the 1980s. When a fellow dissident leader died in an automobile accident, Gamsakhurdia became the indisputable standard-bearer of Georgia's nationalist camp.

During his meeting with Nixon, Gamsakhurdia spoke at length about Soviet plots to undermine him and alleged that his political opponents in Georgia were on the KGB payroll. He also boasted that once Georgia gained its independence from Moscow, Tblisi would turn against Russia and cut it down to size. Gamsakhurdia's bravado did not make a favorable impression on Nixon, who decided that he was a demagogue and a political and intellectual lightweight. Still, it was clear that in Georgia, as in Lithuania, pro-independence individuals and groups were in full control—and that nothing short of an increasingly unlikely Soviet invasion could change that fact.

By 1991, any sense of imperial patriotism was significantly diminished in both Russia and the former Soviet Union.[9] After the stagnation and disillusionment of the Brezhnev period, the turmoil of Gorbachev's perestroika, and the humiliation of the Soviet withdrawal from Afghanistan in 1989, the Soviet people were simply too tired to fight to keep the Union together. Visiting the markets and shops of Moscow, Nixon himself sensed the changed mood of the people, whom he saw as beaten down and disgusted. During his previous visit, Nixon said, Muscovites "were not dressed as well but had much higher spirits." The Russian people were preoccupied with their own survival and that of their families and communities; they did not have the stomach to spend blood (especially that of their own sons) and treasure for the unity of the USSR, which had become little more than an abstraction to them.

But the fact that the increasingly powerful pro-independence movements in Georgia, Lithuania, and other Soviet republics did not push Gorbachev more firmly into the hard-liners' camp did not preclude his finding common ground with another of his powerful rivals, Boris Yeltsin, and saving at least something from the collapsing Soviet Union. While possible, however, that option would have required that Yeltsin accept a subordinate role, at least for a time. But it was not Yeltsin's style to defer his ambition—particularly in view of his intense resentment of Gorbachev. Also, cooperating with Yeltsin was anathema to the conservatives, who would not acquiesce to yet another political dance by Gorbachev—this time to their disadvantage.

Nixon received a strong warning of what was to come from none other than KGB chairman Vladimir Kryuchkov. At the conclusion of their hour-long meeting—which began with Kryuchkov telling Nixon that they were both victims of the liberal media—the former president politely told the KGB chairman that he had benefited from the meeting and that Kryuchkov was not merely a policeman but a geopolitical thinker in his own right. Then, when Nixon stood to offer his host a farewell handshake, Kryuchkov suddenly replied to Nixon's compliment, saying, "Yes. Some people believe I am doing too much thinking. I argue with Gorbachev too often." He added that one day the Soviet president could decide that he had had enough of these arguments and would dismiss him from his post.[10]

Nixon and I discussed the unusual conclusion to the Kryuchkov meeting, which we agreed was probably an attempt to send a message. This interpretation was soon confirmed by a curious episode with Aleksandr Zimin, our KGB handler, who called me in my hotel room after the meeting with Kryuchkov and wanted to see me urgently. After trying to get my assessment of Nixon's reaction to Kryuchkov, which I would not provide beyond sharing the former president's parting compliment to the chairman, Zimin volunteered that Kryuchkov had been quite impressed with the comprehensive nature of Nixon's program in the USSR—that Nixon was meeting not only with leaders in the reform movement and the rebellious republics but with their conservative political competitors as well. Strangely, he then sought to convince me that Nixon should meet Anatoly Lukyanov, who, although officially not a member of the August "Emergency Committee," was alleged to have masterminded the coup with Kryuchkov. Zimin told me that as a student of Soviet affairs, I should consider the possibility that Gorbachev and Yeltsin would eventually checkmate one another, "having exhausted their potential" and that there could then be a need for a "constitutional solution" (presumably with the full support of the KGB) in which Lukyanov, as chairman of the Supreme Soviet, could play a key role in removing Gorbachev from power.

Coming from the mouth of a KGB officer sworn to protect the Soviet state, this was incredible—especially when he confirmed that he was seeing me with Kryuchkov's knowledge and approval and that how widely I shared our conversation—with Nixon and, back in the United States, with Bush administration officials—was "my prerogative."

When I conveyed my conversation with Zimin to Nixon, he immediately understood the significance of Kryuchkov's message—but neither of us was entirely certain what it meant. Was it a signal to the Bush administration that an anti-Gorbachev conspiracy was underway? Or was it disinformation to substantiate Gorbachev's claims that he was not responsible for the hard-liners' actions? Or was it just a clumsy attempt to arrange a meeting with Lukyanov in order to have a greater impact on Nixon's thinking?

We agreed that it would be completely inappropriate for Nixon to seek a meeting with Lukyanov at the suggestion of the head of the KGB. We also agreed that I would share the episode with Ambassador Matlock, which I did. Later, after our return to the United States, I described the Zimin episode in some detail in an article in the *Washington Post*.[11] I also briefed Brent Scowcroft's aide Ed Hewitt and Fritz Ermarth, by then the chairman of the CIA's National Intelligence Council. Nixon himself described the incident in his conversation with President Bush in the White House on April 21.

Nevertheless, the Bush administration did not take this information seriously, perhaps because of its KGB origin. Only two months later, when Jack Matlock received an alarmist message to the same effect from Gavril Popov, a leading pro-reform politician who later became the mayor of Moscow, did the administration decide to warn the Soviet president (obviously to no avail). In retrospect, it is quite remarkable how easy it was to see the emerging anti-Gorbachev plot in Moscow. Yet, Gorbachev could not imagine that people whom he had appointed to key positions could move against him—despite the fact that he was contemplating getting rid of the whole conservative group in his cabinet. It was simply inconceivable to him that they would move first.

•   •   •

The fact that Gorbachev was quickly becoming history increasingly turned the spotlight to his rival, Boris Yeltsin. What kind of leader would Yeltsin be? Would his skill in political infighting and his remarkable chemistry with the Russian people be sufficient to make him a genuine nation-builder? Was his commitment to democracy merely a matter of convenience in his fight with Gorbachev and federal structures, or had the former Party *apparatchik* truly reinvented himself?[12]

A further question related to Yeltsin's choice of methods. Even if the Russian leader was deeply committed to economic and political reform, how would he choose to advance it? Historically, Russian rulers committed to change had often been willing to use the most barbaric of means to achieve their objectives. One of Russia's most effective—and most brutal—reformers was Tsar Peter the Great, who, in 1689, personally took hold of an ax to behead soldiers resisting him. He forced several of his close associates to do the same.

Our first warning sign in answering these questions about the man who would become Russia's next tsar was the difficulty we encountered in arranging a meeting for Nixon with Yeltsin. While I fully expected problems with Gorbachev, I thought Yeltsin would understand that having Nixon as an ally could be very useful to him—particularly at a time when the Bush administration was still giving the Russian leader the cold shoulder.

My contacts in Yeltsin's circle, Russian foreign minister Andrei Kozyrev and Russian Supreme Soviet Foreign Affairs Committee chairman Vladimir Lukin, told me that receiving Nixon was in Yeltsin's interest and that a meeting would be organized promptly. Nevertheless, the meeting was not arranged until the day before Nixon's departure from Moscow—and was then established only after I informed Lukin and Kozyrev separately that the Gorbachev meeting had been confirmed and that we were facing the possibility that, to our great surprise and regret, Nixon would return to the United States without talking to Yeltsin. I added that because we would have no good explanation for why the meeting did not take place, the lack of a meeting would only confirm perceptions in the Bush administration and elsewhere that Yeltsin was an unpredictable eccentric and no match for Gorbachev.

Most Russians with whom we shared our problems in arranging the session with Yeltsin suggested that the trouble simply reflected the inexperience of Yeltsin's staff. Indeed, Yeltsin was not yet the Russian president—he would be elected in June—and still had to make due with his relatively small office as chairman of the Russian Supreme Soviet. Nevertheless, I was concerned to hear our contacts in Moscow say that Yeltsin's office was "disorganized" and that his staff routinely failed to return telephone calls and displayed the type of vulgar arrogance typically seen in the aides of provincial Party officials.

When it took place, the meeting with Yeltsin was equally as chaotic and contradictory as the process that led to it. On one hand, according to Nixon, the Russian leader was sharp, well informed, and fully capable of a serious discussion of complex issues during the forty minutes the two men spent alone. On the other hand, however, the first portion of the meeting—in which I participated—reflected another side of Yeltsin's personality entirely. After offering Nixon a drink (which he did not accept), Yeltsin informed Nixon that he was particularly pleased to meet him because they had so much in common in their backgrounds. I expected to hear—as in Kryuchkov's case—something about his distaste for the liberal media, so I was surprised when the Russian leader began talking about Nixon's grand-father, whom he said had lived for a time as a businessman in Yeltsin's na-tive Yekaterinburg (Sverdlovsk during the Soviet period). Yeltsin then suggested that his grandfather and Nixon's could have known one another. "Maybe we are even relatives," Yeltsin added cheerfully.

As I knew from reading a number of Nixon biographies, neither of the former president's grandfathers had ever traveled outside the United States, let alone lived in Russia. Nevertheless, Nixon sat through Yeltsin's pleasant rambling with a poker face. When the Russian and American groups left the two men alone twenty minutes later, I took the opportunity to ask a member of the Russian group, Deputy Foreign Minister Andrei Fedorov—who, ironically, later became a bitter critic of Yeltsin as a top advisor to his rival, Russian vice president Aleksandr Rutskoi—where Yeltsin got the idea that Nixon's grandfather had lived in Russia. "Beats me," Fedorov an-swered.

Nevertheless, Nixon was very impressed by Yeltsin's charisma, which he considered crucial for any major politician. He also said that he could understand how Yeltsin could be better than Gorbachev in communicat-ing with the Russian people. "Gorbachev is Wall Street and Yeltsin is Main Street," he observed. Finally, Nixon added that no one should worry too much about what he called "this grandfather nonsense." "The man is obviously under tremendous pressure and he still doesn't have a competent staff. I'm sure someone said something to him and he just misunderstood. Anyway, we shouldn't talk about it back in the States. I know Bush and Scowcroft, they would just love to hear about it because it would substantiate their tendency to dismiss Yeltsin. And that would be wrong." The former president's generosity in this regard was striking given his personal desire to know as much as possible about his interlocutors prior to any meeting. Even as a private citizen, he requested briefing papers detailing the backgrounds of those with whom he planned to meet.

Nixon also told me that he promised Yeltsin he would do his best to obtain a commitment from President Bush to receive the Russian leader in the Oval Office rather than "dropping by" to see him, as Bush had done during Yeltsin's first visit to the United States. (Bush on that occasion spoke with Yeltsin for approximately fifteen minutes in Brent Scowcroft's office.) He also told Yeltsin that he would talk to Senator Bob Dole about arranging for a formal invitation for Yeltsin, as Dole's parliamentary counterpart (Yeltsin was then chairman of the Russian parliament).

I agreed completely with Nixon that to the extent that U.S. foreign policy had to focus on personalities, the time had come to start to shift that focus from Gorbachev to Yeltsin. I was less sanguine, however, about Yeltsin's apparent lack of intellectual discipline and his erratic behavior. Neither characteristic made him a promising candidate to lead his country through an enormously challenging historical transition to a profoundly different political, economic, social, and indeed, moral order. I was also concerned about Yeltsin's already noticeable authoritarian streak. Several months later, I wrote in the journal *Foreign Policy* that "without prematurely questioning Yeltsin's commitment to democracy, the Bush administration and Congress should discreetly voice concerns over some of his government's authoritarian practices."[13] Yeltsin's potential authoritarianism was not a big problem as long as the Russian leader's principal occupation was leading a crusade to destroy the Soviet Communist empire, but if he were called by history to preside over the building of a new nation, I was far less certain what one could expect of him.

Nevertheless, I visited Moscow again in June in part to help prepare for the first visit of newly elected Russian president Boris Yeltsin to the United States. This time, Yeltsin was very well received by the Bush administration and the congressional leadership, in some measure because of Nixon's personal briefings of President Bush and Senator Dole.

• • •

After our return to the United States and the Yeltsin visit to Washington, events in Russia and the Soviet Union substantiated our expectations. After Yeltsin's June election as Russian president, which came despite—or perhaps because of—Gorbachev's strong opposition, the Soviet leader again shifted gears and began a dialogue with his rival. This dialogue eventually included leaders of the other republics and led to the preparation of a draft Union Treaty that would have reconstituted the USSR as a confederation. In a conversation monitored by the KGB, Gorbachev also promised Yeltsin that he would fire hard-liners in the Soviet government, including the prime minister, the defense minister, and the KGB chairman.[14] Feeling both betrayed and threatened by the Soviet president, Kryuchkov, Yazov, Pugo, Pavlov, Yanaev, and others placed Gorbachev under house arrest in his Crimean vacation residence and attempted to establish emergency rule on August 18. After what Nixon and I had seen during our Soviet trip, I was neither surprised by the coup attempt nor overly alarmed about its prospects for success. Just a few hours after word of the putsch reached Washington, I predicted confidently first on CNN and then on the MacNeil/Lehrer News Hour that the junta would not survive for more than a week. In fact, it lasted for only three days.

The conventional wisdom in both Russia and the West holds that it was the failure of the coup that ultimately destroyed the Soviet Union. Otherwise, the argument continues, Gorbachev and Yeltsin could have worked out a modus vivendi and established, at a minimum, a loose confederation. Although one cannot conduct a historical experiment, replaying events without the coup, three points are certain. First of all, the principal reason the coup occurred was that its organizers believed that the short-lived cooperation between Gorbachev and Yeltsin during the summer of 1991 would soon result in the dismantlement of the Union. Had the coup not occurred, the new Union Treaty negotiated by Gorbachev was to have been signed on January 20, 1992. But the treaty was no more than a temporary compromise between the center and the republics, and in a nation without a strong legal tradition, few of the signatories would likely have felt bound by its conditions.[15] Although it preserved the Union as a legal entity (with a new name), the Treaty would have fundamentally altered the character of the USSR.

Second, the cooperation between Gorbachev and Yeltsin would likely have been merely a temporary phenomenon: Gorbachev was too tied to the past and Yeltsin too bent on vengeance—and coming out on top—for the relationship to have remained positive. And finally, republican elites throughout the USSR were by mid-1991 firmly entrenched and had come to enjoy their new autonomy. They had learned how to survive within their local political systems without Moscow and, further, that they were better off politically when they were able to campaign against the imperial capital. In the republican capitals, few would have fought to reestablish Russia as their "elder brother."

Interestingly, another reason for the failure of the coup was that its organizers—who, they said, moved boldly because of the danger of Gorbachev's indecisiveness—themselves lost nerve. They had the will to declare emergency rule, and even to call out the troops, but ultimately Kryuchkov, Yazov, and the other plotters could not bring themselves to order the butchery that would have been required for their putsch to have succeeded. Arriving in Moscow two days after the collapse of the putsch, I saw that it was already too late for the techniques of old-style Soviet repression.

Given these conditions, the attempted coup in August 1991 served only to accelerate a process of disintegration that was already well underway. Paradoxically, by irreparably damaging the federal machinery of repression, the coup probably provided a softer landing for the Soviet Union. Had the central government's capacity to strike back not been destroyed, the disintegration of the USSR could have been even more chaotic and certainly much more violent. If anything, the putsch quickly and relatively painlessly relieved the agony of a dying state. The inability of the center to resist the collapse of the empire contributed importantly to avoiding the Soviet Union's third possible future, that of civil war.

Significantly, the coup and its aftermath also demonstrated that the greatest danger to Mikhail Gorbachev's reform of the USSR was not from the conservative faction within the Soviet leadership but rather grew out of the almost unstoppable force of nationalism and the ambitions of republican leaders, most evident perhaps in the case of Russia and its remarkable new president, Boris Yeltsin.

Ironically, while Yeltsin's courageous resistance to the junta made him a hero in Russia, it made him much less appealing in the other Union republics. Once the conservatives were out of power and Gorbachev had been humiliated and stripped of the support of the power ministries, Yeltsin became a commanding presence in Soviet politics and, in the republican capitals, a potential menace.

From the first moment, Yeltsin clearly enjoyed every second of his new stature and power. But his conduct quickly alienated the leaders of the other soon-to-be post-Soviet states, who sought reassurance that once the unifying threat of the federal center had been destroyed, Yeltsin would continue to treat them as equals. Instead, the Russian leader sent them the message that his time had finally come—that everyone in the post-Soviet arena should acknowledge both his predominance and that of Russia as well. Thus, by pushing away the other fourteen former Soviet republics, Yeltsin himself drove the final nails into the coffin of the USSR. He and the Russian leadership killed and buried the Soviet Union with their ambition in a manner not so different from that in which Slobodan Milošević and his colleagues destroyed the former Yugoslavia.

Importantly, many of the leaders of the other republics would likely have been satisfied remaining within a looser, reformed USSR. The Baltic states were on their way out of the Union, as was Ukraine by the fall of 1991. There were also strong separatist tendencies in Georgia, Azerbaijan, and Moldova. But the remaining Union republics did not seek the destruction of the Soviet Union. As Gorbachev writes in his memoirs, for example:

> Nursultan Nazarbayev [the leader of Kazakhstan] was the most consistent advocate of the Union. . . . The leaders of the Central Asian Republics—Karimov, Akayev, Niyazov and Iskanderov, who at the time represented Tajikistan—held similar views. . . . These national leaders showed a genuine understanding of the colossal losses the break-up of the Union would inflict on their peoples. This is not to say that they unconditionally supported every proposal tabled by Union agencies. Each aspired to free his republic from the heavy burden of excessive centralism. Nevertheless it ought to be said that they never lost their common sense and refrained from transforming independence into a fetish, an end in itself, to be pursued regardless of the consequences.[16]

In fact, many in those republics were both shocked and insulted by dissolution of the Union and creation of the Commonwealth of Independent States (CIS) pronounced in the December 1991 Belovezhsky accord among Russia, Ukraine, and Belorussia. Moreover, as the former Soviet leader also notes, from a purely technical legal perspective, the three signatories had no right to destroy the USSR; they could merely withdraw from it.[17]

As Gorbachev implies, however, independence was a "fetish" for Boris Yeltsin, who clearly sought to free Russia from the USSR without regard to its potential cost. The CIS was thus an instrument to destroy the Union (and Gorbachev personally) rather than to protect Russia's interests within the collapsing USSR. A carefully negotiated separation agreement could have included procedures for the division of Soviet assets, including its military assets (such as the Black Sea Fleet, the division of which troubled Russian-Ukrainian relations until 1997), effective collective security measures, and a mechanism for arbitration of territorial disputes. The latter would have been of particular importance to Russia given the 26 million ethnic Russians residing outside the borders of the RSFSR. For example, Yeltsin did not even explore the possibility of linking Russian support for Ukrainian independence to Kiev's agreement to allow a popular referendum in Crimea allowing the overwhelmingly Russian region to choose between Russia and Ukraine.

Today, however, after seven years of independence for the former republics of the Soviet Union, Russian politicians' attempts to persuade leaders of other CIS member-states to reopen some of these questions are understandably perceived—inside and outside the CIS—as Russian neoimperialism. Statements by Moscow mayor Yuri Luzhkov and other nationalist politicians regarding Crimea and its Black Sea port of Sevastopol are a case in point. Yeltsin's haste to tear down the USSR may have cost Russia the opportunity to reach a historic bargain with its fellow republics which, without seriously damaging the rights or interests of the other Soviet successor states, could have made Russia's transition from communism less humiliating and painful and ultimately contributed to the long-term stability of the post-Soviet region as well.

•   •   •

With the death of the USSR as a political entity, the key issue for the United States was how to deal with the new Russia. What were American priorities vis-à-vis the largest post-Soviet nation? It was devastated economically, armed with thousands of nuclear weapons, and led by a former Communist Party functionary with a patronizing attitude toward his country's newly independent neighbors. But at the same time, the new Russia proclaimed a commitment to democracy and sought strategic partnership with America and the West. Assessing U.S. national interests in dealing with the new Russia was the natural place to start.

Nixon and I were fully aware that defining American priorities with respect to a country of such importance—in a period of chaos and rapid change—would be a complex task with no easy answers. Our own disagreements with one another illustrated some of the problems. Nixon, who was more favorably disposed toward Yeltsin than I, thought that there was little practical difference between supporting the Russian president and supporting his country's transition toward democracy. On the contrary, I was afraid that replacing Gorbachev with Yeltsin as America's new favorite would obscure some of the fundamental problems likely to emerge in U.S. relations with the new Russia. At the time, I wrote that "the United States should avoid repeating the same mistake it made with Gorbachev—namely, an excessive personalization of Russian-Soviet politics by focusing on Yeltsin."[18]

Where Nixon and I agreed was in the firm belief that the collapse of the Soviet Union and the birth of a new Russia was an event of monumental proportions, which required a fundamental reassessment of U.S. foreign policy. We also agreed that the American stake in Russia was great, that the time to act was now, and that the consequences of procrastination would be serious and real. "But," Nixon told me, "the most important thing is to think about Russia strategically. Russia is a big enchilada and we cannot afford either to be sentimental or casual in how we approach it." I could not have agreed more.

Chapter Five

•

The Face of the New Russia

It is clear by now that Nixon was right in seeing Russia's chances for further trouble and its potential to grow into greatness from the rubble of the Soviet empire. His approach to Russia may perhaps best be described as romantic pragmatism. Although he was a committed practitioner of hard-headed realpolitik, the former president was a Wilsonian at heart. In fact, Wilson's portrait was one of only two pictures he kept in the Cabinet Room during his time in the White House; the other was a portait of Eisenhower, under whom Nixon had served as vice president.[1]

Nixon identified with Wilson's passionate belief that the United States should stand for more than its narrow self-interest in its foreign policy and that America must combine its power with idealism.[2] On a purely practical level, he was convinced that realpolitik without a human face would appear too cynical to the American people and, as a result, could not be sustained domestically. But throughout his political career, he also believed strongly that the United States had a genuine purpose in the world and was an indispensable force for good. He saw communism as a menace not only because it provided an ideological rationale for the geopolitical challenges to the United States from the Soviet Union and, to a lesser extent, China, but also simply because it was evil.

In contrast, former secretary of state Henry Kissinger approached Russia primarily from a realist perspective. He saw Russia as a huge country which, by virtue of its size and power, has presented a constant problem for its neighbors and the world as a whole. Kissinger's approach to Russia is also based on Russian history, which is certainly not on the side of those who hope for a benign Russia in the future. Although Kissinger and others who advocate the realist perspective acknowledge that no nation is a prisoner of its history, they have typically implied that Moscow's tsarist and Soviet imperial past must be considered very seriously in evaluating Russia's future.

As a classical realist, Kissinger has not been terribly preoccupied with developments within Russia because, as he writes, it is not clear "that even a democratic Russia will conduct policies conducive to international stability."[3] Kissinger is concerned that "even sincere reformers may see in traditional Russian nationalism a unifying force to achieve their objectives. And, in Russia, nationalism has historically been missionary and imperial. Psychologists can debate whether the reason was a deep-rooted sense of insecurity or congenital aggressiveness. For the victims of Russian expansion, the distinction has been academic. In Russia, democratization and a restrained foreign policy may not necessarily go hand in hand."[4] With so many uncertainties in Russia, Kissinger sees Russian foreign policy, not its uncertain domestic evolution, as the focal point of U.S. policy.

As a Wilsonian, however, Nixon cared deeply about the transition underway within Russia. And while he knew that democracy would not guarantee nonaggressive behavior, he was certain that in the long run, the opposite was also true: without democracy, Russia would almost inevitably return to its old expansionist ways.

Like Kissinger, former national security advisor Zbigniew Brzezinski, and other authorities on Russia, Nixon believed that the imperial burden had been an obstacle to Russia's development as a peaceful, prosperous, civil society. Accordingly, Nixon welcomed the collapse of the USSR as good for Russia itself. Nevertheless, he shared my belief that how the collapse was handled—and the extent to which Russia's legitimate interests and sensitivities were taken into account—was of great importance. If empire was incompatible with democracy, the disorderly and painful transformation of the only state the Russian people had known for centuries could be similarly devastating. Thus, we both believed that hardship and humiliation would not be fertilizers for the budding Russian democracy.

•   •   •

It was in this spirit that Nixon addressed a large audience of scholars, journalists, and quite a few officials at Moscow's prestigious Institute for the World Economy and International Relations (IMEMO) during his 1991 trip to the USSR. Nixon's tone was that of a respectful friend rather than an arrogant mentor: "America does not have all the answers. Yours is a country with a long and great history and a unique tradition. You have to sort out things for yourselves. That does not mean measuring success by foreign models, including those of the United States. Your tradition emphasizes spirit, great art, inner growth. . . . I am convinced that while you paid an enormous price for your preoccupation with spiritual values, you enriched all mankind. The United States and the Soviet Union are different, and our solutions may not be applicable to your situation," Nixon observed before advocating more political pluralism, more emphasis on market forces, and more understanding of the republics' determination to make their own decisions.[5]

Even more remarkable for one of the most tough-minded presidents in American history was Nixon's willingness not just to treat Russia with respect, not just to acknowledge that it was entitled to its foreign policy interests—even when those interests were at odds with those of the United States—but to argue strongly and publicly before prominent Russian audiences that Moscow should avoid the appearance of being in Washington's pocket.

In a February 17, 1993, address at the Carnegie Endowment's new Moscow Center, which I chaired at that time, Nixon said precisely that, and made other arguments probably unthinkable for any other American statesman. First, he advised approximately fifty members of the Russian elite— including former acting prime minister Yegor Gaidar, Yeltsin's chief of staff, his top foreign policy advisor, a deputy foreign minister, the president of the Russian Academy of Sciences, and several key members of the Supreme Soviet—that they should not believe in the "myths" that "American democracy can be exported to other nations" and that "all economic problems can be solved by adopting Free Market policies." After assaulting these two articles of faith among Moscow's radical reformers, Nixon really took the gloves off. As he put it, "Russia is a great power. Its foreign policy must serve its interests. Generally Russian interests are the same as those of the United States. But we must recognize that while we are now friends and no longer enemies, that does not mean we will have no differences. . . . Russia must avoid appearing to be in lockstep with the United States in a way that disserves Russia's interests. This would give ammunition to those in Russia who oppose reform and who use foreign policy as a club to beat the reformers over the head."[6]

Nixon delivered the same message during an hour-long meeting with President Yeltsin a few days before his speech, on February 10. After the meeting, Yeltsin said to me, "This was a very big conversation. President Nixon is a real friend. I hope President Clinton listens to him." And Yeltsin's foreign policy advisor, Ambassador Dmitri Ryurikov (who, in the spirit of full disclosure, was soon to become my father-in-law), said that Nixon's approach was a rare instance in which top Americans treated Russians as mature adults capable of figuring out what was good for them on their own, without intrusive guidance from the United States.

Nixon's approach in his speech at IMEMO, and later with Boris Yeltsin, was in stark contrast to President Clinton's conduct during his September 1998 visit to Russia. Speaking at the elite Moscow University for International Relations, Clinton in all seriousness provided detailed, point-by-point instructions to his Russian audience on how their economy should be run. His rationale for this paternalistic attitude was appropriate only for a global schoolmaster: He had to tell the truth ". . . to the [Russian] people so that you're not skeptical when your political leaders tell you things that are hard to hear." The result was a thirty-five-minute speech without a single round of applause.[7]

Several days later in the Latvian capital of Riga, Nixon made a passionate case for more equal treatment of ethnic Russians and other Russian-speakers in Latvia at a working dinner given in his honor by then parliament chairman Anatolijs Gorbunovs. "Alienating Russia may become a self-fulfilling prophecy. If it helps Russian extremists, Latvia would be the first to suffer," he declared.

•　　•　　•

This preoccupation with promoting Russian democracy led Nixon to write his famous February 1992 memorandum urging immediate, massive assistance to Russia. Sent initially to fifty acquaintances, the memo was intended to be made public. Distressed by the lack of real attention to foreign policy during the presidential primary season, the former president charged in the text that "while the candidates have addressed scores of significant issues in the presidential campaign, the most important issue since the end of World War II—the fate of political and economic reforms in Russia—has been virtually ignored. As a result, the United States and the West risk snatching defeat from the jaws of victory."[8]

The same theme dominated Nixon's March 1992 speech at a Washington conference organized by the Richard Nixon Library and Birthplace. The conference (chaired by former secretary of defense James Schlesinger and codirected by Nixon Library director John Taylor and myself) provided Nixon with a platform to launch a high-profile crusade on behalf of Russian democracy, an issue about which he cared deeply out of both his romanticism and his pragmatism.

In his book *The Nixon Memo,* journalist Marvin Kalb reduced Nixon's motives in making his emotional case for Russia during the electoral campaign to a desire for self-promotion and a personal animosity toward George Bush and, particularly, James Baker. Kalb latched onto Nixon's warning in his February memo that "if Yeltsin goes down, the question of 'Who lost Russia?'" would have devastating domestic consequences as a direct attempt to undermine Bush politically.[9] This was not, however, the case.

Nixon was of course aware that his implicit criticism of U.S. policy toward Russia was not helpful to President Bush. But hurting Bush politically was not Nixon's goal at all. Whatever misgivings Nixon had about Bush did not amount to a preference for Bill Clinton or any other Democratic contender for the presidency. What Kalb and similar critics failed to recognize was that Nixon was not a small man playing politics with Russia regardless of the cost. For Nixon, giving Russian democracy a chance was a historic project which he adopted as a personal "swan song" of sorts in his later years. Whatever minor inconvenience he created for George Bush was in Nixon's mind an acceptable price for pursuing what he viewed as America's number-one foreign policy priority. Besides, anyone who was as aware as Nixon was of declining public interest in international affairs would have good reason to assume that suggesting that Bush could do more for Russia could not conceivably undermine his chances for reelection. Bush had an impressive foreign policy record, particularly in the aftermath of the Gulf War, and could not have been damaged that easily.

•   •   •

Ironically, there appeared to be no great difference on the surface between Nixon's advocacy of American engagement on behalf of Russian democracy and the stated goals of the new Clinton administration. In fact, when my article "How Not to Lose Russia" appeared in the *Washington Post* on January 31,1993, I received a call from Strobe Talbott, who had just been appointed ambassador-at-large for Russia and the newly independent states and given the rank of undersecretary of state. Talbott invited me to visit him in his temporary office, where he told me that he had read my article and that he agreed wholeheartedly with my arguments. "We think along the same lines. I cannot guarantee that we will do everything you want, but many things will be done and done soon. Give my regards to President Nixon. I always greatly benefit from his wisdom and would like to arrange a meeting soon."

When I called Nixon to tell him about my conversation with Talbott, he was encouraged but took little at face value and asked for my evaluation of Talbott's intentions and his credentials. Typically, he began with a long introduction of his own: Talbott was among the journalists who cultivated him, he said, and who were cultivated by him in return. Nixon thought that he would have good access to Talbott and, because Talbott was known to be Bill Clinton's close friend, access through him to the president himself. Nixon also considered Talbott to be unusually well informed about Russia for a senior official and thought that he was a bright and well-meaning man. "He's also a good writer. But I like him more than his writing. He wrote all those books about that arms control crap as if it were the most important thing in the world. It's a very different business to write essays about foreign policy and to make it. Does he have the stuff? I'm not sure," Nixon wondered.

It took very little time for Nixon and me to discover that the new administration's foreign policy philosophy and particularly its attitude toward Russia were quite different from ours. There were two fundamental and irreconcilable differences between Clinton's approach to Russia and the approach that Nixon and I shared.

First, the approaches differed in the level to which the United States should become involved in telling Russia how to run its own reform process. Nixon cared deeply about Russian democracy, of course, both because democracy was right and because only a democratic system could create the domestic checks and balances necessary to prevent the reemergence of Russia's imperial habits. As far as Russia's economic reform was concerned, Nixon felt strongly that the transition to capitalism—while indispensable—should be conducted in accordance with local traditions and circumstances and with proper attention to maintaining a social safety net for the victims of reform. He knew that radical reform—"shock therapy"—would risk a powerful societal backlash and could endanger the very survival of Russia's fragile new democracy. To Nixon, giving Russia's democratic experiment a fighting chance was much more important than structuring economic reforms according to the rigid criteria established by international financial institutions.

In the January *Washington Post* article praised by Talbott, I argued that "simply put, salvation of the Russian democracy is too crucial to be left to economists. It is time to put politics first in designing the Russian aid package. The package should be sensitive to political circumstances in Russia and the new administration should be careful not to push the Russian president to do things that may further destabilize the situation unless vital U.S. interests are at stake."[10] Nixon wrote me two days later to express his agreement.

Nixon observed that the International Monetary Fund and the World Bank, both of which had acquired a dominant role in providing aid to Russia, were "populated by people who are unable to think politically. They would not know the difference between what is appropriate for Russia and for Bangladesh. Decisions on how to help Russia should be made at the highest political level by G-7 [Group of Seven] governments, which can put politics above economics and are in close consultation with the Russians themselves."

Despite his compliments for my views, Strobe Talbott's instincts led him and his Clinton administration colleagues who shared his perspective in a rather different direction. Without much deliberation, the administration began to offer instant advice, often amounting to outright pressure on the Yeltsin government, as to how exactly Russia should conduct its economic reform—and even who were the right people for the job.

Understandably, the Russians did not take well to the idea that the United States knew better than Russia itself how to conduct Russian affairs.

Shortly after the Vancouver Summit—from which Talbott called me to explain the administration's policy and to highlight its good chemistry with the Yeltsin team—a top Russian diplomat told me that "among ourselves, we call Talbott 'Proconsul Strobe.' He has all the answers and rarely hesitates to tell us what to do, as if we were small children in need of instruction."

This propensity for what then U.S. ambassador to the United Nations Madeleine Albright would call "nation-building"—an inclination the administration demonstrated in Somalia, Haiti, and Bosnia—was not limited to Mr. Talbott and soon became the trademark of the administration's Russian policy as well. In the process, economics was put above politics to the extent that if the "shock therapy"–style reforms the administration, the IMF, and the World Bank advocated could not be implemented without taking detours from Russian democracy, the Clinton administration did not seem to mind. The administration conveniently labeled Russian opponents of shock therapy "reactionaries" and encouraged Yeltsin to take drastic steps against them. "These guys are just plain nuts. They don't understand that by encouraging Yeltsin's authoritarian temptation they're playing with fire," Nixon told me after Talbott's April 19, 1993, House Appropriations Committee testimony defending the administration's request for funds to support aid to Russia. In that testimony, Talbott was jubilant that "President Yeltsin threw down the gauntlet in Moscow before a parliament that is dominated by reactionaries," effectively welcoming steps by Russia's first democratically elected president in seeking the dissolution of a no less democratically elected parliament.[11] Nixon gave the Kremlin precisely the opposite advice in a confidential March 1993 letter to Boris Yeltsin in which the former president suggested that any steps by Yeltsin to dissolve the Supreme Soviet should be, at a minimum, postponed.

The second difference between Nixon's and the Clinton administration's approaches regarded the appropriate U.S. response to an increasingly assertive Russian foreign policy. Unlike Kissinger, Nixon cared deeply about Russia's domestic evolution. Like Kissinger, however, he believed that it was ultimately Russia's international conduct that mattered most to the United States. In his view, the Clinton administration soon went far too far in "adopting" Yeltsin and in avoiding inconveniencing him even at the expense of important American interests. Ironically, the administration had it completely backward: instead of offering Yeltsin some slack on economic reform—where he needed it to lessen popular dissatisfaction and protect democratization—the administration gave Yeltsin undue consideration in foreign policy matters whenever the specter of Russian nationalism was raised.

As Nixon observed in a thinly disguised rebuke to the Clinton administration in his last article before his death, written in March 1994: "Most important, the U.S. should be candid with Russia when our views do not coincide. We are great world powers and our interests will inevitably clash, but the greatest mistake we can make is to try to drown down differences in champagne and vodka toasts at 'feel-good' summit meetings." According to the former president, "we cannot allow Russia to determine the future of NATO. The alliance—the main security bridge across the Atlantic—is too important to America and to Europe to be sacrificed for the sake of Russian sensitivity."[12] Nixon did not live to see how the Clinton administration proceeded enthusiastically to transform the very nature of the Atlantic alliance in order to convince the Kremlin to accept its expansion. But knowing how little he thought of League of Nations–type collective security organizations, I am sure that he would have agreed with Kissinger in rejecting the administration's intention to use the enlargement of NATO to change the nature of the alliance.

I believe Nixon would also have been nonplussed by Russia's undeserved and unnatural prominence during the June 1997 Denver Summit, at which the traditional format of G-7 summits was abandoned and replaced by the administration's new formula: "The Summit of the Eight." Russian president Boris Yeltsin, previously included only in G-7 political discussions, took part in all of the summit sessions except for one international finance meeting in which his country, still heavily dependent upon loans from international financial institutions, could not have played a credible part.

President Clinton himself celebrated Moscow's new status in Denver by describing its new summit role and its membership in the Paris Club of creditor nations as "evidence of Russia's emergence as a full member of the community of democracies."[13] The U.S. president also expressed confidence that "as long as Russia keeps moving as it is under President Yeltsin and those reformers, and the people of Russia keep supporting the direction they have, I think that you will see more good things ahead."[14] Beyond that, he promised to make an effort to incorporate Russia into the World Trade Organization (WTO) as soon as possible. Even Secretary of State Madeleine Albright, despite her reputation for toughness and outspokenness, pronounced that "the inclusion of Russia is a big step forward" and predicted that Moscow "will become a permanent fixture" at future summits of what has become a de facto G-8.

And Russia's international rise has not been limited to incorporation in economic structures; Moscow has made remarkable advances in the security sphere as well. Although the Yeltsin government's opposition failed to halt the enlargement of the NATO alliance, it succeeded—again, with enthusiastic help from the Clinton administration—in accomplishing something potentially more important: the transformation of NATO from a military alliance into a mutual security organization in which Russia has gained a major voice through the NATO–Russia Permanent Joint Council.

Russian and American legal experts still debate whether the Permanent Joint Council, outlined in the Founding Act on Mutual Relations, Cooperation, and Security between NATO and Russia, will give Russia a voice in alliance deliberations, as President Clinton argues, or a veto, as Boris Yeltsin insists. Much will depend upon Russia's power at the moment. But regardless of whether the Kremlin formally has a voice, a veto, or something between the two, Moscow can potentially influence NATO discussions on issues ranging from international terrorism to peacekeeping in the Balkans and even the further expansion of the alliance. It is possible that Russia, as one of three cochairs of the council, will have a greater impact on NATO deliberations than most full-fledged members of the alliance.

Such accomplishments easily explain Yeltsin's evident jubilance in Denver. What is more difficult to understand is the motivation behind President Clinton's apparent decision to treat Russia's U.S.–sponsored rise in international economic and security organizations as his own personal triumph. Similarly, it is unclear why yesterday's evil empire merited such a dramatic increase in status with so little public discussion and scrutiny in the United States and elsewhere. During Clinton's lengthy press conference at the June 1997 Denver Summit, he was never asked why Russia—a leading debtor nation with a collapsed economy, and a country increasingly run by a corrupt oligarchic regime that only one year earlier was committing atrocities in Chechnya comparable to the war crimes in Bosnia—should be invited into the group of key economically powerful democracies.

Only Japan, obviously disappointed with the lack of progress in its negotiations with Russia for the return of the so-called Northern Territories
(annexed by the USSR after World War II and known in Russia as the Kuril
Islands),[15] has raised any objection to the inclusion of a country clearly un-
qualified by any reasonable standard in the most exclusive club of capitalist
democracies. The administration's response to the Japanese government—
which asked why Russia should be included if the Chinese economic powerhouse is not—was that Russia is a democracy and China is not.[16]

●   ●   ●

The Clinton administration has been determined to call Russia a democracy
almost without regard to the behavior of its leaders or the real workings of
its political system. The administration did this as early as October 1993,
when Boris Yeltsin disolved Russia's democratically elected parliament.
Despite Yeltsin's own admission that he was acting "outside the constitution," the administration assured Americans and the West that Russia was
still a democracy—and actually a better one, since it had rid itself (regret-
tably by force) of a reactionary legislature.

The administration continued those assurances after the adoption of
Russia's postindependence constitution in December 1993. The new constitution, which was for all practical purposes written by Yeltsin's team after
the October shoot-out, dramatically increased Yeltsin's power and reduced
the role of the Russian parliament. It was adopted by popular referendum—
without any consideration by legislative bodies—amid serious allegations
of electoral fraud. The administration's reckless disregard of reality was
again apparent when Yeltsin was reelected in July 1996 after a campaign in
which his election headquarters saw no distinction between the state treasury and its own coffers and evidence of fabricated vote tallies surfaced in
several regions. For years, despite highly incriminating information linking
Yeltsin's close associates to corrupt practices in government, business, and
politics (including the management of the Yeltsin campaign), the Clinton
administration continued steadfastly to proclaim that Russia was marching
toward genuine democracy and full integration into the U.S.–led international community.

In fact, however, the situation in Russia is very different from the
rosy portrait painted by self-congratulatory officials in Washington. As

the distinguished Russian sociologist Liliya Shevtsova has observed: "On the whole, if one thinks about what has changed in the period of post-communist development and what has remained as before, one arrives at the conclusion that Russian society—delivered from communism—has today received a monster-state which may be even more frightening than its predecessor."[17] Of course, whatever may be said about the faults of the new regime, the Russian system is no longer totalitarian and, accordingly, the regime no longer has the same opportunities to control its subjects or to channel its vast resources to aggressive purposes. Nevertheless, to distill the sentiments of Shevtsova and many of her democratic colleagues, Boris Yeltsin has created a system in which Al Capone would be more at home than Thomas Jefferson. Five basic points are crucial in understanding why this is the case.

- First, despite—but also perhaps partly because of—Boris Yeltsin's quintuple bypass surgery, the Russian president's health, intellectual faculties, and moral character have all deteriorated considerably since his heroic resistance to the August 1991 coup attempt from atop a Soviet tank. Also, while Yeltsin has proven himself a master politician, he has no political agenda beyond remaining in power. He has thus successfully created a regime uniquely suited to protecting his presidency but much less capable of addressing Russia's fundamental economic, political, and social problems. Never known as a hands-on chief executive, the ailing Russian leader has become increasingly dependent upon a small circle of associates whose primary function is to guarantee that his rule is unchallenged. Nevertheless, while Yeltsin remains very much in charge, the "Yeltsin era" is already over.
- Second, although Russia has some democratic forms—elections, constitutionally protected press freedoms, and a nominally independent judiciary—it is in reality a semi-authoritarian regime run by often corrupt senior government officials in close cooperation with leading financiers and industrialists. Government and business are inseparably intertwined and, as a result, key government decisions are routinely influenced (if not made directly) by oligarchic clans seeking personal gains. This unsavory relationship

between big business and the state has led to monstrous corruption, which has already survived at least five anti-corruption campaigns and will doubtless outlast more. This oligarchy, despite its growing misgivings regarding Yeltsin's ability to govern, still views him as its principal protector and, accordingly, strives to guarantee his continued presence in office. To an increasing extent, the oligarchy shapes official policy as well—a senior Russian official admitted in 1996 that tax privileges alone transfer nearly $30 billion from state to private coffers.[18]

• Third, as the government of Yevgeny Primakov has demonstrated, the Russian economy is not always moving in the free-market direction. As in the case of its progress toward democracy, much of Russian economic development is little more than a fancy façade put up to encourage support from international lenders and investors. Inflation was brought under control primarily through the nonpayment of billions of dollars in wages and pensions to tens of millions of Russian citizens. To the extent that wage and pension arrears have been paid today, they have largely been paid with multibillion-dollar loans from international financial institutions and, more recently, bond issues. Similarly, while official statistics show over 70 percent of Russia's GDP to be produced by its private sector, even superficial scrutiny reveals that many so-called private companies are in fact owned, or at least controlled, by the government. The Russian economy is much closer to Asian crony capitalism than America's free-market model. The severe financial crisis in August 1998 demonstrated how little has changed in Russia's economy and how weak its new institutions—especially in the banking sector—really are.

• Fourth, there is greater potential for a change of course in Russia than is commonly assumed. After more than ten years of painful upheaval under Gorbachev and now Yeltsin, the majority of Russians have little taste for further dramatic experimentation. Fortunately, they do not seek a return to the past; nevertheless, the degree of popular alienation is very high. According to one June 1997 public opinion poll, only 18 percent of Russians support pro-government parties in the Duma; the vast majority would prefer that opposition parties gain seats.[19] This alienation presents a threat to the regime even while as Yeltsin remains in power, and it could contribute to major shifts in policy when the Russian president leaves office. Political alienation was a clear cause of the dramatic change of government in August and September 1998.

- Finally, Russia is actively seeking to deny the United States world leadership and to create a new global power equilibrium through arrangements with countries dissatisfied with American preeminence, ranging from China to Iran. This threatens to constrain significantly the ability of the United States to shape international events in a manner favorable to its interests. While Russia is eager to avoid conflict with America and its allies, particularly when it desperately needs their economic assistance, Russian views on many important issues diverge widely from American positions. There is also a strong undercurrent of resentment and other anti–U.S. sentiments among the Russian elite and people alike.

As with President Clinton's domestic programs—and scandals—the administration and its supporters have apparently decided that the best defense of its policies vis-à-vis Russia is a good offense, and have tended to portray those who object to its rosy view of Russian political and economic developments as unreformed Cold Warriors and even Russophobes. The administration's uncritical approach toward Moscow is perhaps best summarized by an unnamed senior official interviewed at the Denver Summit: when questioned about the administration's disingenuousness regarding Russia's transformation, the official stated, "I don't really care what Yeltsin does here. What's important is that he is here."[20]

Remarkably, administration officials cover up for not only the Yeltsin government but also the questionable habits and poor health of the Russian president personally. According to General Aleksandr Korzhakov, Yeltsin's estranged former chief bodyguard, for example, during Yeltsin's September 1994 visit to the United States, President Clinton attempted to camouflage the Russian president's heavy drinking at a lunch meeting. "While they were photographing Bill and Boris one more time," Korzhakov writes, "I got up from the table. Irritation was growing within me and I wanted to calm down a little, contemplating the surrounding well-being. . . . At lunch, Boris Nikolayevich ate a tiny piece of meat and emptied several glasses. Even earlier during an aperitif, Clinton realized that something strange was happening to his counterpart, but tried to pretend that everything was okay.

The chief got up from the table slightly unsteady on his legs. I clenched my teeth in fury. The wine had gone to the head of the Russian president."[21] But a Clinton administration spokesman denied that there were any problems with Yeltsin's performance.

More recently, Yeltsin's behavior during state visits to China and Sweden in late 1997 has raised questions about the Russian president's physical health and mental acuity. During the China trip, Yeltsin reportedly said to his hosts—who asked him to extend his successful visit—that he could not remain in China any longer because "I have food only for two days."[22] Later, during the December trip to Sweden, Yeltsin appeared to believe that he was in Finland, inaccurately referred to Japan as a nuclear power, and announced sharp unilateral cuts in Russian strategic nuclear forces, which were promptly disavowed by startled aides and military officials.[23]

The Clinton administration has attempted to defend this behavior as well. Responding to questions about Yeltsin's physical and mental health raised by the Sweden trip, State Department deputy spokesman James Foley said, "We have no reason to believe that he's not at the top of his game. . . . That he's in good health. He recovered amazingly well from the surgery he had." When questioned about the Russian leader's seemingly confused behavior in Stockholm, Foley stated that Yeltsin's conduct did not trouble the administration and that "like many effective politicians, he is sometimes given to spontaneous remarks; he doesn't always limit himself to what's prepared. I think that's the frustration of bureaucrats in every political system, though."[24] It is incomprehensible that a State Department spokesman should believe that his responsibilities include covering up for foreign heads of state.

•   •   •

The administration's approach to Boris Yeltsin's health problems is consistent with its treatment of events in Russia in general. The problem is that after dealing with "the new Russia" for six years, the Clinton administration simply cannot claim ignorance of developments there to excuse its hasty and unsavory embrace of Moscow. As in the case of Yeltsin's erratic behavior, there has been plenty of good reporting on how the Russian democratic experiment is going astray in leading American newspapers, most notably the *New York Times,* the *Washington Post,* and the *Los Angeles Times.*

Powerful Russian voices have also alerted outsiders to the deterioration of Russian freedom. Understandably, when those charges came from conservative former leaders of the Supreme Soviet (disbanded in 1993), from Communist Party chairman Gennady Zyuganov, or from the maverick General Aleksandr Lebed (who was himself suspected of harboring a Napoleon—or perhaps Pinochet—complex), the administration had an excuse to be skeptical of their motives and their validity. But devastating indictments of the Yeltsin regime have not been limited to forces of the past as the Russian government and its supporters in Washington like to pretend.

Some of the harshest attacks on the way in which Russia is ruled have come from politicians on the democratic end of the spectrum. Moscow's mayor, Yuri Luzhkov—a supporter of free enterprise overwhelmingly re-elected in 1996 (with no accusations of fraud)—has said that the manner in which privatization was conducted in Russia was criminal and that it led to "the unlimited criminalization of the economy. And, of course, the government itself." Commenting on corruption in Russia, Luzhkov said that "Today we do not have a problem with bandits, but with the most respectable citizens. They have important posts in the government. In banking structures, in ministries, and so on. Their names are well-known. . . ."[25] Interestingly, Luzhkov's comments appeared in an interview in the Russian newspaper *Izvestiya* published just after a trip to the United States during which he met with President Clinton, to whom he delivered the same message, to no avail.

Another top Russian democratic politician, Grigory Yavlinsky—coauthor of Russia's 500-Day Plan for economic reform in 1990—has drawn attention to the fundamental problems of Russia's transformation. Yavlinsky, now serving as the leader of the reformist Yabloko faction in the lower house of the Russian parliament, the State Duma, has made such statements repeatedly in the Russian press, the American press, and in international venues including meetings of the prestigious World Economic Forum in Davos, Switzerland. In a 1997 article in the *New York Times Magazine,* Yavlinsky wrote: "When President Clinton came to Russia, the Russian people expected to hear something like this: 'We Americans understand the difficulties you are facing. America has been through the Depression, has dealt with corruption and crime. Please do not think that corruption and crime are normal attributes of democracy.' Instead all they heard was unstinting praise for the Government, which the people no longer trust."[26] Perhaps most important, Yavlinsky has put his money where his mouth is: his impeccably pro-democracy, pro-reform Yabloko faction has become the most consistent opponent of the Yeltsin government in the Russian parliament on issues ranging from the war in Chechnya to the budget and tax reform. By comparison, the Communist and nationalist factions in the Duma cooperate increasingly frequently with Yeltsin, including even by participating in the Primakov government, which Yabloko refused to do.

Finally, the U.S. embassy, reporting directly from Moscow to the Department of State, has provided ample supporting evidence of the erosion of Russian democracy. In fact, back in 1995, the embassy played host to an interesting episode in which Thomas Graham, then the embassy political officer, published a lengthy article in the Russian press asserting that Russia was increasingly controlled by powerful political-financial clans that managed the country through behind-the-scenes deals.[27] When the Russian Foreign Ministry protested what it termed U.S. interference in its country's domestic politics, the State Department explained that the article reflected only Mr. Graham's point of view and did not represent official U.S. policy.

Nevertheless, the highly professional and quite disciplined American ambassador in Moscow, Thomas Pickering (now serving as undersecretary of state for policy) had approved the article for publication. Further, Mr. Graham was never disciplined for expressing views so visibly at odds with official policy. As someone who benefited frequently from briefings by Ambassador Pickering, Mr. Graham, and others during visits to Moscow, I am convinced that the Graham article was fully consistent with much of the reporting from the embassy. In fact, a confidential cable sent with Ambassador Pickering's signature to Secretary of State Warren Christopher in March 1995 stated directly that "power in Russia is wielded less by constitutionally defined institutions than by an oligarchy of economic and bureaucratic groups, each with their own political patrons, business clubs, media outlets, private armies, and financial support."[28] That reporting was certainly well known to the highest echelons of the Clinton administration but was never shared with the American people, who were led to believe that Yeltsin's Russia was firmly on the path to democracy.

•   •   •

Of course, from the American standpoint, there is much about the present-day situation in Russia, and particularly Russian foreign policy, that should give grounds for satisfaction. First and foremost, none of the nightmarish scenarios of bloody civil war in a nuclear-armed nation or a Communist or nationalist takeover leading to revanchist territorial designs have come to pass. In this sense, Boris Yeltsin's firm grip on power has been a blessing to the rest of the world.

Also, Russian foreign policy has generally been quite moderate for a surviving core state that has just lost its empire. There have, of course, been many disputes between Russia and its newly independent neighbors—over issues ranging from the treatment of Russian-speakers in the Baltic states to the division of the former Soviet Black Sea Fleet with Ukraine. Nevertheless, while Russia has not been above throwing its weight around when local circumstances permit (such as in the break-away Georgian region of Abkhazia, the similarly independence-minded Transdniester Republic in Moldova, or Tajikistan's continuing civil war), the Yeltsin government has typically acted with restraint. Russia's leaders have clearly been eager to avoid becoming too involved in bloody local conflicts, particularly after the disastrous war in Chechnya. Moscow has also been reluctant to alienate the United States and its allies prematurely, while Russia's economy still depends heavily upon their goodwill.

In other areas, outside the borders of the former Soviet Union, Russia has often taken positions differing from those of the United States. For example, Russia's perspective on Iraq, its international arms trade (particularly with "outlaw states" like Iran and Libya), its position on the transfer of nuclear and missile technology (to Iran and India, respectively), its approach to relations with China, and its views on the conflicts in Bosnia and Kosovo as well as NATO enlargement, were all at odds with U.S. policies. Still, in most cases, after asserting its position, the Kremlin was prepared to compromise or retreat when faced with strong U.S. opposition.

At the 1997 Denver Summit, for example, Russian president Boris Yeltsin supported a U.S.–promoted statement on Bosnia and, after a meeting between Secretary of State Madeleine Albright and Russian foreign minister Yevgeny Primakov, agreed to a compromise enabling a U.S.–supported United Nations Security Council resolution threatening additional sanctions against Iraq. Moscow was later instrumental in persuading Baghdad to comply somewhat with existing U.N. demands for access by inspectors to suspected weapon facilities.

If Russia were not a former superpower with large stocks of nuclear weapons and—more to the point—considerable potential for future greatness, this record of cooperation would probably entitle Moscow to special consideration by the Clinton administration. After all, notwithstanding the Clinton administration's international moralism, repressive domestic policies and rampant corruption have never become an issue in U.S. relations with other "useful" governments such as the Saudi Arabian monarchy, Mobutu's Zaire, or Suharto's Indonesia (until it was hit by financial crisis). It cannot be denied that Russia has gone along with American wishes more often than not since its independence—or that Boris Yeltsin has often accommodated Washington in the face of strong domestic opposition.

But precisely because Russia has both a great past and considerable potential for the future (for good or ill), it should be treated as a "big enchilada"—not because the Clinton administration has kindly agreed to do so out of its generous spirit, but rather because Russia is a genuinely important country and merits treatment as such. Accordingly, rather than focusing almost exclusively on Yeltsin's ability to consolidate power inside Russia and to go along with the sometimes arbitrary priorities of the Clinton administration (such as a unified Bosnian state, which the majority of the population of Bosnia does not seem to want), American policy-makers should give precedence to the fundamental trends in Russia and their implications for Russian foreign policy—and American interests—in the twenty-first century. By this criterion, the Clinton administration's policy toward post-Communist Russia has hardly been a success story.

•   •   •

The sudden collapse of the Soviet Union left the United States without a conceptual framework from which to approach relations with the USSR's successor states. The Bush administration had little interest in treating the new Russia as a matter of great importance or urgency. The Clinton administration was another matter altogether. In quickly adopting Russia's transformation as its own pet project, the new administration articulated an unabashedly Wilsonian approach to international affairs, and to the former USSR in particular, from its beginning. Where Nixon's Wilsonianism was tempered by respect for Russian civilization and careful calculation of American interests, the administration's approach seemed arrogant and capricious—a noble but futile crusade to impose our own ideas and standards around the globe. As the president himself said: "During the cold war, our foreign policies largely focused on the relations among nations. Our strategies sought a balance to keep the peace. Today, our policies must also focus on relations within nations, on a nation's form of governance, on its economic structure, on its ethnic tolerance. These are of concern to us for they shape how these nations treat their neighbors as well as their own people, and whether they are reliable when they give their word."[29]

In the same Wilsonian tradition, the Clinton administration wanted to make Russia safe for democracy and, as a result, was not inclined to separate Russia's domestic situation from its foreign policy. In fact, the administration presented the promotion of economic reform and political democratization as a precondition for the new Russia's emergence as a responsible world citizen. In a typical display of political hyperbole, President Clinton himself stated that "if the economic reforms begun by President Yeltsin are abandoned, if hyperinflation cannot be stemmed, the world will suffer."[30] Thus, in contrast to the Bush administration, President Clinton emphasized that helping Russia should be among the main goals of American policy. He also stated loudly and clearly that his administration has fairly specific views of the reforms the Russian government should undertake.

The administration has often defended its policy toward Russia by arguing that there were no credible alternatives. After all, administration officials have said, we must work with the legitimately elected Russian president. And we all agree that economic reform is essential to the long-term survival of democracy in Russia. And anyway, they conclude, the Cold War is over. Why should we provoke artificial conflicts with our new Russian friends?

There were, however, at least two alternative approaches to the Clinton administration's patronizing affection toward Russia: Nixon's romantic pragmatism and Kissinger's realism. And while neither advocated needless confrontation with Russia over minor issues, each recognized that Russian and American interests must differ, by definition, and that the United States must take strong steps to defend and advance its interests with respect to Russia when necessary.

• • •

It would be grossly unfair, of course, to blame everything that has gone wrong in Russia on the policies of the Clinton administration. Russia is too big, too complex, too well educated, has too much of its own tradition and patterns of operation, and is in effect too much its own universe for any foreign power—or even the world as a whole—to have a decisive impact upon its fundamental choices. Nevertheless, it is also true that a historic window of opportunity existed during the early stage of Russia's transition during which the United States could have given history a little push in the right direction. That opportunity was largely wasted by the administration. Worse, poorly designed and arrogantly implemented American attempts at social engineering served only to contribute to the emergence of an oligarchic system of Russian state capitalism. While Russia remains weak and dependent upon foreign giveaways, that system represents little immediate threat to its neighbors, let alone the United States as the world's sole remaining superpower. But if—or, more likely, when—Russia gets on its feet again, there is not likely to be much gratitude felt toward Yeltsin's Western sponsors.

The Chechen debacle should teach the United States two different lessons in this regard. The first—absorbed only too well by the West—is the weakness of Russia's armed forces and the unwillingness of Russian society to support a costly war even to protect its own territorial integrity. The second lesson—learned, in contrast, by very few in the United States and the West—is the tremendous and almost casual ruthlessness of the Russian leadership, which conducted the war without much discrimination between Chechen military units and innocent civilians, including Chechya's hundreds of thousands of ethnic Russians. All of these civilians, regardless of ethnicity, were Russia's own citizens. The invasion allegedly took place to restore constitutional order and to protect those citizens against "criminal elements." But if the Russian government is capable of treating its own citizens with such inhumanity, on what grounds can we believe that outsiders would have fared any better?

It is an oversimplification to claim that autocratic rule at home always leads to mischief abroad. Russia pursued a far more cautious foreign policy (partly because it was aggressively seeking foreign loans) under the reactionary rule of Alexander III than under his liberalizing predecessor Alexander II. Similarly, Spain under Franco and Chile under Pinochet largely left their neighbors at peace. But Russia is in a different category. It has not and may never be able to reconcile itself with the loss of its superpower status. It has territorial disputes—although they are low-key today—with many of its neighbors. Finally, it has growing global economic interests and a new elite willing to pursue them assertively. All of this is built atop a centuries-long imperial tradition and thousands of nuclear warheads.

How Russia is ruled is not of purely theoretical interest to the United States. It may make a difference—and much sooner than many think—in Russia's current restraint in foreign policy proving to be a lasting trend or merely a short-term interlude. And if Yeltsin's polarizing rule ends in social explosion, the potential consequences for America are difficult to overstate. Realism about the nature of Russia's post-Soviet domestic evolution is vital to American interests.

This is why the Clinton administration's cover-up of Russia's transgressions is not merely innocent sensitivity to a helpful client regime. It is, instead, dangerous mythmaking that may prevent the American people from comprehending an emerging challenge and from taking reasonable precautions while still possible without undue cost or risk.

Chapter Six

•

Russia's Founding Father

The failure of the August 1991 reactionary coup was widely touted as a victory for democracy in Russia. Nevertheless, as do so many historical events, the collapse of the conspiracy had unintended hidden consequences.

After the acceleration of the disintegration of the USSR, the most important of these consequences was probably the birth of Tsar Boris, Russia's new and now uncontested leader. Yeltsin was truly at his best during the crisis: he appeared determined and in control and was appropriately dramatic in his public appearances. The television image of the Russian leader atop a Soviet tank, exhorting his supporters to resist the coup, made him an instant global superstar.

In his recent memoirs, Aleksandr Korzhakov—Yeltsin's former top security aide turned bitter critic—sheds new light on the Russian president's personal contribution to the victory over the junta. According to Korzhakov, Yeltsin's staff had made all the necessary arrangements for the president to flee to the nearby U.S. embassy and request political asylum, but when this option was presented to Yeltsin, he categorically refused to abandon his country.[1] Gorbachev's isolation while on vacation in Crimea made Yeltsin the focal point of resistance to the coup. Had he abdicated that responsibility, his decision would have dramatically altered Moscow's political dynamics and could have allowed the conspirators—despite their pathetic ineptness—to gain the upper hand. Because the time for a successful reactionary takeover was long past, their success would likely have been short-lived—but even temporary success could have been sufficient to trigger major bloodshed or even a civil war. In that sense, Yeltsin indeed saved the day.

This episode highlights an important contrast to the American and many other revolutions: the fact that Boris Yeltsin had no peers with whom to share his heroic status as leader of the opposition. With the Nobel Prize–winning dissident Andrei Sakharov dead and Gorbachev an object of pity during his period of "house arrest" in his Crimean vacation home, Yeltsin appeared to be the sole standard-bearer of the anti-Communist Russian Revolution.

After the coup, Yeltsin's unique role solidified. The Soviet Union was in tatters and the Russian Supreme Soviet, which Yeltsin led before his election as Russian president in 1991 (and whose home, the White House, he shelled in October 1993), was initially very deferential to him. As a result, he had extraordinary opportunities to shape Russia's critical choices as a newly independent nation.

That these choices allowed Russia to avoid a return to communism, the victory of extreme nationalism, or bloody civil war (with the exception of Chechnya)—and brought peace with other post-Soviet nations as well as billions of dollars in Western aid—is to Boris Yeltsin's credit. An intuitive and pragmatic politician, he correctly understood the general direction of Russia's transformation and quickly bound his own career to it.

Whatever else may be said about Boris Yeltsin, he is without doubt a major historical figure with serious achievements to his credit. Among the accomplishments, he completed Gorbachev's job in destroying the Soviet Union. Then, without equivocation, he put an end to Communist domination and enthusiastically embraced the concept of private enterprise. Turning to the Russian people for political legitimacy, Yeltsin relied on popular elections both to stay in power and to introduce breathtaking—and highly controversial—reforms. Despite strong centrifugal trends, he kept Russia's diverse regions together during a painful transition period (again, with the notable exception of Chechnya). And finally, he won almost unprecedented international status for Russia as "a good citizen" through his relatively benign foreign policy. And despite his country's weakness, Yeltsin did gain at least symbolic status for Russia as a major democratic power that was entitled to treatment as an equal by far more developed, genuinely free nations.

Nevertheless, Yeltsin has proven incapable of one crucial step—

becoming a democrat. Worse, the man who claimed to be leading Russia to freedom was revealed to have significant despotic tendencies. Thus, after helping to destroy the Soviet Communist system, Yeltsin played an essential role in replacing it not with democracy, or even a gradual movement in the direction of democracy, but with what amounts to a new form of semi-constitutional authoritarianism with strong links to the new oligarchy. It is an open question whether this new hybrid form of autocracy at the top, autonomy for the regions, and an emerging civil society below will outlast Yeltsin. His form of government is bound to prove transitional as well; the regime is built so heavily around accommodating his interests and style that it would be unsuitable for virtually any other leader, let alone Russia's progress as a nation.

Of course, one may argue that Russia simply could not reject its Communist baggage so decisively in a handful of years by democratic means alone. But no explanation (or justification) can change the basic fact: just as Sakharov feared, democracy was always more of a tool for Yeltsin to accomplish his objectives than an end in itself. Boris Yeltsin liked the idea— and the prestige—of being Russia's first democratically elected president. While trying to preserve the trappings of democracy, however, he was frequently prepared to ignore its essence should his plans, and particularly his personal power, depend upon it.

Revealingly, Yeltsin himself does not mind being called a new Russian tsar as long as it is done with proper respect. The Russian president has even only semijokingly identified himself as "Boris I."[2] And his subordinates have repeated the comparison more seriously. Thus, then deputy prime minister Boris Nemtsov explained at the end of 1997, "I once referred to Boris Yeltsin as 'tsar,' and that was not by accident. The powers wielded by the current president are not inferior to those of a constitutional monarch." Unfinished, he continued: "I call him tsar according to the Russian tradition. But in fact, the president does resemble a tsar, at least outwardly. It would never occur to me to call Mikhail Gorbachev a tsar. While you can apply this title to Yeltsin without a jeer: the scope of his figure allows for it."[3] Nemtsov, who was known as the president's favorite and whose political future heavily depended upon Yeltsin, did not cause any controversy in Russia—or provoke even a pro forma rebuke from his boss—with this description.

In fact, few Russians would consider their president to be a Western-style constitutional leader even though his power was legitimized through elections. Tsar Mikhail, the founder of the Romanov dynasty, was himself chosen by representatives of the people in 1613. After that selection, however, the people's will was no longer seen as the primary source of Mikhail's mandate; his rule was then considered divine and, accordingly, was not subject to challenge. Times are of course profoundly different today, but the tradition of attributing greater legitimacy—and certainly greater authority—to the supreme leader than to legal norms and legislative bodies is still alive. If anything, it has been enhanced by Yeltsin.

Yeltsin's transformation into a new Russian tsar was an outgrowth of his own predispositions, the circumstances in which he found himself, and Russian history. It was perfectly logical for Yeltsin to wrap himself in the banner of democracy while the Soviet Union still existed. The other side— Mikhail Gorbachev and the central government—could rely upon the full resources of the Soviet state at a time when Yeltsin had at his disposal only his own charisma and the Russian people's hostility toward the declining Communist regime and their newly awakened love for freedom.

This is not to suggest that Yeltsin's attitude toward democracy was entirely cynical from the start; it was simply that democracy was the best weapon available to Yeltsin in his fight against the party establishment— and he seemed to be genuinely excited about its unexpected effectiveness. Given Yeltsin's own party background and limited outlook, the Russian leader was unlikely to engage in philosophical deliberations about the nature of democracy in Russia. Similarly, while he had a number of intellectuals as allies and advisors from his beginnings as a key opposition figure, Yeltsin was not close to any of them and, in contrast to America's Founding Fathers, was simply not interested in theoretical abstractions with no immediate use to him.

The problem was that Yeltsin, unlike Alexander II, saw no value in developing the rule of law or in building procedures to facilitate order and the growth of civil society. Instead, Yeltsin constantly adjusted the system to suit his needs through crude manipulations such as replacement of judges on the Constitutional Court who did not support him in his 1993 confrontation with the Supreme Soviet. The current chairman of the Court is Marat Baglai, a Soviet-era legal scholar on whom Yeltsin assumes he can count.

Yeltsin's legal manipulations demonstrate that, unlike Alexander II or Peter the Great, he is not an enlightened autocrat—he is perhaps more accurately described as a benign despot.

At first, Yeltsin's autocratic credentials actually added to his credibility as a formidable leader. When perestroika began to stall, two prominent pro-reform Soviet intellectuals, Andranik Migranyan (now a member of the Presidential Council, an advisory body to the Russian president) and Igor Klyamkin, gave a long and widely quoted interview making a strong argument that only an "iron hand" could ensure the success of reform in Russia.[4] According to Klyamkin, "the transition from a non-commodity economy to a commodity economy, to the market, has never, nowhere, in no country occurred in parallel with democratization. A more or less long rule by authoritarian regimes always preceded political changes." Migranyan was more direct: "Yes, at the present moment I am for dictatorship, for a dictator." From this perspective, even Chilean dictator Augusto Pinochet looked like an almost acceptable solution because he was an anti-Communist and a supporter of free enterprise. Measured against such a yardstick, Yeltsin's authoritarian tendencies looked like an asset.

Much of what has gone wrong in Russia's democratic experiment is attributable to the Russian president. "Certainly no small part of the responsibility for the lost opportunity of democratic development lies with Yeltsin himself. It was precisely he who made a choice which was definitely not in favor of democracy," writes prominent Russian analyst Liliya Shevtsova.[5]

Despite Yeltsin's enthusiastic public support for democracy, his past as a Party apparatchik was often more evident in his behavior. For example, it was surely as a regional Party functionary that Yeltsin learned to divide all those whom he encountered into two groups—superiors, who were owed obedience, and subordinates, of whom obedience was expected. He thus had no framework for partners or colleagues.

At the end of 1991, Boris Yeltsin had no superiors save rapidly declining Soviet leader Mikhail Gorbachev—and he did not believe that any of his subordinates were anywhere near his own level. As he told Nixon in my presence in 1992 while discussing his emerging disagreements with the Russian Supreme Soviet, "These midgets really have decided that they are somebodies. We'll have to find a way to teach them a lesson."

The consequences of the despotic side of Yeltsin's personality ranged from amusing (if occasionally disturbing) incidents to more fundamental problems. For example, when he became annoyed with presidential press secretary Vyacheslav Kostikov's jokes during a boat trip in Siberia, the Russian president ordered Kostikov thrown overboard. The presidential command was implemented by three senior officials: the chief of presidential security, the administrative director of the Presidential Administration, and the presidential chief of protocol. Only after Kostikov was allowed to climb out of the water did Yeltsin show his kind side—he offered his press secretary vodka to prevent him from catching cold.[6]

Even Yegor Gaidar, who served as acting prime minister and was Yeltsin's favorite for some time, acknowledges the domineering side of the Russian president's character. As Gaidar writes, "Yeltsin is intolerant of human weaknesses and is capable of patronizingly humiliating people. It never happened to me personally, but it did occur with others and I have to admit honestly feeling painful discomfort for both the excessively fawning servant and his condescending master."[7]

Although Yeltsin's arrogant capriciousness may seem to be merely a superficial flaw, the Russian president's attitude toward his associates created serious problems in his administration and had real policy implications. It was an obstacle to orderly decision-making, to the timely flow of information to the president, and to the full consideration of policy options. According to Korzhakov, Yeltsin considered it "offensive" to receive telephone calls on Saturday and Sunday—even from his key aides.[8]

Nixon and I experienced the peculiarities of Yeltsin's decision-making during the former president's final visit to Russia in March 1994. Nixon had originally planned the trip for the fall of 1993; his visit was postponed to the spring, however, after Yeltsin took one of his frequent unplanned and unexplained vacations in the wake of the October shoot-out with the Supreme Soviet. Then, in December 1993, the unexpected success of Vladimir Zhirinovsky's Liberal Democratic Party of Russia and the Communist Party added a new key dimension to the rescheduled trip: Nixon wanted to take a personal reading of Russia's opposition leaders, especially Zhirinovsky. At his request, I cleared this objective with the White House, and ultimately Nixon himself received President Clinton's personal blessing in a telephone call prior to his departure.

We realized, of course, that it would be best for Nixon to meet with Yeltsin first—for reasons of protocol—and that he should meet with Zhirinovsky, Communist leader Gennady Zyuganov, and former vice president

Aleksandr Rutskoi only afterward. Rutskoi was the most controversial, as he had just been released from prison after being amnestied by the new Duma over Yeltsin's strong objection. Several days before Nixon's arrival, however, we were informed that the meeting with Yeltsin could take place only on the last day of the trip as Yeltsin had decided—despite earlier assurances—that he wanted a light schedule after an upcoming long vacation weekend. In fact, the meeting would not even be in Moscow; Nixon was to travel to the Russian president's residence in the Black Sea resort of Sochi.

It was impossible for Nixon to postpone the visit—he had scheduled meetings with Ukrainian president Leonid Kravchuk in Kiev and German chancellor Helmut Kohl in Bonn immediately following his scheduled departure from Russia. The sessions with Kravchuk and Kohl could not be changed, because they had already been canceled when the fall 1993 trip to see Yeltsin was postponed due to his becoming "unavailable" as a result of what we were told was an unexpected vacation. Consequently, Nixon had to see Russia's opposition leaders before Yeltsin or give up on the meetings entirely, which would profoundly undermine the fact-finding nature of the trip. Nixon made the same decision he had taken vis-à-vis Mikhail Gorbachev in 1991: he put the investigative objective of the trip ahead of a meeting with the top leader.

Of course, Nixon wanted to do everything possible to avoid alienating Yeltsin. Arriving in Moscow shortly before President Nixon, I informed our official host—Security Council secretary Oleg Lobov—of our plans. I assured Lobov that Nixon would certainly find a way to make it clear that his meetings with opposition leaders in no way detracted from his strong support for the Russian president. While Lobov was obviously not happy to hear that Nixon would meet with Zhirinovsky, Zyuganov, and Rutskoi before Yeltsin, he did not raise a strong objection.

During the arrival ceremony at Moscow's Sheremetevo international airport, Nixon pointedly mentioned his intention to meet with opposition leaders several times. Taking into account that Lobov had been Boris Yeltsin's friend and confidant for twenty years and that our plans were also known to the Russian leader's top aides, we assumed that Yeltsin would be made aware of Nixon's intentions and that we would be informed if those plans created a serious problem. In fact, we received assurances to this effect from our Russian hosts. So we were quite surprised when Yeltsin suddenly exploded in responding to a question about his meeting with Nixon during a photo opportunity on Red Square on March 9. The Russian president, who had just returned from a long weekend at his dacha, angrily announced that not only would he not receive Nixon but that he would order other Russian officials not to see the former president as well.

As former press secretary Vyacheslav Kostikov reveals in his memoirs, Yeltsin's outburst on Red Square was entirely spontaneous. The Russian president did not consult any of his aides before canceling the meeting with Nixon. In fact, Oleg Lobov learned of Yeltsin's decision just as we did—through inquiries from the press. As Kostikov notes, "Yeltsin's reaction was obviously inadequate" and "totally out of proportion to the 'offense'."[9] In fact, as Kostikov also mentions, one bemused group of analysts speculated that Yeltsin's action was in fact orchestrated by the Clinton administration in order to embarrass Nixon and congressional Republicans.[10]

Kostikov dismisses this explanation as excessively Machiavellian and as evidence of Russia's tradition of conspiratorial thinking. Based upon my own information, from several sources, I am also satisfied that there indeed was no conspiracy directed from Washington. Instead, knowledgeable officials told me, the explanation for Yeltsin's unexpected outburst was nothing more than the Russian president's drinking at his dacha over the long weekend resulting from the March 8 International Women's Day holiday in Russia.

Knowing Yeltsin's habits, Lobov was reluctant to interrupt his superior's rest with the unwelcome news that Nixon planned to see Rutskoi and other opposition leaders. Other key Yeltsin aides also knew better than to bother him with anything short of an emergency, particularly when the project was someone else's—in this case Lobov's—responsibility. As a result, the Russian president learned of the meeting with Rutskoi not from his advisors, who could put the session in perspective, but from televised press reports of the session. The damage was compounded by the fact that Yeltsin had been drinking for some time upon hearing of the meeting and that, as usual, he was not in routine contact with his national security aides. So, when a reporter unexpectedly asked the Russian president a question about his scheduled meeting with Nixon the morning of March 9, Yeltsin responded emotionally that "after those whom Nixon was meeting with here, it is impossible. . . . It is impossible in Russia to act as one wishes."

Later, Yeltsin sought a public reconciliation with Nixon and eventually issued an invitation to the former president to visit Moscow again just prior to Nixon's death in April 1994. Although the incident generated headlines in Moscow and Washington, it did no great harm to Nixon—who in a way enjoyed the unexpected spotlight on what could have been a fairly routine trip—or to U.S.–Russian relations. For both Nixon and me, however, the episode was a troubling example of the Kremlin's decision-making practices—that is, of Yeltsin's propensity to make important pronouncements, sometimes with fairly serious consequences, on a whim.

•   •   •

Although the Nixon episode was somewhat embarrassing for Russia, Moscow paid much more dearly for Yeltsin's drinking in other cases. This is perfectly illustrated by the Russian president's infamous September 1993 statement in Warsaw—after a bout of drinking with Polish president Lech Walesa—that Russia had no objection to Polish membership in the NATO alliance. Despite the almost immediate retractions and reinterpretations of this statement by the Russian government, the statement lent new momentum to the enlargement of the Atlantic alliance, which eventually proved unstoppable.

Yeltsin's regular habit of public criticism of even the most important members of his cabinet—up to and including then Prime Minister Viktor Chernomyrdin—is part of the same mind-set. Like the Russian tsars, Yeltsin sought to avoid the blame for his government's policy failures by placing himself above the fray as a benevolent ruler under whom all would be well if it were not for his incompetent underlings. Also like the tsars, Yeltsin tried to ensure that none of his associates should become too important in their own right. Yeltsin's attitude was perhaps most graphically stated by Tsar Paul I, who said, "In Russia, only the person to whom I am speaking is big. And he is big only so long as I am speaking to him."[11] Thus, as Kostikov writes of Yeltsin, "In general, the president did not like to have bright people around him. In this he resembled an actor. He wanted all of the brightness of the spotlights, all of the applause, to belong only to himself."[12] While there have been quite a few bright and dynamic people associated with Yeltsin at different times, such as Boris Nemtsov, those individuals have rarely been admitted to the president's inner circle. Similarly, Yeltsin has made it clear that they should not be considered political heavyweights in their own right—he was more comfortable dealing with aides than with allies or partners.

This seems to be the principal explanation for Yeltsin's sudden firing of Chernomyrdin after the prime minister's successful meetings with Vice President Albert Gore in Washington in early 1998. I was among a small group of American business and foundation executives who met with Chernomyrdin in Blair House at the end of his talks. The prime minister seemed self-confident and relaxed and sounded like a political powerhouse rather than a senior bureaucrat. This new image, which Chernomyrdin projected on a number of other occasions, including on Russian television, was quickly conveyed to Yeltsin by zealous underlings and had a decisive impact on the president's decision to dismiss him. As Michael Specter wrote, the prime minister's main fault was that "after five years of dedicated service [he] was starting to look a bit too much like a leader to suit the first freely elected president of Russia."[13] By August, however—having already shown everyone who was the boss—Yeltsin was willing to take Chernomyrdin back after firing Sergei Kiriyenko, Chernomyrdin's short-lived successor.

The real result of Yeltsin's insecurity, however, was to undermine the effectiveness of the government as a whole and to set its officials against one another in attempts to redirect the president's ire—and especially his public criticism. Under these circumstances—as in Russia's Imperial Court—it is not surprising that a number of important decisions were based on Number One's mood and palace intrigues rather than the elaborate policy formulation processes of a modern state.

The peculiarity of Yeltsin's leadership is further exacerbated by his regular bouts of depression, which frequently follow victories in crises. After magnificent triumphs over his political opponents, Yeltsin has often been suddenly overcome by painful self-doubt—almost to the point of paralysis. Yeltsin himself writes that he endured "the debilitating bouts of depression, the grave second thoughts, the insomnia and headaches in the middle of the night, the tears and despair" just months after his heroic performance in August 1991 as he faced daunting obstacles in his attempt to introduce radical economic reforms in his devastated land.[14] Describing the difference between his crisis and noncrisis behavior, Yeltsin writes: "In emergency situations, I'm strong. In ordinary situations, I'm sometimes too passive.

Sometimes I don't look anything like the Yeltsin everyone has grown used to seeing. I mean, I can fly off the handle in a stupid way, like a child. That is probably a weakness."[15]

Coupled with his propensity for excessive drinking (at least before his fall 1996 heart surgery), these cycles of depression were incompatible with acting as a hands-on chief executive—particularly during a time of great transformation in Russia. On one level, Yeltsin was aware of his limitations: "I am not the head of the executive branch but rather the head of state," he said in 1992.[16] But in reality, Yeltsin was always uncomfortable with reigning but not ruling. He reserved all major decisions to himself, which, given Yeltsin's reliance on intuition rather than analysis and the absence of an orderly policy formulation process, meant that decisions were by definition often unpredictable, whether made by the chance of his mood or under the influence of one or another among his inner circle.[17] Had Yeltsin in fact been content with the father-of-the-nation role that Ronald Reagan performed so successfully—had he let others run the machinery of the Russian state—his country's government could perhaps have functioned fairly smoothly. But Yeltsin wanted to have it both ways—to have absolute power while maintaining distance from the affairs of government and refusing responsibilty for its failures.

Problematic for Russia in the best of times, Yeltsin's desire to decide everything but take responsibility for nothing became increasingly dangerous as the Russian president's health deteriorated. Yeltsin apparently failed to understand the "scale" of Russia's August 1998 currency devaluation and, in the early days of the Primakov government, reportedly ordered Central Bank chairman Viktor Gerashchenko to ban the use of dollars in Russia—resulting in widespread alarm among Russians and foreign investors, neither of whom were easily calmed. One American journalist described Yeltsin as "a tired old king who cannot control his unruly court and whose impulsive pronouncements have created so much havoc that no one in government can get anything done."[18]

More ominously, it was not just that Yeltsin could not reconcile himself to such notions as the separation of powers or even delegation of authority within the executive branch. Although he did not fully realize it himself, the Russian president's temperament—consciously or not—required the existence of enemies to justify his continuance in office, with extraodinary powers, regardless of his own record or popularity. In this respect, Gennady Zyuganov's Communists and Vladimir Zhirinovsky's nationalists are useful to the Russian president because they generate a sense of danger from which only he can save the country. Dividing the nation into "us" and "them" in order to present himself as the only savior has become Yeltsin's favorite political technique. Thus, in terms of his emotional predisposition, the Russian president more closely resembles Lenin and Stalin—albeit in a much milder version—than a Western-style leader seeking consensus within the law.

Three personality traits made it impossible for Yeltsin, the great destroyer, to become the founding father of Russian democracy. First, remarkably, the first Russian president lacks any political philosophy of his own. Nowhere in his two books, the memoirs of his associates, or my own encounters with Boris Yeltsin have I seen evidence of serious thinking about what kind of Russia Yeltsin sought to build. Second, he has an inordinate sense of himself, manifest in his assessment of almost all events through their effect on him personally as well as his virtually irresistible urge to seize and hold personal power. Finally, despite his rejection of the Communist past, Yeltsin has stayed true to one key element of the Leninist legacy—the belief that ends justify the means and, specifically, that Russia's rulers are entitled to rape the ruled into a better tomorrow.[19]

The gravest flaw in Yeltsin's leadership has been his lack of clearly defined policy objectives and a stable team in his administration to implement those objectives with or without the president's personal attention and involvement. On taking Russia's helm, Boris Yeltsin had next to nothing in this regard beyond his rejection of Russia's Communist past, a vague preference for democracy and partnership with the West, and a strong desire to get rid of Mikhail Gorbachev.[20] So, acting as was natural to him, Yeltsin opted to focus on leading political battles rather than formulating a substantive program for change in Russia. As Yeltsin writes with remarkable frankness in his memoirs, "I had an urgent need to share the total responsibility of running the country with someone, to assign to someone else the long-term planning and selection of courses of action and personnel, leaving me free to conceive all the tactics and strategy of the immediate political struggle."[21]

This preoccupation with political tactics at the expense of substantive

policy explains the regular drastic changes in the composition and orientation of Yeltsin's team. In 1991–92, Yeltsin relied heavily on radical reformers such as State Secretary Gennady Burbulis and Acting Prime Minister
Yegor Gaidar. Then, from 1993 to 1995, he became dependent on a shifting
constellation of conservative military and security officials, particularly his
own chief bodyguard, Aleksandr Korzhakov, whom he described as "a very
decent, intelligent, strong, and courageous person. While outwardly he
seems very simple, behind this simplicity is a sharp mind and an excellent
and clear head."[22] In 1996, Yeltsin executed another sudden and profound
turnaround and again favored the radical reformers—this time in the per-
sons of Anatoly Chubais and, in 1997, Boris Nemtsov, whom Yeltsin raised
from governor of Nizhni Novgorod to first deputy prime minister. By the
end of 1997, however, the political fortunes of the reformers were again
fading as Yeltsin turned to Prime Minister Viktor Chernomyrdin, who had
been in their shadow for most of the year. Then in early 1998, Yeltsin
zigzagged again, sacking both Chubais and Chernomyrdin and appointing
the untested and radical Sergei Kiriyenko as Russia's new prime minister,
only to replace him less than six months later with Chernomyrdin and,
when the Duma rejected his candidacy, with the even-more "anti-radical"
Primakov.

Although each of these personnel changes had major policy implications, there is less to each of them than meets the eye. Rather than repre-
senting real policy goals on Yeltsin's part, they more accurately reflect the
Russian president's remarkable ability to sense which tools will best serve
his political needs of the moment. While the jump from generals to radical
economists would be next to impossible for a politician with a clear policy
agenda, it was much less difficult for Yeltsin, who sought primarily to enhance his personal power. Thus, in 1991–92, he rode the wave of reaction
against the Soviet state by bringing the most radical economic and political
reformers into his camp. When the Russian people became disillusioned
with reform and the struggle with the Supreme Soviet threatened Yeltsin's
own hold on power in 1993, he discarded the reformers and picked up the
best tool he could find in a fight for his life: the Russian military and security services. Only in early 1996, when it became clear that Yeltsin would
need something more if he were to be reelected president in June, did he
get rid of the economically and politically conservative power ministers in
favor of a new group—the bankers and media barons then allied with Ana-

toly Chubais, who could finance and publicize the massive campaign effort Yeltsin required to fight back from single-digit approval ratings. In late 1997 and early 1998 Yeltsin seemed to favor Viktor Chernomyrdin over Chubais and his circle and then summarily sacked both (and many other ministers) in March 1998 and turned to Kiriyenko. Soon, however, a new financial crisis persuaded Yeltsin to bring Chubais back into government part-time as a special envoy to negotiate another multibillion dollar IMF-led rescue package. When the package failed to stop Russia's economic meltdown, Chubais was fired again without even a presidential phone call.

The casual manner in which Yeltsin made the historic decision to appoint his shock therapy government in the fall of 1991 illustrates the Russian president's ability to make tactical judgments without examining their policy consequences; it was particularly devastating to the cause of democratic reform in Russia. After the failure of the coup, Yeltsin knew that he wanted a young, pro-reform team; he had already come to the conclusion that old-timers—such as former Russian prime minister Ivan Silayev, who coordinated Soviet economic policy at the time—were not sufficiently bold or innovative for the enormous task of reorienting the Russian economy toward the market. Unduly optimistic about the possibility of immediate and massive Western aid, Yeltsin also wanted an economic team that would have the confidence of major Western governments and international financial institutions and therefore would be more likely to win significant Western economic assistance. This consideration argued strongly against drawing his economic strategists and spokespeople from the ranks of the nomenklatura.

But beyond this general predisposition, Yeltsin had neither a specific program nor a particular individual or group of individuals in mind to serve as his key economic advisors. At the time, the most obvious choice seemed to be the thirty-nine-year-old economist Grigory Yavlinsky, whose 500-Day Plan for Soviet major economic reform Yeltsin had originally supported. Yavlinsky's reformist credentials were also well established in the West and particularly in the United States, where he had worked closely with the team of Harvard University economists and political scientists under the leadership of Graham Allison, then dean of the John F. Kennedy School of Government.

Despite his qualifications, however, Yavlinsky was not at all acceptable to Yeltsin at the personal level. Yavlinsky argued that the far-reaching

economic reform required in Russia would be much less disruptive if some
type of joint economic space could be retained among the newly independent former Soviet republics. That this argument was also advanced by
Gorbachev—and could even be used as a rationale to keep the Soviet president in office—made Yavlinsky instantly suspect in the eyes of Yeltsin and
his entourage.[23] In addition, Yavlinsky's impeccable credentials as a reformer were matched by his status as a real intellectual with a propensity
for nuanced thought. He was not given to speaking in bumper-sticker-style
clichés. As a result, as one former Yeltsin aide told me, the Russian president had no personal chemistry with Yavlinsky and often had difficulty following his arguments or simply became bored during his encounters with
the young economist.

Finally, and perhaps most important, even before Russian independence
Yavlinsky had an element of the same "star quality" possessed by Yeltsin
himself. Despite his youth and political inexperience, he had his own following and a strong sense of himself as an independent political actor with
his own objectives. This essentially disqualified Yavlinsky from serving as
Yeltsin's economic tsar. After all, there could be only one real tsar in Russia—and Yeltsin was it.

Instead, Yeltsin gave responsibility for the Russian economy to another
young academic, Yegor Gaidar, whom he appointed first deputy prime minister. When I met Gaidar myself in 1993, I was struck by how—in the tradition of many Russian intellectuals—he had traveled from one extreme to
the other in his economic views without stopping in the middle. He had
gone from defending the centrally planned economy to believing in free
markets and had become a greater monetarist than Milton Friedman in the
process. But I got nowhere trying to engage the then former acting prime
minister in a discussion of how to apply general market principles to the
specific political and economic circumstances in Russia.

Georgi Arbatov, the well-known director of the Institute of the USA
and Canada at the time, had a similar impression. "Gaidar is a capable
scholar and an honest man. But I think there is something sectarian in him,
something of a fanatic neophyte who, having been fully immersed in Marxism, dives into something opposite—an extremely conservative Western
economic theory—without the slightest personal experience in the practical
economy."[24] When I compared notes with Henry Kissinger, who had also

come to know Gaidar, the former secretary of state observed that the architect of Russia's radical economic reform reminded him of a true-believer assistant professor in a small college who enthusiastically adopted new economic and political concepts but lacked the intellectual depth to use them creatively.

What helped Gaidar with Yeltsin was that, in contrast to Yavlinsky, his arguments were not burdened with complexity and self-doubt. Although a scholar like Yavlinsky, the younger Gaidar—thirty-five years old in fall 1991—was less prominent in his academic achievements. Unlike the coauthor of the 500-Day Plan, however, the future acting prime minister had spent a number of years outside the academic world as a Party publicist and had directed the economic departments at the Party's leading journal, *Kommunist,* and by 1990 its premier daily newspaper, *Pravda.* Working in the field of public relations, Gaidar learned to reduce complex economic arguments to easily digestible points for mass distribution and to present them with mandatory optimism. Yeltsin also believed that the physically unimposing Gaidar could be the president's advisor, or his instrument, but would never be a potential competitor.

Basing his decision to appoint Gaidar on these criteria, Yeltsin gave relatively less weight to substantive questions of economic policy. He would later discover the consequences, as he admits in his memoirs, in which the Russian president notes that Gaidar and his ministers—most also intellectuals—"were done in by their inability to implement even their own programs" and that they would "just crash through everything as if they wanted to tear apart with their bare hands the entire decrepit system of rank and top-down management."[25] They had no real understanding of how the Soviet economic system worked, what exactly they were trying to destroy, or what it would take to build the new market economy.

But like the tsar in appointing his ministers, once Yeltsin had selected Gaidar, the Russian president left his new economic policy chief free to act virtually without supervision. Thus, Gaidar and his team of untested, inexperienced intellectuals had nearly full control of Russia's economic reform during the economy's most critical moment. Yeltsin established no self-correcting mechanisms within the presidential administration to provide analytical scrutiny of Gaidar's policies and had no advisors with other perspectives. As a result, the Russian leader's involvement in the economic

reform process was essentially limited to the selection of Gaidar, his defense against criticism, and, when Gaidar's policies finally made Yeltsin
himself too vulnerable, his dismissal.

Ironically, two of the president's protégés led the opposition as well.
Despite his status as a master political tactician, Yeltsin is a rather poor
judge of character. The Russian leader has often found new "favorites" on
the spur of the moment and promoted them to positions of power and pres-
tige only to suffer bitter disappointment upon discovering that the individuals he selected were not up to the job. Even when Yeltsin correctly
determined who would be most useful to his cause at the moment, he routinely disregarded the longer-term consequences of his intuitive but ill-
considered senior appointments. One of the Russian president's most
fateful mistakes in this respect came in June 1991, when he selected the
Afghan war hero and Soviet air force general Aleksandr Rutskoi as his
running mate in Russia's first direct presidential elections.

It is now apparent from a variety of sources—including Yeltsin's own
memoirs—that Yeltsin did not give much thought to the qualities he should
seek in selecting an individual who, he surely hoped, would be Russia's
first democratically elected vice president and, at least in theory, the sec-
ond-most-powerful person in the country behind Yeltsin himself. He knew
that his principal advisor and political strategist Gennady Burbulis was very
eager for the job but, in Yeltsin's view, Burbulis lacked charisma and could
not bring additional votes to his very popular master. "How can I take Burbulis?" Yeltsin complained to Korzhakov. "When he appears on TV his
face, eyes, and manner of speaking would alienate potential voters."[26]

The idea to select Rutskoi appears to have come from Yeltsin's speech-
writers, who approached Korzhakov with the suggestion that the war hero's
military credentials and good looks would appeal to "patriotic voters"
(Russian nationalists) and women, respectively. Yeltsin instantly clung to
the proposal, summoned Rutskoi to his office, and offered him the number-
two spot. With tears in his eyes, the grateful Rutskoi promised to justify
Yeltsin's confidence in him and, as Korzhakov writes, "to serve as a guard
dog in front of his office."[27]

The trouble was that Yeltsin himself did not know whether he wanted
Rutskoi to be his guard dog, his attack dog, or to have any other role in the
government. (In fact, Yeltsin probably wanted a lap dog as vice president

more than anything else—as demonstrated by subsequent events.) Rutskoi, a former Yeltsin critic who became the leader of a pro-Yeltsin Communist splinter group, was a man of considerable ego and ambition who took his elevation to the second-highest position in the Russian Federation quite seriously. He was shocked to discover after the presidential election that there was no substantive place for him in the Yeltsin government. "They have picked me to squeeze as a lemon and then to throw me away because they do not know how to treat people with opinions of their own," a bitter Rutskoi told me later, in 1992. Rutskoi even admits in his memoirs that he considered resigning from his post just days after the end of the failed August 1991 coup. Having played a major role in organizing the defense of the Russian White House, finding allies among the Soviet military establishment, and arresting the members of the junta, Rutskoi was not even invited to the victory party organized by Yeltsin and his entourage.[28]

At the same time, Rutskoi was under constant attack by Burbulis, who believed that Rutskoi had "stolen" the vice presidency from him and Burbulis's protégé, Yegor Gaidar. Gaidar, in his memoirs, relates an attempt by Rutskoi to organize a reconciliation between himself and the Burbulis-Gaidar team to rebuild ties destroyed by sharp disagreements over economic shock therapy. Invited to a conciliatory meeting, Gaidar did not exactly pick up the proffered olive branch; instead, he decided to respond in language "accessible" to the vice president. "Sasha," he said, "you don't understand anything about economics. So why do you become involved in it?"[29]

When an irreconcilable conflict between the president and the parliament erupted in 1993, Yeltsin turned to General Korzhakov and the power ministers, who became his inner circle. It was not just that circumstances forced Yeltsin to make a deal with the devil to maintain his power; rather, once he found that shock therapy and the reformers were not a magical "silver bullet" to eliminate serious opposition to his rule, he was forced to look for a new political tool to maintain his hold on the country. His own imposition of radical economic reforms on an angry parliament and a reluctant population logically forced Yeltsin to rely upon repressive instruments to keep the opposition in check.

It was this iron fist that Yeltsin used to beat down the Supreme Soviet in October 1993 after the parliament refused to obey his decree disbanding the body, which even he admitted to have been unconstitutional. After several days of upheaval in Moscow, Yeltsin ordered tanks to shell the Russian White House, which was then the seat of the parliament. He later used the incident to ensure that the new parliament, especially its opposition-dominated lower chamber elected in December 1993, stayed down. The Russian president also did not hesitate to use military force in Chechnya, where he began a full-scale war in December 1994. Thousands of civilians were killed indiscriminately to put down the Chechen resistance—including vast numbers of ethnic Russians living in the Chechen capital of Grozny. The intervention was staged in the name of protecting the rights of those very people slain so carelessly.

Later Yeltsin's changing political fortunes brought about the demise of the power ministries and the return of the radical reformers. Faced with single-digit approval ratings and visibly deteriorating health in early 1996, the Russian president had only three options: to step down without running in the June elections, which would not have been an easy decision for a man addicted to absolute power who (because of his contribution to the collapse of the USSR and his responsibility for the Russian blood spilled in Chechnya) feared far worse treatment from his successor than that he had given Gorbachev; to cancel the presidential elections (as suggested by Korzhakov), which would have made him totally dependent upon the questionable long-term loyalty of the security services and critically damaged his image in the West (and the money pipeline that went along with it); or to find a way to buy as much of the election as possible and steal as much as necessary. It was the ability of Anatoly Chubais—who had been dismissed from the government only months before for his failure to resolve the problem of Russia's wage and pension arrears—and his banker allies to deliver the preferred third option, which led to Yeltsin's latest change of direction. Thus, the Russian president's decision to turn to Chubais was hardly proof of a rediscovered commitment to economic and political reform.

Until the late 1997 and early 1998 cabinet reshuffles, most Western officials and commentators were very encouraged by Boris Yeltsin's reliance on the new team of reformers led by First Deputy Prime Ministers Anatoly Chubais and Boris Nemtsov. There was a tendency to believe that the Russian president's decision to appoint the reformist group represented a new commitment to economic and political change in Russia. While such an interpretation would have been defensible in 1992—when Yeltsin selected

Gaidar and the first reformers, including Chubais—too much happened between 1992 and 1997. Predictably, by the end of 1997, Yeltsin had reduced Chubais's and Nemtsov's powers and complained of the excesses of market reforms.

The quest for personal power became a consistent and dominant theme of the Yeltsin presidency. The first time I met Yeltsin, I was struck by his self-centeredness, indeed, his self-obsession. Of course, most major leaders have a strong sense of themselves; Richard Nixon certainly took himself seriously. What is unusual about Yeltsin is the extent to which his heroic vision of himself is devoid of any meaningful purpose beyond his own political fortunes. Once the Soviet Union had been destroyed and his rival Gorbachev had lost, Yeltsin became a near-absolute leader in search of a mission.

Because he did not have much interest in substantive policies and was, by his own admission, suspicious by nature, he took any disagreement with his actions not as legitimate criticism of his policies but as a direct challenge to his authority and even his manhood. In fact, at this stage, when his ministers came under attack in the parliament or the media, that would encourage Yeltsin to stick with them as long as the personal chemistry stayed right. He was convinced that sacking an unpopular minister could be taken as a sign of contemptible weakness rather than commendable intent to improve the effectiveness of government. As he told Nixon and me during a meeting in 1992, "they pretend to be shooting at Gaidar, but they are really aiming at me." Gradually, Russia's more Machiavellian politicians came to understand that direct attacks on a cabinet member were counterproductive—they served only to bind Yeltsin more closely to the target. Palace intrigue, they learned, was usually much more effective.

Driven primarily by personal interests, Yeltsin could not survive without adhering to another Leninist principle—the notion that the ends justify the means. As Yeltsin himself told Nixon (whom I accompanied) in 1992, "You cannot build a new Russia wearing white gloves." What he did not realize was that after decades of totalitarian immorality, it was precisely "white gloves" that Russia needed most. Deliberately disregarding his country's need for a new political legitimacy based upon law and morality meant inflicting damage to the Russian democratic experiment even more grave than the potential costs of the most unattractive compromise with the opposition.

Yeltsin's willingness to do whatever was necessary to advance his personal interests manifested itself even before the October 1993 crisis. As Korzhakov reports (without denial from the Yeltsin camp), the Russian president had earlier ordered the security services to make arrangements to dissolve the parliament if it should vote to impeach him in March 1993. The appropriate decree was signed, security personnel with poisonous gas were pre-positioned close to the parliament building, and buses to remove the deputies were gathered nearby. It was only the failure of the impeachment vote that saved the parliament for another six months.[30]

When Yeltsin finally decided to get rid of the parliament in late September, a number of his liberal advisors objected to what Kostikov admits "from the formal legal point of view meant a *coup d'état*."[31] Even Gaidar was concerned with "the disproportionate strengthening of presidential authority and the collapse of the whole system of checks and balances."[32] Reservations based less on principle and more on the fear of provoking a shootout with an unpredictable outcome were expressed by then prime minister Viktor Chernomyrdin and chief of the presidential administration Sergei Filatov. But Yeltsin's mind was set. Neither the constitution nor the reluctance to spill the blood of fellow Russians was much of a constraint to him.

Today's rampant corruption in Russia also owes much to Yeltsin's personality and attitudes. While he has already ordered numerous "successful" anti-corruption drives since taking office, few senior officials have lost their jobs—let alone been prosecuted—as a result of illicit conduct. Those who have found themselves in trouble with the law have done so usually after first losing the president's favor (for unrelated reasons). Thus, alleged financial irregularities were simply an excuse when Yeltsin fired Security Minister Viktor Barannikov in 1993. As Kostikov explains, Yeltsin is perfectly willing to forgive indiscretions on the part of loyal servants. It was questions regarding Barannikov's loyalty and suspicions about his contacts with Supreme Soviet chairman Ruslan Khasbulatov and Aleksandr Rutskoi that in reality lead to his downfall.[33]

Although there have been no serious allegations that Yeltsin is himself corrupt, a growing body of information suggests that his family members have benefited financially from their close relations with the Russian president. None of these charges have been proven, but they do tarnish the luster of the former man-of-the-people who now crisscrosses Moscow in a long cortege of limousines. Yeltsin's imperial persona was similarly illustrated almost immediately after the August 1991 coup when he ordered the construction of a new presidential aircraft and began to acquire a collection of luxurious new residences. Another "tsarist gesture," traveling throughout Russia to dispense hundreds of millions of rubles in gifts to whomever he sought to impress, became a fixture of his political campaigns.[34]

Most American commentators initially accepted at face value Yeltsin's September 1997 announcement that he would not seek reelection, which the Russian president has repeated several times subsequently.[35] However, Yeltsin has stated repeatedly in the past that he would not run for president again. He has never considered himself bound by these announcements and few in Russia have taken them literally. For example, in a September 3, 1997, Russian newspaper article analyzing Yeltsin's pronouncement that he would not run for president in the year 2000, one commentator proposed three explanations for his statement: that Yeltsin wished to discourage premature speculation about who will be president in 2000, that he was "testing the water," and that he was indeed planning to step down. "You can really understand that," the writer continued, "his age, his grandchildren . . . Nonetheless, this assumption seems so fantastic that we will not waste any time on it."[36]

During a 1992 meeting with Yeltsin at which I was present, Nixon complimented the Russian leader on one of his earlier public pronouncements that he would not stand for reelection upon the expiration of his first term as president. Nixon called the statement "a masterstroke," which sent the message to Yeltsin's opponents that he could afford to pursue unpopular policies. At the same time, Nixon added, the announcement put his political enemies on the defensive and would be to Yeltsin's advantage even should he eventually decide to run again. The Russian president smiled broadly. "Of course, of course," he answered gleefully. Yeltsin was pleased to show that he, too, was a member of the exclusive club of world leaders and could speak its language.

In retrospect, it is apparent that Yeltsin was not just playing political games in making his 1992 announcement that he would not run. The Russian president was already exhausted by the burden of power and frustrated with the constant struggle with the Russian Congress of Peoples' Deputies. According to the memoirs of former presidential security chief and confidant General Aleksandr Korzhakov, Yeltsin openly told Korzhakov in a moment of despair in early 1992 that he "[did] not have the stomach for a second term and [needed] a successor."[37] Nevertheless, when the time came to make the actual decision, in late 1995, what Yeltsin really could not stomach was surrendering power to someone else. His family and his entourage had little difficulty persuading him that there was no alternative to his running again.[38] The Russian financial crisis has likely changed this calculus. On top of Yeltsin's declining health and a constitutional provision limiting the president to two terms (which could be reinterpreted by loyal judges under happier circumstances), Yeltsin's new extreme unpopularity—including among the elite—makes it very unlikely that he will run again in the year 2000. But so long as he remains in office, the lack of strong alternative domestic power centers ensures that Yeltsin will continue to have a profound, if no longer commanding, impact on Russian politics. Russia may have to wait until the post-Yeltsin era for its laws to take precedence over its tsar's needs.

Chapter Seven

•

The New Oligarchy

Boris Yeltsin was deadly effective as a destroyer; he made a major contribution to ending both Soviet communism and the Russian Empire. In building the new Russia, however, Yeltsin's record has been mixed. His greatest economic achievement—the massive privatization program which, according to former first deputy prime minister Anatoly Chubais, removed 70 percent of Russia's gross domestic product (GDP) from state control in five years[1]—was based on shattering the complex network of economic interdependencies among the republics of the Soviet Union. And it imposed tremendous new hardships upon the already impoverished Russian people.

Privatization has also been a great transformation. It has brought an end to the notorious central planning system of the Soviet Union and to the state's near-total control of the economy as well. It has created an entirely new social stratum of multimillionaire entrepreneurs. It has given many Russians the opportunity to start their own businesses and provided many more with a chance to decide for themselves whether they would like to work for the government or in the new private sector. And it has drawn foreign investment to Russia on a scale not seen since the period of the New Economic Policy (NEP) of the 1920s. Most important, however, privatization has helped ordinary Russians by filling store shelves, which were nearly empty at the beginning of Yeltsin's rule, with consumer goods and foodstuffs. It is no overstatement to say that privatization has made Russia into a profoundly different country: Russia is ruled in a different way and exhibits increasingly different social values, including attitudes toward work, from those evident during the Soviet period. With this record, it is understandable and possibly even inevitable that the architects of privatization should be lionized by many in the West as symbolic of Russia's transition to democratic capitalism.

Yet, even Russian president Boris Yeltsin, privatization architect Anatoly Chubais, and former reformist deputy prime minister Boris Nemtsov acknowledge that economic reform in their country faces serious challenges. Nemtsov has stated that "Russia now has to choose one of two ways—bandit capitalism or democratic, peoples' capitalism."[2]

Russia does indeed face this choice. But the danger of corrupt oligarchic rule and what Nemtsov has called "the semi-gangsterish accumulation of capital"[3] did not emerge as an inevitable product of dark forces of Russian and Soviet history or the special circumstances of Russia's post-Communist evolution. The pervasive and inefficient central controls, poorly motivated labor force, and suppressed individual initiative of the Soviet period have, of course, had an influence on Russia today. So have the unique conditions of Russia's transition—the economy devastated before the process even began and, in contrast to Central Europe, the lack of any social or political force capable of leading an effort to build capitalism from below.

Anyone who visited Russia in late 1991 or early 1992 would have seen a country on the brink of disaster. The store shelves were literally empty—shops routinely lacked butter, milk, fish and meat, and fresh vegatables. There was a sense of despair and of urgency in Moscow's food stores, where there was often nothing available but canned vegetables and poor-quality sausages. I became particularly worried in one shop close to Red Square that Nixon visited to examine Moscow's food situation firsthand in May 1992. At first, his reception was very friendly; several customers recognized the former president and requested his autograph. They complained about the empty store shelves and asked Nixon to tell the truth about their suffering on his return to America.

But the mood quickly changed. The large knot of people around Nixon provoked other shoppers, who were unable to approach the service counters. Then there were angry voices: An elderly man shouted that Russians did not need Americans first to destroy the Soviet Union and then to come to Moscow to gloat. And a middle-aged woman tried to ask the former president for money. I could see that our security escorts, two ex-KGB men—former employees of the Ninth Main Directorate, the rough equivalent of the U.S. Secret Service—were becoming increasingly nervous. One of them, who had been Soviet president Mikhail Gorbachev's last key bodyguard, asked whether I could find a way to quickly but delicately remove Nixon from the building—which I did.

To me, the incident in the store was a small illustration of the explosive potential accumulating in Russian society. Seeing that potential firsthand during this trip and previous trips encouraged Nixon to lobby the U.S. government to do more for Russia and triggered his criticism of the Bush administration for lacking the courage and vision to help the Russian democratic experiment. Within Russia, the easily perceptible tension naturally motivated Boris Yeltsin to look for people and policies that could help him to defuse the explosion quickly. So obvious was the desperate need to proceed with major economic reform that the Congress of People's Deputies, the same body that Yeltsin would dissolve by force in October 1993 after it turned against reform, gave the Russian president extraordinary powers to implement economic reform by decree. This new authority was of course in part a reflection of the generally deferential attitude toward Yeltsin throughout Russia after his spectacular performance in facing down the August 1991 putsch. But it was also a function of widespread consensus in Russian society that the status quo was unacceptable. This consensus provided Boris Yeltsin with a mandate for radical change.

Yeltsin could rely on no such consensus, however, regarding what kind of economic reform was necessary. Worse, there was no political party or institution to mobilize support for a transition to the free market, let alone a coherent set of ideas about how such a transition could be accomplished.

Within the politically relevant portion of the spectrum of Russian opinion at the time, the best-known advocates of market-oriented change were grouped around Grigory Yavlinsky, coauthor of the 500-Day Plan for Soviet economic reform embraced by Yeltsin but ultimately rejected by Soviet president Mikhail Gorbachev. Yeltsin's problem with the Yavlinsky circle— beyond the young economist's ego and high profile, both of which irritated the Russian president—was their claim that radical economic reform could be conducted without inflicting intolerable pain on the general population provided the Soviet state were to simultaneously assure an adequate social "safety net" to protect the citizens who would be most severely affected.

This was unattractive to Yeltsin because it would have required time for pa-tient negotiations with the parliament to develop appropriate legislation. Equally problematic for the Russian president was the assumption in the Yavlinsky camp that it was impossible simultaneously to destroy the com-plex system of economic relations between enterprises in the various re-publics of the USSR and to manage a tolerable transition to a capitalist economy. This view made Yavlinsky and his followers useless to Yeltsin, who by the fall of 1991 was preoccupied with snatching the Soviet Union away from Gorbachev even at the cost of its destruction. And since Yeltsin had persuaded himself that the other Soviet republics were so dependent on Russia that, as he told Nixon in March 1991, they would eventually "crawl" back to their elder brother, the temporary disintegration of the union did not seem to him to be too high a price to pay for attaining supreme power in Russia and, ultimately, in the post-Soviet territory.

Yeltsin could not afford to rely upon reform proposals that depended upon even the short-term survival of the union. Because Yeltsin could real-istically control only Russia, he needed a plan to save Russia alone. More-over, being by nature an impatient autocrat, he did not like gradualist approaches contingent on parliamentary support.

The alternative plan was provided by a group of academics headed by Gennady Burbulis's protégés, Yegor Gaidar and Anatoly Chubais. As aca-demics, neither Gaidar nor Chubais—nor most of their close associates—had had any previous experience in government service. Similarly, none had held management positions in the economic sector or had any signifi-cant background in finance. As a result, their understanding of the Russian economy was largely theoretical. Worse, because economic data in the USSR were highly classified state secrets, they—like the vast majority of Soviet academic economists—did not fully comprehend the Soviet Union's economic condition.

In the absence of such knowledge, the views of the Gaidar-Chubais group were shaped to a large extent by Western economic literature and their personal contacts with Western colleagues. Given the appeal of West-ern books and articles as forbidden fruit—and the historical tendency of Russian intellectuals to go to extremes—it is not surprising that pro-reform Soviet economists were tempted to adopt Western economic formulas wholesale, without much attention to specific Russian conditions. And be-cause quite a few Russian intellectuals had an understandable urge to reject anything connected with not only communism but also Marxism and socialism during the last days of the Soviet Union, Milton Friedman was much more attractive to them than John Maynard Keynes.

Gaidar and his colleagues also shared the attitude of many Moscow intellectuals toward the non-Russian republics of the Soviet Union and did not have much respect for other Soviet nationalities, except for the Westernized Baltic states. As one of Gaidar's close associates put it to me in January 1992, "Who cares about these 'Chuchmeks' [inferiors or subhumans]. Russia will only be better off without them." Of course, there were important objective reasons why by the fall of 1991 Russia had little choice but to make some of its key economic decisions unilaterally; most important, Moscow did not have control over the other emerging independent states' economic policies. But the young reformers' predisposition to say "to hell with the rest of the Union" contributed to their disinclination to coordinate their economic policies with Russia's newly independent neighbors during the transitional period, even on a short-term basis. As Ukrainian president Kravchuk told Nixon and me in June 1992 when I pointed out that Ukraine's radical economic break with Russia would be detrimental to both countries, "Moscow preaches economic cooperation in general, but whenever we try to coordinate anything in particular, we encounter great obstacles, and often they come from precisely those who are viewed in the West as champions of economic reform."

This attitude toward the other newly independent states temporarily raised the stock of Gaidar and his colleagues with Yeltsin, as did their emphasis on destroying the old economic structures right away—even before they could be replaced with the new free-market foundation. The proponents of what became known as shock therapy did not intend to harm the Russian people. As Harvard economics professor Jeffrey Sachs, a principal advisor to Gaidar and his colleagues at that time, later told me, he knew that radical reforms were bound to bring pain to the majority of Russia's citizens. Nevertheless, he believed that quick major surgery with a chance of recovery would be preferable in the long run to mild and ineffective treatments over many years. Referring to an old Russian proverb that calls for measuring seven times before making a cut, Gaidar himself later wrote that "at the end of 1991, there was no time left to measure even twice let alone seven times. We had to cut into a live body."[4] Still, in the Russian revolutionary tradition (from which the newly anti-Communist intellectuals were not immune), Gaidar was much more concerned about doing what he believed was right than with winning support from the people. As he told me in 1993, after he had been removed from his government post, "You cannot do what is necessary by following the peoples' wishes or by allowing those who are unable to adapt to dictate government policy." So long as Boris Yeltsin was willing to support him, it did not matter much to Gaidar if those who were "unable to adapt" were the majority of the population. One need not search in Gaidar's informative and basically honest memoirs for evidence of anguish over his decision to inflict pain on his fellow citizens. It is not there.

Using the extraordinary powers granted to Boris Yeltsin by the Russian parliament on November 1, 1991, to implement economic reforms, the Gaidar team quickly proceeded with its privatization program. The program was approved unanimously by the Presidium of the Supreme Soviet on December 27, two days after the resignation of Soviet president Mikhail Gorbachev and Yeltsin's installation in his Kremlin office. Five days later—on January 2, 1992—prices were freed on 80 percent of wholesale and 90 percent of retail items. Privatization and the price liberalization became two central pillars of Yeltsin's reform policy.

Within several months, radical economic reform began to generate a powerful political backlash. The virtual elimination of price controls predictably led rapidly to hyperinflation. The considerable savings accounts amassed by Russians during the Soviet period—when widespread shortages of foodstuffs and consumer durables encouraged savings—were eliminated almost overnight. Cruelly, the collapse of the ruble occurred before price liberalization was able to fill store shelves with food and consumer goods. Instead of having plenty of money with nothing to buy, Russians suddenly discovered that they had no money when the products they had long sought finally became available. In statistical terms, Russia's gross domestic product and per capita income declined by some 50 percent in the period 1991–94 while prices increased 1200 percent.[5] Although these figures do not include Russia's considerable unreported income hidden from tax collectors, they indicate that the country experienced an economic catastrophe much more severe than the Great Depression in the United States.

Predictably, as the general population lost whatever resources were available for investment, privatization soon came to mean the rapid transfer of state property to Soviet-era economic managers and underground entrepreneurs with hidden reserves of hard currency, gold, and other valuables. As a rule, property was transferred not to the highest bidders or to strategic investors who planned to put their own money into enterprises to restructure their operations and increase efficiency and long-term profitability. The principal beneficiaries of privatization were the remnants of the old *nomenklatura* and speculators out to make a quick ruble.

One need not have been a Communist to be appalled by this outcome of radical reform. Andrei Sakharov's widow Yelena Bonner, an early supporter of Gaidar, observed that the effects of the Gaidar economic program on the Russian people "make the concerns of traditional dissidents appear trivial by comparison."[6]

Gaidar and Chubais were well aware that the "voucher privatization" program in which Russian citizens received vouchers entitling them to a token share of state property would lead to "inevitable and large-scale speculative redistribution of these checks" to a small group of well-connected and well-financed individuals. Yet they were willing to pay this price in the name of a "radical reduction of the share of state property."[7] So rapid was this process that in two years the private sector became responsible for over 50 percent of Russian economic output, a share greater than that in a number of Western European countries. It was never adequately explained why so much had to be done so quickly, without real preparation, for privatization to be considered a "success." It was almost as if Gaidar and Chubais had inherited the mind-set of Stalinist-era managers overseeing the collectivization of agriculture, who considered a rapid increase in the percentage of peasants living on collective farms much more important than improving—or even maintaining—levels of agricultural output.

Was there another way? Gaidar and his team denied that there were any alternatives, but Nixon and I thought otherwise. Our idea, shared by many leading pro-reform Russian economists and Western business leaders alike, favored a combination of stopgap stabilization measures, a more gradual and systematic approach to major economic reforms emphasizing the elimination of monopolies, industrial restructuring, and the aggressive pursuit of foreign investment, particularly as a source of capital for small and medium businesses in the agricultural and consumer product sectors. Like China, Russia needed to make a concerted effort to build private enterprise from below.

We also believed that the measures should be based on legislation (however imperfect) rather than presidential decrees of questionable legality. Yeltsin, however, was persuaded by the young reformers that such systematic change—which would take time and require dialogue with the Parliament—was not necessary. He took it as an article of faith that radical reforms would unleash the Russian economy's productive forces and that the worst would be over in less than one year. Yeltsin promised this publicly to the Russian people on numerous occasions: in February 1992, for example, he said, "I am convinced that by the end of 1992 we shall see light at the end of the tunnel, and in 1993 we shall begin to get out of the crisis."[8] He reiterated this assessment privately to Nixon in my presence during a Kremlin meeting on June 4, 1992.

During the same meeting with Yeltsin, Nixon—who had traveled to Moscow in his capacity as honorary chairman of the Fund for Democracy and Development, a nonprofit organization that provided humanitarian assistance to Russia—outlined his ideas on how the United States could help the Russian economy, including a proposal to arrange a "safety cushion" for the Russian government in the event that economic deprivation led to rioting or other social disorder. After consulting a number of U.S. corporate executives, the former president suggested to Yeltsin that American private emergency assistance could be mobilized very quickly. He also expressed hope that if large-scale assistance became necessary, the U.S. government could be persuaded to join the private humanitarian effort.

Although Nixon thought that a humanitarian aid program on the scale of the Marshall Plan was unlikely, he believed firmly that the United States could use its international leadership to organize a modest campaign helpful to Russia during the most traumatic phase of its transition. He also thought that the American government could persuade international financial institutions, particularly the IMF, to relax their then stringent lending criteria in order to allow Russia to receive loans while creating opportunities for economic growth by temporarily continuing limited subsidies to select, basically sound state enterprises and even increasing investment in promising government sectors such as the oil and gas industries. Because Nixon was not confident that the IMF or the World Bank—both of which focused appropriately on macroeconomic issues—would be capable of managing what was first and foremost a political and social crisis in Russia, the former president favored the creation of a special body under the G-7 nations to administer assistance to Russia. He was particularly concerned about the role of the IMF and the World Bank because he believed that the reforms that might make the most sense from a narrow economic standpoint could never be implemented by democratic methods—and that in the long run building democratic institutions in Russia was more important to U.S. interests than macroeconomic indicators.

Finally, Nixon emphasized to Yeltsin the dramatic potential for foreign investment in Russia. After discussions with several American business leaders, he hoped that if Russia were to open its doors to foreign capital, the level of foreign investment in Russia could realistically reach up to $100 billion over a five-year period. This was probably overoptimistic given the level of uncertainty in Russia, which was surely a deterrent to foreign investment. Still, even a more modest inflow of capital would significantly improve Russia's economic situation by providing the Russian state with additional tax revenues, creating millions of new jobs for the highly qualified workers no longer needed in its ailing military-industrial complex and stimulating a genuine interplay of free-market forces.

Nixon and I discussed the ideas included in the plan with a variety of Russian economists and senior political leaders including Grigory Yavlinsky and other reformist economists to senior officials in Yeltsin's government. While none of them were responsible for the contents of the plan or agreed with it in every detail, all felt that Nixon was on target in his approach to Russia's economic crisis.

In the end, however, Nixon's plan never came to fruition. This was in part due to the fact that the Bush administration was simply not prepared to invest its political capital in assistance to Russia during an electoral campaign dominated by the refrain "It's the economy, stupid." It was also a consequence of the situation developing in Russia. Although conditions remained quite bad and the polarization of Russian society was only deepening, the Russian people were too exhausted and too preoccupied with their day-to-day survival to stage large-scale riots, protests, or other forms of stronger resistance to the regime. Simultaneously, Russia's younger and better-educated citizens were sufficiently encouraged by the new opportunities in their country to stay out of the streets. This reduced the urgent need for Washington to proceed with an expensive and controversial aid package for Moscow.

The position taken by Gaidar and his reformist colleagues also worked against the implementation of the plan, particularly its crucial foreign investment component. Precisely because Gaidar was, like Yeltsin, an instinctive advocate of drastic and polarizing approaches, he did not want to "rock the boat" further by allowing massive foreign investment. To put it simply, he believed that a widespread public impression that Russia's state property was being transferred into the hands of foreigners would be a political kiss of death to economic reform and quite possibly the Yeltsin government as well.[9]

No less important, Gaidar and his team needed to use the redistribution of state property for their own domestic political ends (to create a powerful constituency supporting further reform) and could not afford major foreign involvement in the Russian economy. Gaidar explained to me that he and his colleagues drew inspiration from the example of tsarist prime minister Petr Stolypin, who issued a decree in 1907 allowing more successful peasants to withdraw from Russia's rural agricultural communes and become independent property-holders. These so-called "strong peasants" soon became political supporters of the tsarist regime and ultimately played a major role fighting against the Bolsheviks during Russia's 1917–22 civil war. The absence of any real organized domestic constituency for radical economic reform drove Gaidar to attempt to create supporters for his policies through similar means—this time, the redistribution of state property. His "strong capitalists"—again created by decree, though not given a name— were intended to become the backbone of Russian political and economic change.

But there were differences between Stolypin's reforms, which are very popular among Russian reformers today, and the path taken by Gaidar. Most important, a distinct group of prosperous peasants who eventually became "strong peasants" already existed when the tsar's chief minister drew up his plan. They were simply waiting for an opportunity to break the chains of the communes and to develop their full potential. No similar group existed in the Russia of 1991–92; seventy years of communism had insured that there was no readily available class of small capitalists and entrepreneurs ready to make it big. But Gaidar was undeterred—he believed he could create such a group or, more accurately, that the government could establish one by decree. Thus, ironically, the initiation of Russia's radical market reform was accompanied, even facilitated, by an ambitious effort at social engineering.

As suggested above, Gaidar's decision to attempt to create a political base of Russian capitalists affected the Russian government's ability to attract foreign investment. Because Russia's new capitalists had very little capital, they were opposed to foreign participation in the Russian economy on anything approaching equal terms. Furthermore, foreign investment could not be drawn into Russia overnight—especially without a real legal basis. Because the initial steps of the Gaidar team almost immediately alienated the Russian parliament, that legal basis, including such key elements as property rights for foreign firms, was almost impossible to obtain.

Events could have proceeded differently, Communist Party chairman Gennady Zyuganov told Nixon during the former president's last trip to Russia in March 1994, had the legislation on foreign investment been presented to the parliament by a government enjoying popular confidence. I, for one, was never persuaded that protecting foreign investors would have been more controversial than Yeltsin's other emergency measures imposed by decree in late 1991 and early 1992. Widespread positive attitudes toward the West immediately following the collapse of the Soviet Union created a window of opportunity for the Yeltsin government to open Russia to investment. But the Gaidar team failed to exploit that chance, and Russia's most radical economic reformers ironically became protectionists.

One reason Gaidar and Chubais believed that Russia could afford to postpone opening its doors to foreign investment was Moscow's growing access to IMF and World Bank funds. Russia became a member of the IMF on June 1, 1992; by August 5, the IMF had approved the first billion dollars to support the Yeltsin government's macroeconomic reforms.[10] The loans, however, benefited Russia's emerging oligarchy more than they did the Russian people. Futhermore, abundant evidence demonstrates that a significant portion of the issued credits were either mismanaged or diverted into private offshore bank accounts. And credits from the IMF and the World Bank were no substitute for large-scale foreign investment in Russia's transformation.

Russian and foreign critics of shock therapy in Russia often blamed the IMF for being too preoccupied with macroeconomics at the expense of other priorities in Russia, such as allowing state investment in still viable industries and protecting the country's fragile democracy from political backlash against harsh reform measures. Although this criticism is partially justified, it is important to remember that the young reformers more often than not welcomed IMF pressure for change as a domestic political alibi for the firmly monetarist policies favored by Gaidar and his colleagues.

The reformers' zeal was illustrated in the wake of the December 1993 parliamentary elections, in which the nationalists and the Communists scored unexpected gains. Commenting on the troubling defeat of Russia's reformist politicians and, by extension, the Yeltsin government, Deputy Secretary of State Strobe Talbott—probably the greatest patron of Russia's reformers in Washington—acknowledged that the evident unpopularity of the government's reform program suggested that Russia needed "less shock and more therapy."[11] Revealingly, then Russian finance minister Boris Fedorov—who returned briefly to government as the tax service chief under Kiriyenko—immediately protested Talbott's comment and termed his remarks a "stab in the back" of the reform.[12]

Russia's pro-market reforms proceeded without an adequate legislative foundation, without a candid explanation to the Russian people of the likely hardships, without popular support, without signficant new investment (foreign or domestic), without a credible mechanism to ensure the meaningful restructuring of the privatized (more often than not transferred at nominal prices to management) government enterprises, and finally, without giving the vast majority of the population a real stake in the reform process. Under the circumstances, it is not surprising that Gaidar and Chubais could not count on the backing of existing social groups or that in the absence of such support they attempted to create a new class of property-owners who could be relied upon to support radical change because of its great personal benefits.

Three distinct but interconnected groups were the principal beneficiaries of privatization and, as a result, became key components of Russia's post-Communist business and, ultimately, political elite. The first group was composed of managers who quickly turned their administrative control into de facto property rights and even true ownership of their enterprises. The managers' acquisition of shares or controlling stakes in their companies was facilitated by the abolition of dozens of Soviet-era industrial ministries, which were either transformed into huge monopolies—such as Gazprom, the successor to the Soviet gas ministry—or individual enterprises.

Firms like the gigantic Gazprom and its counterpart in the oil sector, Lukoil, inherited control over enormous natural resources with considerable market potential outside Russia and, despite low investment, have done relatively well. Although the government retained a major stake in these energy giants, their management was more or less independent of government control. Most enterprises, however, gained only theoretical autonomy, because without money, other resources, or established commercial suppliers (as opposed to suppliers dictated by Soviet central planners), they remained almost totally dependent upon the state for survival. New semiprivate companies in the declining military-industrial complex, and the manufacturing sector in general, were at best struggling to stay afloat; they had lost many of their suppliers and customers alike in the disintegration of the USSR and, since the Russian treasury was already strained to the breaking point, they could not count on any meaningful new investment. At best, these ailing enterprises could hope for minimal subsidies barely sufficient to keep their doors open and their workers out of the streets. Even under these circumstances, however, the so-called red directors were able to enrich themselves very quickly and became the virtual owners of their factories and mines in the absence of laws regulating the new market conditions. More important, the *bespredel*, or "everything goes," environment in which Russia found itself meant that the managers could easily divert funds from their firms to newly established personal Swiss and other foreign bank accounts without much fear of punishment.

The second group to benefit from privatization emerged very quickly, literally from nowhere: the new commercial bankers. Unlike the managers of major companies like Gazprom and Lukoil—who had long and distinguished records in Soviet industry—most of the bankers had no background in finance. Instead, they had an instinctive understanding of the new opportunities created by the collapse of the old economic order, skills in cultivating important connections that would provide them with access to government accounts (the only source of funds, as no significant private accounts were available at the time), and a sense of how to turn *bespredel* to their advantage. They were entrepreneurs rather than managers.

In the Soviet environment, the bankers could not realize their potential because private entrepreneurship was treated as a felony and punished with long prison terms. Some of today's bankers actually did serve time in labor camps after being convicted of "economic crimes." Most, however, labored in other professions ranging from organizational science (LogoVAZ head Boris Berezovsky) to theater production (Most Bank founder Vladimir Gusinsky) to official foreign trade (Oneksimbank chairman Vladimir

Potanin). As has often been demonstrated in revolutionary wars, when yesterday's farmers and teachers rapidly become today's famous generals, the new tycoons had hidden talents of which they themselves were likely not aware until their hour had come.

It is difficult to see any redeeming value in the the third component of the emerging elite—Russia's new organized crime lords. Soviet-era underground enterpreneurs were not alone in moving swiftly to exploit the *bespredel* created by privatization *à la* Gaidar and Chubais; outright gangsters were also quick to see the magnitude of the potential gains. At first, the crime bosses limited themselves primarily to protection rackets by providing a "roof," or *krysha*, for their unhappy customers. Before long, however, they began to use their money and, more important, their muscle to become co-owners and even sole owners of increasingly important enterprises. Because many of these enterprises also served as "sponsors" of severely underfunded local law enforcement agencies, particularly in Russia's poorest regions, the local godfathers soon became untouchable. Some fixed parliamentary elections and, as members of the State Duma, acquired immunity from prosecution.

In an environment in which no laws existed to regulate the new relations among commercial entities, and courts and law enforcment agencies were frequently corrupt, it soon became routine to settle business disputes through intimidation and assassination. Rarely were those responsible for these acts brought to justice, and when they were, the offenders were almost without exception small fry without high-level political connections. In remote regions, the situation was even worse; local leaders often used criminal enforcers to protect their personal business and political interests. While the federal government did not condone this pervasive violence, Yeltsin and his pro-reform advisors never gave the battle against organized crime sufficient priority to reexamine the economic reform process.

A dramatic example of this trend is the meteoric rise of Anatoly Bykov in the Krasnoyarsk region. A well-known gang leader, Bykov was accused of using numerous contract murders, extortion, and bribery to reach the heights of power in local business and politics. Bykov not only became chairman of the board of the huge Krasnoyarsk aluminum factory, but also acquired control of a regional television station and, in December 1997, was elected to a regional legislature.[13] A remarkable—but not atypical— aspect of Bykov's rise was the extent to which he was aided by key local officials and even by the police. One former chief of the Krasnoyarsk region police, General V. Ageyev, did not dispute Bykov's criminality and acknowledged that, on orders from above, local law enforcement agencies created a united front with the mafiosi against foreign shareholders in the Krasnoyarsk aluminum factory.[14] Later, when Bykov emerged as an important supporter of General Aleksandr Lebed's successful bid to become governor of Krasnoyarsk, the argument was made that while Bykov operated outside the law, he was essentially a surrogate for the security services in a battle with even worse criminals who could not be stopped by legal means. By then, Bykov was considered "respectable" enough for Lebed to welcome his endorsement. As *Izvestia* put it in an extensive article on Bykov, "Criminality is marching straight into power. . . . Not only the authorities but even common sense is demonstrating total paralysis when confronted with the Russian criminal world."[15]

The three groups obviously had diverse backgrounds, philosophies, and interests. The managers, for example, were more conservative and more committed to continuing state subsidies. Their interests were represented in the Russian government by officials such as former factory director Yuri Skokov, former construction manager and later provincial party secretary Oleg Lobov, and the then deputy prime minister for energy and former Soviet gas minister Viktor Chernomyrdin. They were solid citizens who mistrusted economic experiments. As a rule, they were also capable administrators. Because the new bankers had to build everything from scratch, they favored radicalism and experimentation. Also in contrast to the industrialists, they and their champions in government—Gaidar and Chubais— were opposed to inflationary government spending (that is, the subsidies favored by the industrialists), which they viewed as detrimental to financial stability regardless of how justified it may have been to protect particular industries or on general humanitarian grounds. Organized-crime leaders had little interest in economic policy at all provided no one interfered with their efforts to grab everything within reach and to penetrate legitimate businesses.

Nevertheless, the groups shared two important common interests. First, all three depended upon access to government money. This was more obvious in the case of the industrialists, who relied almost entirely on federal funds, but was no less true of the bankers, whose well-being—or even survival—was contingent on their ability to obtain government accounts. In

fact, government agencies were not-so-secret shareholders in many banks
and even held controlling interests in some of Russia's new and supposedly
private financial institutions. Like the industrialists and the bankers, criminals also wanted access to state funds. More important, just as the managers
and bankers, organized crime leaders sought a closer relationship with the
authorities. At the most fundamental level, they needed to avoid prosecution
for their illicit activities. The more ambitious also saw an opportunity to use
corrupt law-enforcers against their rivals.

Second, faced with skyrocketing inflation and mounting political instability further aggravated by shock therapy, none of the three groups was interested in investing its profits inside Russia. According to estimates of
Grigory Yavlinsky, $22 billion flowed out of Russia in 1996 alone.[16] In con-
trast to America's nineteenth-century robber barons, to whom they were
frequently and erroneously compared in the West and even in Russia, the
new Russian business leaders became rich primarily by redistributing the
existing assets of the state rather than by building new railroads and steel
mills or drilling oil wells. Worse, they exported their newfound wealth
rather than reinvesting it in Russia to create new wealth for the benefit of
the entire nation. Given that the vast majority of Russians were not invited
to participate in this bonanza and that, unlike the old Soviet elite, the "new
Russians" delighted in conspicuous consumption, it was almost inevitable
that the Gaidar-Chubais reforms would generate strong popular backlash.

Leaving aside widespread resentment of the new Russians, it was only
to be expected that there would be considerable opposition to any economic
reform that sought profound change in the way the Soviet economy was
run. Post-Communist parties had already benefited from the dislocations
and suffering caused by the transition to a market economy in Central Europe, where the tradition of free enterprise was much stronger than in Russia. And former Communists returned to power for a time after only a few
years of economic experimentation even in Lithuania, the pioneer among
Soviet republics in the struggle for independence.

Nevertheless, it was not inevitable that the backlash against political
and economic transition should become so strong in Russia or that it should
take such extreme and ugly forms. Russia's problem was that Boris Yeltsin
and his entourage were attempting dramatic reform without much regard
for public opinion and, particularly, public suffering. Simultaneously, Russia's opposition forces increasingly turned to the slogans of the past and

seemed determined to outdo the government in intolerance and radicalism rather than offering a responsible, moderate alternative in the social-democratic tradition like Central Europe's post-Communist parties.

This predicament arose for several reasons. First among these was the absence of a democratic tradition in Russia, where, for example, compromise was often seen as a demonstration of weakness. Despite the collapse of Soviet communism, the Russian people continued to believe in a political "absolute truth" that only the ignorant or the simply evil would fail to recognize and support. This pulled Yeltsin's critics onto the self-destructive path of what would become known as "irreconcilable opposition." Second was the absence of any established political parties beyond the most retrograde remnants of the Communist Party, the particularly hard-line faction opposed to perestroika. It was because of this situation that the old-style Marxist-Leninists—many of whom turned in a nationalist direction—became the organizational focus of the opposition.

Third, the disorderly and often violent disintegration of the Soviet Union transformed many Russian politicians into superpatriots virtually overnight. Some, such as Ilya Konstantinov, were former dissidents and early supporters of Yeltsin whose political philosophy turned almost 180 degrees after the collapse. An early anti-Communist who refused to be co-opted by the Soviet system, Konstantinov became a founder of the National Salvation Front and entered into a loose alliance with the Communists. After a fall 1992 debate with the intelligent and witty Konstantinov on Russian television, I asked him privately about this apparent contradiction. Intriguingly, despite being considered one of the greatest villains of what liberals called the "Red-Brown Camp" (the tactical alliance of Russian Communists and nationalists) at the time, he remained highly critical of the Communists. "I am still an anti-Communist," he said. "And I have major disagreements with the Communist Party. But when the Motherland is sinking, you cannot be too particular about who helps you to man the lifeboat. We have to deal with the enemies of the Motherland first and will settle our differences with the Communists later."

There were, of course, other voices in the opposition. There were old perestroika supporters such as Gorbachev's right-hand man, Aleksandr Yakovlev, and former Moscow mayor Gavriil Popov, who tried to create a social-democratic movement. There was the accomplished agricultural manager Nikolai Travkin, at that time second in popularity only to Yeltsin,

who led the middle-of-the-road Democratic Party of Russia. Finally, there
was Grigory Yavlinsky, who, in alliance with two other liberal intellectuals,
foreign affairs scholar and former ambassador to Washington Vladimir
Lukin and Leningrad scientist Yuri Boldyrev, created the Yabloko Party, a
pro-reform alternative to the Yeltsin government that advocated more measured economic changes domestically and a philosophy of "enlightened patriotism" in Russia's foreign policy.

But all three centrist movements had a difficult time developing a genuine popular following. The social democrats were terribly burdened by their
historical link to Gorbachev, who had become extremely unpopular throughout Russia. Travkin's Demoractic Party suffered from internal disputes and
could not define a coherent and comprehensive alternative philosophy; it opposed the government tactically, but not strategically. Yabloko did better but,
with its rational and nuanced positions and its emphasis on respect for the
law and democratic procedures, it had difficulty developing wide appeal in
an impatient country wracked by systemic crises, lacking a middle class, and
eager for instant solutions to its problems. The fact that Yabloko's Grigory
Yavlinsky was a half-Jewish intellectual did not help either.

Another reason for the marginalization of centrist groups in Russian
politics was that the extraordinary political polarization of Russian society
left moderates without a meaningful role. Had Yeltsin, Gaidar, and Chubais
accepted what every politician in the West takes for granted—namely, that
voters cannot be forced to make major sacrifices against their will and that
imperfect but democratically sustainable reforms are better than more radical changes imposed autocratically—they would likely have found many
opportunities for dialogue with those elements of the Russian political spectrum who were supportive of reform but uncomfortable with shock therapy.
In the end, the moderate politicians and their constituents had to choose between joining one of the two unattractive extremes or becoming politically
irrelevant.

Still, if these moderate groups had succeeded in creating a united front,
they might have been able to compete with the Communists and extreme
nationalists in defining the nature of opposition to the Yeltsin government.
However, they were stymied in their efforts, to the extent such efforts were
undertaken, by Russia's political tradition, which emphasized two alternatives: blind obedience, or anarchy and discord. Russian intellectuals had

been notorious since the nineteenth century for their inability to set aside their differences and create genuine alliances of equals; if there was no pre-eminent leader, each was at war with all. To this day, Russia's moderate and pro-reform groups have been unable to cooperate in large part because of the unwillingness of any of their leaders to give up the top spot.

The Yeltsin-Gaidar-Chubais govenment provided the irreconcilable op-position with a great deal of ammunition. But the government was not alone; Russia's lack of democratic tradition, the extreme circumstances of the Soviet collapse, the absence of a middle class, and the weaknesses and mistakes of the Russian intelligentsia all cooperated to strengthen the oppo-sition.

The opposition rallied around two figures, Ruslan Khasbulatov and Aleksandr Rutskoi. Neither Khasbulatov nor Rutskoi was a born extremist. Khasbulatov, a former economics professor, strongly supported Yeltsin as his number-two in the Russian Supreme Soviet prior to Yeltsin's election as president in June 1991. In a May 1992 meeting with Nixon, Khasbulatov, who was already a bitter critic of radical reform, went out of his way to em-phasize his support for foreign investment and a good relationship with the United States. He was still careful not to criticize Yeltsin personally. Rut-skoi was also very positive about America and the West; when I first met him in January 1992, when he was the vice president, he proudly informed me that he was leaving the office immediately after our meeting to visit an exhibit of photographs of John F. Kennedy. "It is sacred for me to be a part of this show in Moscow," Rutskoi told me. More concretely—like many other senior officials at the time—Rutskoi had created his own fund to pro-mote humanitarian assistance and foreign investment. He was certainly not a philosophical opponent of capitalism or the West. Nevertheless, the logic of the opposition struggle, their wounded egos, and the arrogance of the Yeltsin government in its dialogue with the parliament drew both Rutskoi and Khasbulatov into the ranks of the irreconcilable opposition.

The defeat of the Rutskoi-Khasbulatov camp in October 1993 was un-deniably good news in Russia and for the West alike. The unreformed Communists of the Supreme Soviet and extreme nationalists of the Na-tional Salvation Front were much more radical than Central Europe's so-cialists. Athough it is impossible to know how far they may have turned Russia back toward communism and against the rest of the world, the risk was serious. Western satisfaction with Yeltsin's victory over the Communist-nationalist opposition alliance was both natural and wise.

It was, however, much less wise to portray the Yeltsin victory as a triumph of democracy, as was done by President Clinton, German chancellor Helmut Kohl, and a number of other Western leaders. By emphasizing the overwhelming priority of proceeding with radical reform despite strong social opposition, Clinton, Kohl, and other Western leaders appealed to the Russian president's worst authoritarian instincts and ultimately contributed to a series of events detrimental to democracy in Russia.

Despite Yeltsin's victory over the Supreme Soviet, the nationalists and the Communists did not have to wait long for their revenge, which came at the polls during the parliamentary elections of December 1993. Ironically, the government's overwhelming defeat at the hands of the Communists and Vladimir Zhirinovsky's extreme nationalist Liberal Democratic Party of Russia did not humble its leaders. Speaking in the aftermath of the elections, on December 28, Deputy Prime Minister Chubais boasted that the reforms were indeed successful because 67 to 70 percent of Russia's former state enterprises had been privatized. Russia's industrial and agricultural production decreased dramatically. Its gross domestic product was shrinking. Inflation was up sharply. But to the architect of privatization, economic policy was firmly on course because so many enterprises had been transferred at least nominally into private hands.

But Gaidar, Chubais, and their followers apparently concluded from their electoral defeat that not only the disbanded Congress of People's Deputies but *any* parliament was bound to oppose radical reform. Their response was thus to ignore the legislature as much as possible, particularly since the new constitution (approved in the same voting) gave the president enormous powers. Quoting a March 15, 1789, letter from Thomas Jefferson to James Madison, Gaidar claims in his memoirs that "the tyranny of legislatures is the most formidable dread at present, and will be for long years."[17] However, in taking Jefferson's statement out of its context, Gaidar failed to mention that Jefferson was not arguing for the creation of an overbearing Yeltsin-style executive; rather, he was advocating the Bill of Rights in order to protect the individual from the tyrannical tendencies of government in general.[18]

The radical reformers (who were regularly praised as democrats by the Clinton administration) began to feel that their only salvation was in build-

ing a new authoritarian regime. In a December 31 presentation to his supporters at the pro-reform Interaction club, Gaidar admitted that the opposition forces were in the ascendance again after the elections. Thus, he and
others at the club agreed, the only available means to avoid a fascist
takeover in Russia was a transition to "enlightened authoritarianism" based
on an evolving oligarchy, a new political and business elite that would be
created deliberately by the government. Those present at the gathering were
apparently optimistic that this elite would join the government in promoting
"liberal democratic" positions and would not develop its own agenda.[19]
Thus, instead of accepting the fact that the tragic events of October 1993
and the resurgence of the radical opposition in the December parliamentary
elections meant that something had gone fundamentally wrong with shock
therapy, the proponents of radical reform concluded that, since society
would not support reform, they had to create a new oligarchy as their political base.

But then prime minister Viktor Chernomyrdin reached a very different
conclusion: "We should face the truth and admit that many people voted
against the hardships and mistakes of the current reforms. The election defeat is a personal rejection of Gaidar. The same goes for Chubais. They have
a lot to think about now."[20] Shortly thereafter, Gaidar was forced to resign.

Despite Gaidar's dismissal, Chubais was saved by the personal intervention of the Russian president and was later even promoted. Later, under
his stewardship, the Russian government organized the soon-to-be-infamous
"loans for shares" auctions through which major banks provided loans to the
federal budget in return for the right to manage auctions of shares in state-
owned firms if the credits were not repaid. Because the government never intended to make good on the loans—and because the auctions were
transparently organized to transfer the shares to the very same banks at rock-
bottom prices—the "loans for shares" form of privatization quickly became
scandalous. Even Chubais ally Aleksandr Kazakov, head of the State
Property Committee during 1996, admitted that the policy was a disaster.
"We provided the loopholes through which dishonest hands reached in from
both sides," he said.[21]

Loans-for-shares privatization further contributed to the symbiotic
relationship between the oligarchy and the state. While increasing the dependence of the oligarchy on government largesse, it simultaneously encouraged the oligarchy to seek greater control of the government in order to

reduce the risks of the dependency. Finally, it consolidated the relationship between Chubais and Russia's top bankers, whom he was later able to mobilize to ensure Boris Yeltsin's reelection as president in 1996, and thus led (after Yeltsin's victory) to the so-called *semibankirshchina,* or "rule of the seven bankers."

Despite the severe consequences of Chubais's privatization, many Western analysts argue that it was the only path open to Russia. There were, however, at least two alternatives, as has been demonstrated by the cities of Moscow and Nizhni Novgorod, each of which won substantial autonomy from the federal government in conducting privatization. In Nizhni Novgorod, former governor Boris Nemtsov relied heavily on the economic advice of Grigory Yavlinsky and, unlike the national government, did indeed attempt, although not always consistently, to sell state property in fair auctions.[22] Nemtsov won this freedom from central control because of his demonstrated commitment to reform and his reluctance to be frank about the differences between his policies and those implemented at the national level by Chubais and Gaidar.

In Moscow, Mayor Yuri Luzhkov created what may be considered a more rational and effective variant of Chubais's crony-based state capitalism by convincing Boris Yeltsin to "tell Chubais to leave Moscow alone" and taking control of local privatization efforts himself.[23] In Luzhkov's city, no major activity has taken place in the private sector without participation by the city government. Although this has encouraged widespread suspicion that the mayor and his closest associates have personally shared in the proceeds, it has—unlike the loans-for-shares scheme—brought substantial revenue into the city's coffers to the direct and visible benefit of Moscow's residents.

Significantly, both Nemtsov and Luzhkov won easy reelection to their respective posts; in fact, Luzhkov brought in over 90 percent of the vote in an election widely perceived to have been both free and fair.[24] In contrast, at the national level, the Gaidar-Chubais reforms provoked a powerful political backlash both in December 1993 and again in December 1995. In each of the two elections to the State Duma, the Communists and their allies were the clear victors; in the latter election, Gaidar's Russia's Democratic Choice party was unable even to exceed the 5 percent threshold necessary to win parliamentary seats through proportional representation. Chubais became perhaps Russia's most unpopular official.[25]

Chapter Eight

•

Whither Russian Democracy?

No simple formula exists to explain the current Russian political system. Russia is not a liberal democracy; however, it is also very different from the totalitarian regime of the Soviet period. In fact, Russia's present system is a complex and contradictory synthesis of democratic, oligarchic, and authoritarian elements. It is also still in transition, and nothing is predetermined about the eventual outcome of its evolution. Liliya Shevtsova observes that "as Russian society slowly determines whether the country will move further in the democratic direction, return to authoritarianism, or turn toward a new oligarchy, it is clear that there will be no one-dimensional answer to questions regarding Russia's future. The absence of conditions favorable to the development of democracy in Russia is counterbalanced by a combination of factors which hamper the establishment of an authoritarian regime and particularly a dictatorship."[1]

On the democratic side, Russia has now experienced several fairly free presidential and parliamentary elections based on universal suffrage. It has an elected two-chamber parliament which, despite its imperfections, is by no means a Soviet-style rubber-stamp body. On this point, even the parliament's harshest critics would agree. As a matter of fact, the two houses do have influence on the policy process; the speakers of both the State Duma and the Federation Council participate with the president and the prime minister in meetings of the so-called "big four" and are separately consulted by the government in an attempt to find common ground in solving

Russia's pressing political and economic problems. Each also played an important role in the appointment of Prime Minister Yevgeny Primakov.

More broadly, with the exception of extremist Communist and fascist groups, all parties are allowed to participate in the political process. At the same time, the introduction of private property and the emergence of major private and semiprivate companies has created a steady source of considerable nongovernmental funding for political campaigns. And despite their dependence on the government, Russia's tycoons, and especially entrepreneurs in regions far from Moscow, have learned to hedge their bets through contributions to a variety of political groups, including even the Communists.

Russia's judiciary is also officially independent; there is no longer any Communist Party of the Soviet Union—or any other nationwide "supreme" body—to give orders to judges. The Constitutional Court has the right to overrule even the president himself. The fact that Yeltsin is not in full control of Russia's legal machinery was demonstrated most clearly in February 1994, when the parliament voted over Yeltsin's strong opposition to grant amnesty to Aleksandr Rutskoi, Ruslan Khasbulatov, and other participants in the October 1993 parliamentary resistance to the president. More significantly, notwithstanding direct orders from the president, Yeltsin's own attorney general, Aleksei Kazannik—who yielded his parliamentary seat to Yeltsin in 1989 to enable him to become a member of the USSR Supreme Soviet—determined that he had no constitutional alternative to releasing the amnestied politicians. He set the rebels free from prison and promptly resigned.

Finally, Russia's "subjects of the Federation," as its eighty-nine regions, republics, and provinces are called, enjoy considerable autonomy. Six years after Russian independence, all of their governors and legislatures have been elected at least once and, accordingly, have won new legitimacy and greater power to stand up to the central authorities. Even in Moscow, the seat of the federal government, Mayor Yuri Luzhkov has shown that a popular and self-confident local leader can win considerable autonomy—including on such sensitive matters as privatization. Collectively, the regions have also gained increasing influence through the Federation Council.

Many developments, however, are less encouraging. Elections are free, but not truly fair. With the exception of the Communist Party, newly established political parties are in the earliest stages of development and have shown little progress. The Russian parliament has influence but little real power—and when he wishes, Yeltsin often feels free to ignore it. The courts have not become truly separate from the executive branch in practice. While the fact that a variety of federal and local agencies seek to influence their decisions gives them a modicum of latitude in reaching verdicts, this independence goes only so far—especially in the provinces, where the courts oppose local authorities only rarely.

After a brief interlude between the collapse of Communist Party control and the emergence of new owners, the media, particularly broadcasters, are now again under the influence of outside interests. Television, radio stations, and newspapers are now largely controlled by powerful business clans or, in the regions, by lesser entrepreneurs, who blatantly use the Russian media to promote their own objectives. Further, because the media are both so unreliable and, without the weight of the Soviet state behind them, so powerless, they can be safely ignored by both the authorities and by the Russian people, who do not pay much attention to what they see, hear, or read. In fact, since literally anything—including the most serious allegations—can be arranged for a price, to the extent that people care about political news, the majority are interested less in whether particular charges are true or false than in what is behind the charges. Thus, whether it is General Korzhakov accusing leading pro-reform television commentator Yevgeny Kiselev of being a long-term KGB informer,[2] or Kiselev's influential television station NTV charging Korzhakov with plotting a coup, or NTV raising questions about Anatoly Chubais's alleged unsavory insider deals, the truthfulness of the charges often appears to be secondary to speculation regarding on whose behalf and with what effectiveness they are made.

In part because of Russia's generally underdeveloped political parties and semidependent media, civil society remains weak and, contrary to earlier optimistic expectations, shows few signs of improvement. In fact, society has even seemed to move backward in some areas: there is almost no evidence today of the growing civic spirit evident at the end of the Gorbachev era. Instead, cynicism is pervasive in today's Russia. There is a sense of profound disconnection between the rulers and the ruled, and a widespread belief that public opinion has at best minimal impact on how the country is governed. Worse, years of *bespredel* (conduct without constraints) have blurred the difference between right and wrong. The focus is no longer on who is right but who is on top.

THE RUSSIAN FEDERATION GOVERNMENT

President

- head of state
- elected by popular vote
- serves a four-year term
- can issue binding decrees
- can dissolve parliament
- controls funds and perks for parliament and courts

Presidential Administration

- president's Kremlin staff
- oversees government work on behalf of president
- works with regions

Cabinet of Ministers

- prime minister appointed by the president with approval of the Duma
- ministers appointed and dismissed by the president with recommendations from the prime minister and with no Duma role

Federal Assembly

State Duma

- lower house of parliament
- consists of 450 deputies
- 225 elected from single-mandate districts
- 225 elected through proportional representation
- serves a four-year term
- passes legislation, approves budget and taxes

Federation Council

- upper house of parliament
- consists of 176 deputies; two representatives of each of Russia's regions (except Chechnya)
- usually regional governor and head of regional legislature

Constitutional Court

- hears cases involving the constitutionality of laws, disputes between regions and the federal government or between branches of government
- judges nominated by the president and appointed by the Federation Council

Supreme Court

- Russia's highest court for civil, criminal, and administrative cases
- judges nominated by the president and appointed by the Federation Council

Russia's 89 regions (88 excluding Chechnya) have elected governors and regional legislatures; power-sharing agreements regulate their relations with the federal government.

There are more fundamental problems with Russian democracy as well. It is widely acknowledged, for example, that the 1996 presidential elections suffered from serious irregularities, including open contempt for campaign spending limits by the Yeltsin camp and the massive use of state funds for campaign expenses by the president's team. According to Grigory Yavlinsky, "spending limits are routinely ignored" and the Yeltsin campaign is estimated to have cost at least $500 million, or possibly even $1 billion—hundreds of times the official $2.9 million limit.[3] Simultaneously, all of Russia's major television stations were controlled either by the government or by powerful business leaders collectively known as Russia's "oligarchs." Together they created a united front to reelect Yeltsin; the president of NTV, Igor Malashenko, even acted as an official advisor to the Yeltsin campaign without taking a leave of absence from his NTV position.

Russia's electorate was denied a meaningful choice through time-honored Russian and new and sophisticated Western political techniques. Shevtsova has summarized this point well: "Parliamentary and especially presidential elections in Russia have become a test of sorts for the political class which it has successfully passed by demonstrating a talent for political manipulation. From now on, the Russian political elite does not need to fear democratic procedures—it has learned to use them to its own ends."[4]

One major element of this manipulation was the artificial polarization of the 1996 presidential campaign. Ironically, this strategy was even more effective in the West than within Russia itself. The purpose of this effort was to create a stark choice between Communists and anti-Communists, between dictatorship and democracy, between the past and the future, and between neoimperialism and a moderate foreign policy. This strategy was very successful for Yeltsin and his supporters, but soon after the Russian president's reelection it became apparent that the supposed choice was phony. The Communists had never had a chance and their leader, Gennady Zyuganov, knew it. In fact, in my two conversations with Zyuganov during the campaign, the Communist candidate was preoccupied with explaining that he would not do anything drastic when the other side won. As an American business executive who joined me for a June 1996 meeting with Zyuganov later commented, "The guy is completely beaten up. He has no spirit. All he cares about is not giving the government an excuse to ban his party after the elections."

In fact, by the time of the 1996 presidential campaign, there was only

one truly influential political party in Russia: the "party of power," the loose
alliance of officials and business and political leaders from across Russia's
political spectrum united by their status as beneficiaries of Yeltsin's reforms. I am convinced that the quite practical Gennady Zyuganov was well
aware in early 1996 that the party of power would never let him—or anyone else who could conceivably challenge the results of privatization—rule
in Russia. Thus, Zyuganov was less running for president than trying to affect the balance of forces inside the ruling coalition and, moreover, to become a part of it. He wanted to build himself up so that he could cut the
best deal possible through political maneuvering.

Although Communists were the largest and the most influential parliamentary party, according to 1996 opinion polls, only 31 percent of voters
favored the restoration of Soviet-style socialism—and it was precisely this
unreformed socialism with which the Communist Party (which had a strong
orthodox wing) was identified in the public eye. Even among those who reported voting for the Communists in parliamentary elections, only 68 percent favored a return to the past; 22 percent opposed going back to the old
system. Similarly, among those who voted for ultranationalist Vladimir
Zhirinovsky's Liberal Democratic Party, only 34 percent supported bringing
back socialism, while 44 percent opposed it. The prominent sociologist Yuri
Levada summarized the political lay of the land early in the presidential
campaign: "The idea of restoring the past is supported by less than one
third of the electorate—and less than unanimously even by the Communists' own electorate. This distribution of positions will undoubtedly influence the struggle of opinions both inside and outside the parliament."[5]

The December 1995 parliamentary elections, in which the Communists
drew the most votes of any party, were less a triumph by the Communists
than a rejection of the Yeltsin government. Looking back at the government's record in 1995—continuing economic decline, the scandalous
"loans for shares" auctions, billions of dollars in wage and pension arrears,
and the disastrous war in Chechnya (launched in December 1994)—it could
hardly have been surprising that Russian voters were eager to send a message about their dissatisfaction with official policies. And since it was well
known that under the 1993 constitution the Duma was not likely to be particularly significant, especially with the military and security services under
the president's firm control, protest voting seemed unlikely to have dangerous consequences.

The radical reformers' party—Russia's Democratic Choice, led by Gaidar—was not attractive in this context. Despite its opposition to the war in Chechnya, the party did not sever its ties with the government; one of its key leaders—Anatoly Chubais—was even first deputy prime minister. And the memories of shock therapy, instituted by the Gaidar team, were still too fresh to be disregarded by unhappy voters. As a result of these factors, and the fact that it competed in 1995 as a semiopposition party without the financial and organizational support of the authorities, Russia's Democratic Choice was unable to achieve the 5 percent threshold for proportional representation in the Duma. Nevertheless, nine of its candidates, including Gaidar himself, were elected from single-mandate districts. In contrast, Yabloko, which had an indisputable anti-government record, increased its representation in the Duma from twenty-five to forty-five deputies and became the principal voice of the democratic opposition in parliament.

Thus, the Duma elections were not a sign that democracy and capitalism in Russia were in mortal danger. Aleksandr Tsypko, a thoughtful critic of government policies, was right on target in writing in the *Washington Post* after the Duma elections that "the overwhelming majority of the Russian population is dissatisfied with market reforms and privatization not because they are inveterate enemies of private property but because they, like other people, want prosperity and jobs today. Russians cannot understand the sense of reforms that give them nothing but poverty, uncertainty and crime without limit. They cannot support a privatization program that in exchange for 20 or 30 years of work gives them a voucher valued at $9—not even enough to dine out in Russia today."[6] And President Yeltsin got the message. Once the outcome of the elections became clear, he removed Chubais from his cabinet.

But Chubais's dismissal was too little, too late to boost Yeltsin's popularity. Opinion polls at the end of January 1996 indicated that his approval rating—a mere 5 percent—was far below that of other potential presidential contenders. Zyuganov led the list with 17 percent support but was followed closely by Grigory Yavlinsky with 15 percent and the maverick—but still anti-Communist—General Aleksandr Lebed with 14 percent.[7] The polls did not suggest that Yeltsin was the only, or even the most logical, candidate capable of saving Russian democracy from the Communist threat.

But the Russian president was undoubtedly the overwhelming preference of those for whom the irreversibility of privatization—and, more generally, the maintenance of the status quo—was the highest priority. Of course, all of the candidates were aware that threatening another large-scale redistribution of property was the political equivalent of playing with fire. As Zyuganov told me in March 1996, "any attempt to revise the outcome of privatization would mean civil war, and only a crazy person would take this risk." But Zyuganov's credibility among the newly rich was low. Moreover, many "new Russians" feared that even if the Communist leader meant what he said, the conservative wing of his party could either force him to reverse privatization or remove him altogether. Conversely, the new elite did not trust Lebed or even Yavlinsky because they had not participated in previous privatization schemes. Accordingly, their hands were clean and—despite many other differences—they did not hide their intentions to put an end to crony capitalism. The new Russians harbored similar suspicions against Moscow mayor Luzhkov, who, despite his own cozy relations with some tycoons, liked to promote himself as a populist outsider. The new elite plainly felt both too meteorically successful and simultaneously too vulnerable to take chances with any leader who did not have a strong personal stake in protecting their fortunes. Because they knew how easily they had won their riches, they recognized how quickly they could lose them.

There was only one conceivable candidate beyond Yeltsin who could have satisfied the magnates—Prime Minister Viktor Chernomyrdin. But Chernomyrdin's popularity was only slightly greater than Yeltsin's own, and the prime minister was considered a lackluster campaigner as well. Most important, as a calculating politician brought up in the Soviet bureaucratic system and not disposed to taking risks, Chernomyrdin knew that it was the president who controlled the huge machinery of the state, particularly under Russia's new constitution. The prime minister would have had little chance to prevail against a sitting president. Also, the last thing the establishment wanted was a divisive struggle between two official candidates. Accordingly, notwithstanding his political vulnerabilities and failing health, only Yeltsin could carry the government banner.

The die was cast on Sunday, February 4, in the Swiss resort town of Davos at a meeting of the World Economic Forum. The annual gatherings of the international business and political elite at Davos were particularly appealing to Russians—in addition to providing opportunities to establish useful contacts and to exchange information, the sessions also had the ex-

citement of novelty and gave the Russians a sense that they, yesterday's no-
bodies with little exposure to the outside world, were now able to rub
shoulders with a global who's who. To celebrate their new membership in
the international elite, some Russian bankers had brought costumed Gyp-
sies and even a bear (which, to the discomfort of the Swiss police, they attempted to walk along the city streets) to the 1995 conference. At the
February 1996 meeting, however, they had much more serious business to
conduct: they had to win Western support for their respective political
groupings. With his new clout as a Duma leader with presidential ambitions, Gennady Zyuganov was among the stars of the meeting. His message
was one of moderation, responsibility, and goodwill toward foreign investors. Conversely, Anatoly Chubais, now officially a private citizen but in
reality still a senior advisor to Yeltsin, predicted doom and gloom if the
Communists should come to power. Grigory Yavlinsky was also present to
promote his candidacy and articulate his plan for reform.

But the real action was behind the scenes. Between forum sessions, a
group of top bankers met with Chubais to discuss election campaign strategy. The meeting was unprecedented in two respects: first, the oligarchy
presented a united front when in the past some of the meeting participants—for example, Most Bank president Vladimir Gusinsky and Logo-
VAZ chief Boris Berezovsky—had been considered mortal enemies, and
second, never in the past had Russia's tycoons attempted so ambitiously to
determine Russia's political future.

Chubais acted as the de facto chairman of the meeting. He was on good
terms with each of the participants, and his credibility was enhanced by his
removal from government. "He was in the same boat that we were. Yeltsin
had abused him and there was no love lost between the two. Whatever he
had to say in the president's support was strictly business, exactly like with
us," a participant in the meeting later explained to me.

Those taking part in the gathering were disturbed by Zyuganov's
rather positive reception in Davos. "It dawned on us that the West would
embrace whoever came to power in Russia. It would sell us down the river
for a better profit margin. Perhaps Zyuganov would keep his promise not
to proceed with a full-scale renationalization. But he could kill us just as
well simply by taking the state accounts out of our banks. We could not afford to take chances on this," a member of the group commented. Asked

why the bankers could not support Yavlinsky, he said that "Russia was not ready for a half-Jewish intellectual. Besides, he wasn't one of us. Also, Chubais couldn't stand him and he was setting the tone."

Later, when infighting eventually began between Chubais and some of the bankers, a few American journalists described the Davos deal as a "Faustian bargain" for the reformist politician and suggested that Chubais nobly held his nose while cutting a deal with the tycoons to save Yeltsin and the reform process.[8] This description misses the mark, however. First, there is simply no evidence that an arrangement with the tycoons was distasteful to Chubais in the slightest. He was, if anything, the mastermind of the Davos pact in cooperation with Berezovsky. Second, the magnates were hardly strangers to him. They were to a large extent the creatures of his own privatization policies. They were not an unexpected side effect of privatization, but Chubais's own manufactured political base with which he was finally in a position to make a difference.

At the close of the Davos sessions, the tycoons had reached an agreement with Chubais. All were willing to make an attempt to ensure Yeltsin's reelection. As Berezovsky reportedly declared, "If capital acts in concert with the government and is supported by the media, it should be enough to determine the outcome of presidential elections."

The techniques used by the Yeltsin campaign in 1996 closely resembled Yeltsin's approach to his battle with the old Congress of People's Deputies in 1992–93: demonization of the opposition, polarization of the electorate into two hostile camps, marginalization of moderate politicians, and characterization of the struggle as an apocalyptic conflict between good and evil, future and past, freedom and slavery, prosperity and economic collapse. But there were important new elements as well. The support of the bankers provided the Yeltsin campaign with virtually unlimited funds. And since the banks handled most government accounts, there was little risk in financing the campaign out of the state treasury. Only the tycoons and their operatives would know.

The national media, especially television, were almost entirely controlled by the government and the banks and quickly became a major instrument in the Yeltsin reelection drive. All pretense of objectivity in reporting was abandoned in the name of saving the nation from a Communist comeback. According to a study by the European Institute on the Media, Yeltsin received 53 percent of the media coverage to Zyuganov's 18 percent (the second-highest figure). Moreover, the stories on Yeltsin were overwhelmingly positive, while those about Zyuganov were almost as overwhelmingly negative.[9] The need to stop the Communists could not, however, explain why credible non-Communist candidates with popularity ratings higher than Yeltsin's own—such as Yavlinsky and Lebed—were almost totally ignored in television coverage of the election until it became expedient. But why this happened was hardly a mystery.

Official control of the media became transparent when Oleg Poptsov, an old Yeltsin supporter who headed Russian Public Television (ORT), was unceremoniously dismissed after maintaining the network's balanced coverage of events despite pressure from above, including criticism from Yeltsin himself that the channel showed too much "*chernukha*," or "dark stuff."[10] Conversely, Igor Malashenko, the president of Gusinsky's Independent Television channel (NTV) turned from a vitriolic critic of the president before the Davos deal to a senior advisor to the Yeltsin campaign without giving up his duties at the network. In addition to coordinating media support for Yeltsin, Malashenko was also responsible for unofficial communications with Deputy Secretary of State Strobe Talbott in Washington. Malashenko and Talbott were longtime friends and colleagues of sorts since the perestroika days when Malashenko, then a public relations aide to Gorbachev, helped *Time* magazine—where Talbott was then a columnist—gain access in the Soviet Union. In 1996, as senior officials in Moscow told me, Malashenko's assignment was to coordinate the Clinton administration's role—indeed, its interference on Yeltsin's behalf—in Russia's presidential elections.

These efforts did bear fruit. By mid-April, the president's standing in the polls equaled that of Zyuganov. Meanwhile, all of the remaining candidates—underfunded, and neglected by television—had fallen behind. Just as Chubais had hoped, the election was shaping up as a race between Yeltsin and Zyuganov. But the polarization of society was not without cost: angered by continuous television propaganda, blatant government pressures to force voters to support Yeltsin (including instances in which employees were told to sign petitions supporting Yeltsin's candidacy or risk losing their jobs or even the closing of their offices),[11] and threats to dissolve the Duma, many Communists and nationalists began to discuss preparations for a campaign of civil disobedience. Zyuganov did not encourage this sentiment publicly, but, as he acknowledged in a private conversation with me in

March, he gained valuable political leverage because of the visible willingness of his supporters to go into the streets—if not to the barricades—to protest against the Yeltsin government.

The bankers were quite concerned by this turn of events. Polarization and confrontation that threatened the stability of society was not in their interest. Zyuganov and his people, on the other hand, became increasingly convinced that since the Communists would under no circumstances be allowed to win, their best option was to try to cut a deal before the elections to create some kind of government of national unity. After extensive communication among the Yeltsin and Zyuganov camps and several tycoons, there was a remarkable outcome: thirteen leading bankers signed a letter calling for "a search for political compromise" and "mutual concessions." The letter ended with a warning that those on both sides who sought to "raise political tension" should "understand that the nation's entrepreneurs have the resources and the will necessary to have an impact on politicians who are either too unprincipled or too uncompromising."[12]

The message was loud and clear. The business elite was ready to have the Communists in the government as long as they were the junior partner, promised to play by the rules, and made a contribution to social stability. But Chubais and his radical reformer allies had other ideas. With Yeltsin's victory now in sight, they saw little rationale for accepting an arrangement that would almost certainly mean their own lasting political exile.

When I talked to Zyuganov in March, he emphasized the possibility of forming a coalition government. The Communist leader said that he could work with Chernomyrdin and expressed respect for Yavlinsky. "He is a talented and responsible economist who could play a major role," Zyuganov said of the latter. "As a finance minister?" I asked. "Yes, perhaps even more than that," was his answer. But Zyuganov had a completely different view of Chubais: "We cannot cooperate with the people who are responsible for creating economic disaster and bringing about great suffering by the people." Thus, for Chubais and his brand of radical reformers, the idea of a broad coalition government was almost worse than a Communist victory. It could have demonstrated that reform could continue without Chubais and his associates and may have led the tycoons to shift their support to a new group of officials. The West may even have discovered—as it already had in the case of previously ousted radical reformers such as Gaidar and Foreign Minister Andrei Kozyrev, who was fired shortly after the December

Duma elections—that Russia's future did not depend on any particular individual, even Anatoly Chubais.

Similarly, Chubais's objectives would have been harder to achieve under any coalition government. Rather than broadening the circle of individuals and groups working with the Russian president, he sought to consolidate the radicals' influence on Yeltsin. To achieve this, he needed not only to prevent the creation of any coalition but also to purge the existing cabinet and presidential administration of more conservative officials such as Yeltsin's chief bodyguard Aleksandr Korzhakov, Korzhakov's close ally Federal Security Service chief Mikhail Barsukov, and their friend First Deputy Prime Minister Oleg Soskovets, who could block the radicals' ambitions. Neither further social polarization nor even the risks to Yeltsin's health inherent in imposing the burdens of a demanding campaign on an already weak man seemed too high a price.

But the gamble paid off for Chubais. Yeltsin had always naturally preferred confrontation to accommodation and, by May, his campaign had gained enough momentum to make the president the undisputed front-runner. This of course also discouraged the bankers from further efforts to negotiate a compromise with the opposition.

Once Yeltsin was clearly on top, his campaign intensified its efforts to split the opposition vote. To ensure that those non-Communist voters who could not bring themselves to vote for Yeltsin would not support Zyuganov, Russia's national television channels suddenly gave increasingly frequent and favorable attention to Aleksandr Lebed on the orders of the Yeltsin campaign. The campaign team also actively cultivated Lebed, and Yeltsin himself even hinted that Lebed could one day become his successor. In addition to pulling nationalist voters away from Zyuganov, these "dances" with Lebed were also intended to block his much-discussed potential alliance with Yavlinsky and another democratic candidate, eye surgeon Svyatoslav Fedorov.

Similar approaches were made to Yavlinsky, who was unconvinced. Yavlinsky suspected (correctly, as Lebed's own later experience shows) that while Yeltsin would be prepared to offer him anything on the eve of the elections, the Russian leader would soon return to his habitual capricious and autocratic ways once the balloting was over. The management of Yeltsin's campaign also disgusted him. Accordingly, Yavlinsky was unwilling to discuss joining the cabinet without a binding commitment from the

Russian president that the government would be granted real authority to determine the nation's policies and work toward genuine reform.[13] Such a commitment would have been out of character for Yeltsin and was ultimately unnecessary because of Lebed's willingness to cooperate. On June 6, Yavlinsky admitted in a press conference that his negotiations with Lebed and Fedorov had gone nowhere. He also charged that the forthcoming elections appeared "unequal and unfree."[14]

Whether or not the elections were free, their outcome was successful for Yeltsin and Chubais. Yeltsin led in the first round on June 16 with 35.2 percent of the vote; Zyuganov trailed by slightly more than 3 percent with 31.95 percent. Because neither had achieved a majority, they were required to compete in a second round of polling two weeks later. After the late support of Yeltsin's campaign team, Aleksandr Lebed was also a big winner—he garnered 14.7 percent of the vote[15] and, on June 19, he was appointed secretary of the Security Council and a security aide to Yeltsin. His old enemy Defense Minister Pavel Grachev was soon forced to resign from government.

Chubais's good fortune continued through the night of June 19, when he skillfully used the incriminating arrest of two of his associates on the campaign staff—who had been caught carrying $500,000 in cash out of the Russian White House (the principal government office building) in a box—to accuse Korzhakov, Barsukov, and Soskovets (the last of whom actually had nothing to do with the incident) with attempting a coup d'etat.[16] The arrest and detention of the two Yeltsin campaign staffers (who were quickly released on orders from above[17]) by Korzhakov's Presidential Security Service was linked to statements by Korzhakov earlier in the spring suggesting that the election be postponed and was quickly characterized as the beginning of an attempted *putsch*. That no coup was in the making has by now been fully established. No charges were ever brought against the alleged conspirators.

In fact, Korzhakov and Barsukov had earlier persuaded Yeltsin to allow an investigation of alleged thefts from the presidential campaign headquarters. The two went beyond their mandate, however, and, in an effort to discredit Chubais, began to look into numerous irregularities in the funding of the campaign. It was in this connection that they detained Chubais's colleagues and discovered in their possession a box filled with money the two had received from Deputy Finance Minister German Kuznetsov.[18] Both

Korzhakov and Barsukov had to be aware that such transfers of government funds were pretty routine; after all, as Korzhakov himself writes, Kuznetsov openly maintained an office at Yeltsin's campaign headquarters.[19] But by risking the exposure of Chubais's money-laundering machine, the security chiefs were also risking exposing the illegality of the entire Yeltsin campaign effort on the eve of the decisive second round of the elections. The consequences could have been drastic.

Apparently deciding that the best defense is a good offense, Chubais, on learning of the arrest, hastily arranged a meeting of key associates at Berezovsky's club in downtown Moscow. In addition to Chubais and Berezovsky, the gathering included Boris Yeltsin's daughter Tatyana Dyachenko (who acted as a campaign advisor), the banker Gusinsky, then governor Boris Nemtsov, and several others. Each understood both the dangers and the opportunities presented by the incident; they decided to act quickly. In the middle of the night, Gusinsky's NTV interrupted its regular broadcasting to report on the arrest, which it characterized as the beginning of another putsch.[20] In addition to fearing that he could lose the services of his effective campaign organizer Anatoly Chubais, Yeltsin was persuaded by the arguments of his then chief aide, Viktor Ilyushin, that he should do nothing to disrupt the operations of the re-election effort. Ilyushin said, "Boris Nikolayevich, right now if you wanted to you could catch a minimum of 15 to 20 people around the President Hotel [the location of Yeltsin's campaign headquarters] carrying money out of the building in duffle bags" and explained that otherwise "we cannot organize the elections."[21] The next day, an angry Yeltsin fired the alleged conspirators. "If someone among those fired gets the crazy idea to use force, it can be suppressed by one move of General Lebed's little finger," Chubais threatened.[22] It was an ugly and self-serving farce.

Several days later, Yeltsin suffered a heart attack. Despite his disappearance from public view, the bulk of the media, including Russia's major television networks, pretended that nothing had happened and dampened speculation about the president's odd inactivity on the eve of the crucial second-round vote. On July 3, Chubais and the bankers were rewarded for their hard work: the Russian president was reelected with 53.82 percent of the vote to Zyuganov's 40.3 percent.[23]

On September 5, the Russian government finally announced officially that President Yeltsin's condition required heart surgery. Between the time of his preparation for surgery and the end of his recuperation period in January 1997, the Russian president was largely disengaged from the business of government. Nevertheless, on October 17, the weak Yeltsin fired General Lebed, who had taken the promises made to him prior to the election too seriously and had begun to act as if he were the country's second-most-important official. Lebed was quick to blame his dismissal on Chubais—by then serving as the powerful chief of the Presidential Administration—whom he described as a "regent" controlling the ailing Russian leader.[24]

While Yeltsin was able to remain in power, it would have required an extraordinary degree of naïveté, deception, or—more likely—a combination of both, to proclaim his victory to be a triumph for Russian democracy, as the Clinton administration soon did. The point is not whether it would have been preferable to elect Zyuganov, Lebed, or, for that matter, even Yavlinsky as president. What Russia needed most from its first post-Soviet presidential elections was not a particular outcome but rather respect for the law, for due process, and for the choices of the Russian people—no matter what those choices might be. More than anything, Russia's citizens needed to see that the ends do not justify the means—that the road to liberal democracy cannot be paved with cynical deceit. The 1996 presidential elections taught precisely the opposite lesson.

Some Russians, particularly journalists who felt a need to explain how and why they had again become party propagandists, claimed that their conduct was justified by the overwhelming need to prevent a Communist victory. Since the Communists would not allow freedom of the press, they argued, it was morally justifiable to deprive them of fair coverage. Only the most rigid moralist would deny theoretical validity to this argument in an economically devastated and politically humiliated nation without a democratic tradition that could soon elect a bloody tyrant.

But this argument simply cannot be applied to Russia's circumstances in 1996. First, whatever his failings as a democrat or a reformer, Zyuganov was no Hitler or Stalin. He could have attempted to turn the clock back in Russia, but creating a totalitarian dictatorship was never on his agenda and, more important, was never within his power, even as Russian president. Second, if the elections had been conducted honestly from beginning to end, the chances were good that Zyuganov would have lost in the second round to one of the non-Communist candidates other than Yeltsin. Finally, there is something profoundly disingenuous about recklessly polarizing society for five-and-a-half years, being insensitive to the impact of reform on the majority of the population, and showing contempt for the constitutional process, only to claim that the danger of the predictable backlash created by that very behavior justifies further departures from democratic procedures.

The damage done by the electoral charade was not limited to Russia's democracy. Moscow's ability to conduct economic reform was also affected. Because the Communists and their allies felt after the election that they had been cheated, they and their Duma majority were much less willing to work constructively with the government than they might have been under other circumstances. And, as has been demonstrated by Russia's entire post-Soviet experience, economic reform can go only so far on the basis of presidential decrees. What Russia desperately needs is legislation—which only the Duma can produce—on property rights, taxation, and corruption. That legislation was later made even more unlikely by the spring 1997 appointment of Anatoly Chubais as one of two first deputy prime ministers with tremendous authority over economic matters. Chubais personified both the excesses of privatization and the abuses of the presidential campaign in the eyes of the opposition, and his presence in the cabinet ensured that the Duma majority would not do the government any favors.

No less important, economic reform also required an end to Russia's emerging crony capitalism. But after the election, the bankers had every reason to feel that they had been responsible in large measure for Yeltsin's victory and, accordingly, that they were entitled—indeed, that they had been explicitly promised—further redistribution of state property in their favor. They also believed that they deserved a major role in the affairs of state. Because the president was not physically capable of exercising leadership after his victory, an oligarchy arose in which some of the tycoons, such as Boris Berezovsky and Vladimir Potanin, went directly into the government (as deputy secretary of the Security Council and first deputy prime minister, respectively), while others received alternative forms of compensation from the state. No sound budget, privatization, taxation, or anticorruption policies were possible under those circumstances.

Russia lived under oligarchic rule between June 1996 and March 1997, when Boris Yeltsin finally returned to the Kremlin with his physical health visibly restored after recovering from successful quintuple coronary bypass surgery on November 5, 1996. Because no one—not even the Russian

president's then constitutional successor, Prime Minister Chernomyrdin—
could guess when and in what condition Yeltsin would return, the various
powerful financial-bureaucratic clans opted for a conservative strategy in
their relations with one another: "live and let live." Anatoly Chubais and
Boris Berezovsky, both of whom were personally close to the Yeltsin family, and particularly to the president's increasingly influential daughter,
Tatyana Dyachenko, were on good terms and together protected the interests of their affiliated financial groups in government.

The bankers and their government allies could not rule alone, however,
and had to share power with Russia's huge energy companies, especially
Gazprom and Lukoil, which were close to Prime Minister Chernomyrdin, a
former Soviet gas minister. They reached an unwritten understanding that
the so-called reformers in the government, represented by chief of the Presidential Administration Anatoly Chubais and new First Deputy Prime Minister Vladimir Potanin would not introduce financial measures, including
tax collection, contrary to the interests of the energy giants.

The process through which the oligarchs divided up the wealth of the
Russian state can be seen clearly through the early 1996 acquisition of the
Sidanko oil company by Potanin's Oneksimbank (allied with Chubais) for
slightly more than $20 million. Just how grossly the firm was undervalued
is demonstrated by a November 18, 1997, agreement in which British Pe-
troleum purchased a 10 percent stake in Sidanko for $571 million—more
than twenty-eight times the original sale price of the entire company.[25] Similarly, Boris Berezovsky paid some $100 million for the Sibneft oil com-
pany and later claimed to have been offered $1 billion for the firm after
Yeltsin's reelection.[26] The other tycoons benefited from equally lucrative
deals.

Figures alone do not fully demonstrate the bankers' remarkable gains.
Because official funds were generally managed through "authorized" commercial banks rather than the Central Bank or the state treasury, the tycoons
were often able to purchase companies with the government's own money.[27]
As Mikhail Berger of *Izvestiya* writes, "In any given situation, it is certainly
well known that at a number of banks 90 percent of the money with which
they operate in the market was received as a free gift as 'authorized money'
for the budget."[28] Thus, even minimal investments by the tycoons were not
always necessary. Under such circumstances, intimate connections with senior officials were much more important to success than business acumen.

No meaningful campaign against corruption could be undertaken so long as fortunes were made on the basis of personal ties. If General Korzhakov is to be believed, even members of the Yeltsin family were prepared to sell favors. When I talked to senior Russian officials at the time, they often described their colleagues who would not accept bribes with a certain amazement. Those who were not on the take were viewed as the exceptions rather than the rule. Indeed, it would be hard to expect that a government minister with a salary of $1,000 dollars per month would give companies what are essentially gifts worth hundreds of millions of dollars without seeking something for himself in return. In fact, because connections were everything, even meetings with senior officials came at a price. For the average Russian businessman, a half-hour appointment with a deputy minister of finance could cost around $20,000.

The problem with the oligarchic system during Yeltsin's illness was that it was not only undemocratic and corrupt but also ineffective. Because it was an ad hoc, informal arrangement rather than an organized political system, Russia's oligarchy had only a very loose structure and no single recognized leader. Beyond protecting their gains from privatization and demanding greater influence over official decision-making, they had few interests in common. Preoccupied with the struggle for power and resources within the government and in the economy, they were unable to initiate fundamentally new policies. However, as Yavlinsky told me in a private conversation, the oligarchs were also sufficiently frustrated with Boris Yeltsin's erratic leadership and favoritism to play by the rules—so long as they were applied equally and did not threaten the existing division of formerly state-owned property. That was unlikely under Yeltsin's arbitrary regime.

The lack of a recognized leader during Yeltsin's illness also meant that there was no one to conduct a dialogue with the Duma, so the legislative process ground to a halt. Because the weak federal state was unable to collect taxes from the oligarchs or, for that matter, from lesser business leaders protected by local authorities in Russia's regions, the country's mounting wage and pension arrears could not be paid without massive foreign loans. The arrears—which, despite Yeltsin's campaign promises, were increasing rather than decreasing—contributed to further social turmoil.

Because of these and other problems, there was a growing sense in the country, including among the ruling elite, that the oligarchic system was not working properly. Public support for Yeltsin had dropped to preelection levels—7 percent—while opposition leaders Aleksandr Lebed and Gennady Zyuganov were up to 23 percent and 22 percent, respectively.[29] Andranik Migranyan, a proponent of enlightened authoritarianism during the perestroika period, wrote, "An exit from the current very deep systemic crisis is impossible on a path of unlimited free competition and with a 'minimalist state' acting as a night guard, which is the model of the society's functioning for the radical reformers—followers of the ideals of classical liberalism. Five years of painful convulsions in not only the economy but all spheres of life have proven the lack of perspective of this path of development. . . . The path out of the current crisis is in the creation of a model of a corporatist state in which organized business, represented by several major financial-industrial groups, and organized labor, cooperate constructively under the firm control of the state, which imposes rules of behavior for business as well as for the labor movement and severely punishes all violators of those rules."[30]

Calling what was happening in Russia "the worst example of oligarchic rule," Migranyan concluded that what was required was a "radical shift in relations between the state and business to the advantage of the state in order to destroy the system of oligarchic rule established in Russia." In his view, this "was becoming a question of life and death for the further development of Russia as an industrially developed nation." His article, published in the official government newspaper and signed by Migranyan in his capacity as a member of the Presidential Council, an advisory body to Boris Yeltsin, reflected a strong sense among Yeltsin's entourage that the oligarchy had gone too far and major change was in order. But it also reflected something else: that Yeltsin was recovering, that he was once again ready to take over, and like Russia's tsars before him, that he wanted to make sure that the temporary rule of the boyars in his absence would come to a swift end upon his return. For Boris Yeltsin, showing who was the boss was always a top priority.

Upon his return to the Kremlin in March 1997, Yeltsin proceeded with a drastic cabinet reshuffle. Chubais was moved from the Presidential Administration to become first deputy prime minister and minister of finance. To balance his influence, Boris Nemtsov was also appointed first deputy prime minister and was given the minister of energy portfolio as well. Although Viktor Chernomyrdin remained prime minister, he would be responsible for maintaining the continuity of the government and for dealing with the parliament, while his two energetic and assertive deputies—soon labeled the "young reformers"—would establish economic policy.

Despite his recovery, Yeltsin was less and less able to play a major role in day-to-day government and, as a result, control over the flow of information to the Russian president became very important to the country's competing political-financial alliances. Thus, while Yeltsin returned as the ultimate arbiter of disputes, the oligarchs hoped for a continuation of business-as-usual.

Yeltsin's appointment of Chubais and Nemtsov was initially well received by the tycoons. Chernomyrdin and Chubais, still head of the Presidential Administration, met with the leading bankers on March 4 and assured them that the government had no intention of "changing course." At the same time, the bankers took the lead in calling for Chubais's return to the cabinet.[31] They clearly believed that they would be able to continue to conduct their affairs as they chose without interference by the state.

But Yeltsin and the young reformers had something else in mind. From their perspective, the oligarchs had become too wealthy and too powerful—and made too many demands of the government. They had to be cut down to size. Nemtsov was particularly outspoken about the government's new agenda: "The country is now facing a choice. Last year it was between the prison and the barracks. Now it is between mafia capitalism and a normal market in a democratic society without a giant gulf between the rich and poor."[32] He also assaulted the oligarchs' influence over the machinery of the state: "The most vile element of oligarchic capitalism is the 'privatization of power.' "[33] These bold statements were followed by promises to force the giant energy companies, Gazprom, Lukoil, and the electrical power monopoly Unified Energy Systems of Russia, to pay their fair share in taxes and to give greater weight to the interests of the state (their principal shareholder) in making management decisions.

This appeared quite commendable on the surface, although the energy monopolies considered it unfair. First of all, the monopolies argued, they were victims of large-scale and chronic nonpayment by their customers. Second, taxes in Russia were established essentially arbitrarily and were particularly high on energy producers. Also, since the energy monopolies were perceived to be closer to Prime Minister Chernomyrdin than to the young reformers, suspicion flared that the new initiatives reflected Chernomyrdin's declining fortunes in the Kremlin's continuous power struggles. The bankers were not similarly inconvenienced.

The auction of the Russian telecommunications monopoly Svyazinvest in July 1997 changed everything, however. In what the young reformers claimed was a straightforward deal, 25 percent plus one share in the giant firm was sold to a consortium including Vladimir Potanin's Oneksimbank, George Soros, and other foreign investors for $1.87 billion.[34] But Potanin's rivals, the other bankers, were outraged at what they called government favoritism toward Oneksimbank. They pointed out that Vladimir Gusinsky's Most Bank had managed the Svyazinvest sale for the government and that in the past, that role would have guaranteed the deal for Most. They also called attention to a meeting in France among the vacationing Chubais, Gusinsky, Berezovsky, Potanin and others during which they claimed an understanding had been reached that the deal would go to Most Bank for $1.7 billion. Similarly, they alleged that Potanin, while still first deputy prime minister, had promised that Oneksimbank would not bid for the Svyazinvest shares when he initiated government preparations for the auction. Finally, they accused Oneksimbank—which had huge government accounts, including a State Customs Committee account in which there was $1 billion on deposit every day—of using the government's own money to buy the shares and thus invalidating the sale as an auction to the highest bidder.[35] These were the opening salvos in what became known as "the bank war."

The young reformers argued that the oligarchs' charges were totally false. Chubais accused the bankers of threatening all-out war against the young reformers—and even threatening his life—in the run-up to the auction. Boris Nemtsov made similar statements, while President Yeltsin, unwilling to allow the power of the state to come under assault, defended his loyal ministers. "It is the state which will now begin to determine the main directions of economic activity," Yeltsin said. "In recent years, major corporations have been formed in our country. Private owners have emerged. The government does not intend to interfere in their legitimate activities. However, the state will not tolerate any attempts to pressure it by representatives of business and banks. They must serve society and act for the good of the people of Russia."[36]

Despite Yeltsin's support, Chubais had big problems. First, with his own help, the banks had won control of a large portion of the mass media. Boris Berezovsky effectively controlled the prestigious Ostankino TV, while Gusinsky owned NTV and Mayor Luzhkov—no friend of Berezovsky—considered Chubais the far greater threat and ran Moscow's new Center-TV.[37] More important, again with assistance from Chubais, the oligarchs had learned how to use the media to devastating effect during the 1996 presidential campaign. Because the overwhelming majority of the tycoons were opposed to Chubais after the Svyazinvest auction, with the obvious exception of Potanin, the young reformers were outgunned on Russia's newspaper pages and particularly on television screens.

Similarly, the young reformers had no real support in the Duma, with the exception of Gaidar's tiny Russia's Democratic Choice faction. The progovernment Our Home Is Russia faction was much closer to Chernomyrdin than to Chubais and would take few risks to defend the first deputy prime minister. Despite their public attacks on the government, the Communists were quietly working with the prime minister on a number of issues, as was Vladimir Zhirinovsky's Liberal Democratic Party; nevertheless, even without the link to Chernomyrdin, neither would have been likely to support the unpopular Chubais. Finally, Yabloko, which proved to be the most consistent opposition to the government in the Duma, rejected the young reformers' arguments. As party leader Grigory Yavlinsky put it, "Anatoly Chubais is the architect of the corporate system of power, which is by and large a criminal one."[38] Although Yavlinsky was respectful of Boris Nemtsov's intentions after working closely with him for several years in Nizhni Novgorod, he dismissed the junior first deputy prime minister's ability to affect change and humorously referred to Nemtsov as "the tsar's deputy for revolution," suggesting that his appointment was a populist guesture unlikely to have policy consequences.

Most important, as one of the architects—if not the architect—of Russia's oligarchic system, Chubais had little support in society outside the oligarchy itself. This was in large measure due to the fact that below the level of the prosperous banks and energy giants, at the base of Russia's economic pyramid, little positive change had occurred since Russian independence. Despite initally promising signals, small business development had failed to gain momentum under the constant pressure of organized crime and a business environment oppressive to those not well connected. As Irina Khakamada, Russia's leading small-business official, complained in late 1997,

". . . in the system of priorities among the economic and political elites in Russia, small business occupies the last place."[39] Similarly, Russia's tiny middle class was developing much more slowly than expected, particularly outside Moscow.

Having fractured his alliance with the tycoons, Chubais had only two major sources of support left. The first, of course, was Boris Yeltsin, who had already shown once that he was willing to drop Chubais when he demanded his resignation after blaming Chubais for the government's poor performance in the December 1995 parliamentary elections.[40] Ironically, because Yeltsin, as a tsar, could not allow himself to yield to outside pressure, the more Chubais was attacked by others, the less the president was inclined to let him go.

Almost equally important to Chubais were his Western connections, especially his links with the International Monetary Fund (IMF), the World Bank, and the Clinton administration. For quite some time, Chubais had successfully cultivated an image in Moscow and the West that he served as an indispensable channel for Western financial support of the ailing Russian government. In the absence of any other reliable bases of support, he and his associates worked hard during the bank war—particularly after Russia was hit hard by 1997's Asian economic crisis—to demonstrate that Chubais's departure from government would cost Russia billions of dollars and could in fact trigger economic collapse and social upheaval. Chubais also benefited from his connections with public relations–savvy Western economists who served as consultants to the Russian government. Some, such as Harvard's Jeffrey Sachs, eventually left their advisory position in disgust and criticized Moscow's corruption and errors.[41] Others, however, became virtual members of the Chubais team and continued to promote its activities on returning to the West. Anders Aslund, an economist with Washington's Carnegie Endowment for International Peace, is perhaps the best example; his analysis of Russian developments seemed to correlate almost perfectly with Chubais's presence in or absence from the Russian government. Thus, after Boris Yeltsin fired Chubais at the beginning of the 1996 presidential campaign, Aslund wrote that "Russia needs a change of government; unfortunately, the Communists are the only alternative." Similarly, despite cataloguing the "successes" of Russian reform in an article entitled "Why the Doomsayers Are Wrong About Russia" at the beginning of 1998—when Chubais served as first deputy prime minister—Aslund gloomily said that Russia was facing a "total collapse" in October, after Chubais lost his post as Yeltsin's liaison to international financial institutions.[42]

Throughout his career, Anatoly Chubais enjoyed the perfectly timed approval of loans from international financial institutions and strong indications of support from the World Bank, the IMF, and the Clinton administration alike. For example, on February 22, 1996, just days after Chubais established his team to support the Yeltsin campaign, IMF managing director Michel Camdessus announced the approval of a $10.1 billion IMF loan to support Russia's economic reform process. Remarkably, the loan was issued with a warning that if Boris Yeltsin were to be defeated in the June elections, the IMF reserved the right to review the conditions of the loan.[43] Similarly, in mid-December 1997, when First Deputy Prime Minister Chubais desperately needed money to pay Russia's growing wage and pension arrears in the wake of the budget-busting interest-rate hikes and flight of foreign capital from Russia resulting from the earlier Asian economic crisis, the IMF suddenly released a $700 million tranche of the same loan, which had been held up for months because of Moscow's continuing poor tax collection performance. Simultaneously, the World Bank approved two $800 million loans to the Russian government, the Second Structural Adjustment Loan and the Second Coal Sector Adjustment Project, almost immediately thereafter. The World Bank funds were accompanied by an unusually enthusiastic statement from World Bank vice president Johannes Linn, who said that the loans illustrated the World Bank's "clear recognition and full endorsement of the measures that are currently being implemented" by the Russian government.[44] Neither Yeltsin nor Chernomyrdin would have dared to promote their government's economic policies to their people in such euphoric terms.

In mid-1998, the Clinton administration encouraged the IMF to lead a $22.6 billion rescue effort negotiated by the specially designated private citizen Anatoly Chubais (who then headed Russia's electricity monopoly, United Energy Systems). Although the Russian government has argued that its crisis was caused by Asia's financial troubles, leading Russian economists disputed that assessment. As the liberal economist Andrei Illarionov said, "the relationship between Russia's economic problems and the world financial crisis is a myth."[45] Illarionov claimed that the Russian government's own failed policies were the principal cause of the near disaster.

The bailout package came with strict conditions, particularly in the area of improving Russia's tax collection; however, as Grigory Yavlinsky has explained, it is very difficult to implement an effective but fair tax collection system in an economy in which 75 percent of transactions are conducted through barter.[46] There is simply no cash for tax payments and unlike many Russian enterprises, the government cannot take goods instead.

Because of this—and because of Chubais's prominent role in the IMF talks—the Duma was predictably unprepared to play along. As a result, the Russian government was under great pressure to resort again to rule by decree, despite its questionable legal status. Simultaneously, the aggressive new tax chief Boris Fedorov—himself under investigation for embezzlement[47]—pursued tax-defaulters associated with "unfriendly" clans, such as the natural gas monopoly Gazprom (politically tied to Chernomyrdin), much more vigorously than "friendly" firms like Chubais's United Energy Systems. This could only worsen Russians' perceptions of their government's arbitrary rule and deepen the existing divisions in Russian society.

The 1998 IMF bailout also conclusively demonstrated to many Russians that the Clinton administration was determined to help Boris Yeltsin to stay in power no matter what. As the pro-reform columnist Aleksandr Bekker wrote, the administration had shown that "Boris Yeltsin's political survival is now worth almost any number of billions" of dollars.[48] Of course, Clinton administration officials have argued that the administration was not supporting Yeltsin personally but rather reform and stability in Russia. However, given that only 11 percent of Russians said at the time that they considered Yeltsin's record as president to be fundamentally positive—and 51 percent favored his resignation before the end of his term in office[49]—there is a real danger that, on the contrary, continuing to prop up Yeltsin and the circle of radical reformers around Anatoly Chubais could in fact contribute to the dangerous destablization of Russian democracy by precipitating policies that constrain economic growth and alienate the bulk of Russian society. Russia's August–September 1998 political crisis illustrated this danger.

The problem with the support provided to Russia by the IMF and the World Bank was that it was sufficient to help the Russian government to avoid outright disaster, but—without creating the conditions for economic growth, including a substantial increase in both domestic and foreign investment—it could not put the Russian economy on track. This, too, became clear in the fall 1998 crisis.

The ongoing series of scandals in 1996 and 1997 involving the first deputy prime minister and several of his close associates also undermined Chubais's effectiveness. The scandals included:

- A $2.9 million unsecured interest-free loan to a think tank established by Chubais from tycoon Aleksandr Smolensky (Stolichny Savings Bank, now SBS-Agro) in January 1996. The funds were allegedly used to invest in Russian government treasury bills.[50] Stolichny was a major beneficiary of privatization.
- A resolution passed in the State Duma by a vote of 235 to 19 accusing Chubais of failing to declare his full 1996 income and failing to pay $95,000 in taxes on time.[51] His declared income was $296,000; 2 percent of the sum was attributed to his government salary and his work on the Yeltsin campaign.[52]
- The cancellation of a $14 million Agency for International Development assistance contract with Harvard University's Institute for International Development in June 1997. Two consultants to the Harvard project, Jonathan Hay and Andrei Shleifer, were accused by the U.S. government of using their positions for personal gain through investments in Russia. Chubais defended the pair and claimed that they were victims of American opponents of reform in Russia. A Chubais ally soon announced his intention to hire Hay.[53]
- The dismissal of his protégé Alfred Kokh from his post as chairman of the State Property Committee in the wake of the Svyazinvest auction. Kokh received a $100,000 payment from a Swiss firm linked to Oneksimbank for an unpublished book on privatization in Russia.
- His own acceptance of a $90,000 payment from a publishing house affiliated with Vladimir Potanin's Oneksimbank. Four of Chubais's aides also received $90,000 each for the unpublished history of Russia's privatization process. The three aides still in government were fired by Yeltsin.[54]
- The exposure of Chubais's link to the Montes Auri investment company, headed by Alfred Kokh after his dismissal from government. The firm allegedly made sensational profits investing in Russia's

stock and bond markets with inside information from Chubais and Potanin (while still in government). Montes Auri was also tied to the organization through which Chubais received the $2.9 million loan from Stolichny Bank.[55]

- His decision to fly to India on a special government jet just days after Yeltsin issued a decree limiting such flights to the president, the prime minister, the Duma speaker, the Federation Council chairman, the secretary of the Security Council, and the foreign minister. Chubais claimed that the trip had been approved prior to the decree.[56]

As in the case of other officials accused of corruption, because Russia's parliament had no subpoena power and its attorney general had no real authority to investigate senior officials, nothing was proven conclusively about Chubais's alleged misdeeds. But in Russia's cynical social climate, the number and nature of the scandals ensured that a cloud of suspicion surrounded Chubais. At a minimum, the first deputy prime minister appeared—contrary to his original image—to be a man of reckless arrogance. Even his colleague Boris Nemtsov, who had been a consistent defender of Chubais, eventually acknowleged that the unpopular official's conduct demonstrated that he was capable of "great stupidity."[57] Chernomyrdin was reliably reported to be very irritated with his deputy's missteps—and particularly with the book deal.[58] And regardless of whether Chubais's problems arose from stupidity or criminal behavior, it became increasingly uncomfortable for Yeltsin to keep him at the helm of Russia's economic policy. Chubais soon lost his portfolio as finance minister (November 1997) and, in a sure sign that the move was not purely symbolic, was replaced by the independent Yabloko Duma Budget Committee chairman Mikhail Zadornov rather than by one of his many protégés.

Nemtsov also did not remain untouched. His popularity was weakened by not only his support for Chubais but also his brave attack on the energy monopolies, which ultimately ended with a compromise that did not fundamentally affect the companies' de facto control of state-owned shares in the firms. His equally unrealized promises to eliminate housing subsidies were exploited by Luzhkov and other rivals to expose the first deputy prime minister's "indifference" to ordinary people. Nemtsov's own writing also led to an embarrassing episode when it was discovered that he received $90,000 for his tiny paperback *Provintsial* from a company owned by Sergei

Lisovsky—one of the two Chubais aides arrested leaving the White House with $500,000 in cash. Lisovsky's firm was not known as a publishing house, and printed only 25,000 copies of the book, which retailed for under $1.[59] The publication of the book thus appeared to be another payoff rather than a legitimate business venture. The second young reformer was stripped of his concurrent ministerial position—as energy minister—and, tellingly, was also removed from his post as a government representative on the Gazprom board of directors.

Chubais and Nemtsov were likely already on thin ice with Yeltsin after having spent much of their limited political capital with the Russian president by insisting on the dismissal of Boris Berezovsky from his post as deputy secretary of the Security Council in September 1997. Although Yeltsin agreed to the dismissal after being convinced that Berezovsky had allowed his private interests to affect his public duties, members of his entourage later told me that the president resented being pressured by the young reformers, particuarly because some members of his family—including his daughter Tatyana Dyachenko and son-in-law Valery Okulov (general director of Aeroflot, controlled by Berezovsky) were still friendly with the tycoon. Because Berezovsky's firing was announced while Chernomyrdin was out of Moscow—and without prior consultation with his nominal superior, Security Council secretary Ivan Rybkin—the final strike against him by Chubais and Nemtsov alienated many of their colleagues in government. The prime minister was especially offended; his aides began to speak of the young reformers with growing disapproval.

By the time of his 1997 end-of-the-year radio address, the Russian president was again critical of Chubais's economic policies: "all we've done is swap [Communist] Party slogans for macroeconomic ones," he said. He also called for "replacing confrontation with dialogue" between the executive branch and the legislature.[60]

This atmosphere of cooperation bore fruit in Yeltsin's generally hostile relationship with the Duma. The lower house passed a compromise law on the government that gave the parliament a new voice in the appointment of certain cabinet ministers (excluding the power ministers, whose unquestioned loyalty Yeltsin no doubt still considered important). With the support of Zhirinovsky's Liberal Democratic Party and a number of Communist deputies—and despite the unanimous opposition of Yabloko—the Duma gave its preliminary approval to the 1998 budget in two votes.[61] There was even some progress on the very contentious issue of land reform, specifically with regard to the constraints on the right to sell privatized land.

This unprecedented spirit of relative harmony and constructive cooperation did not last long. The nonconfrontational political environment virtually guaranteed that the Russian president would soon tear the system apart only to patch it together again in a slightly different form. In declining health, Yeltsin was giving less and less attention to the everyday functions of government and was almost driven to create another crisis that only he could solve in order to show that he was still master.

Yeltsin and his entourage had also become resentful of prime minister Viktor Chernomyrdin, who seemed increasingly to be a real second-in-command with an independent power base and who appeared to have obvious presidential aspirations. Chernomyrdin was dismissed less than one month after his return from meetings with Vice President Gore in Washington with little or no prior warning. In another careful balancing act, Yeltsin also used the opportunity to rid himself of the controversial Chubais (whom, only months earlier, he had promised to keep until the end of his term in 2000) and Chubais's longtime conservative opponent Interior Minister Anatoly Kulikov. Although the Russian president soon appointed Chubais to head the giant electricity monopoly Unified Energy Systems (EES), he again balanced Chubais, selecting his nemesis Boris Berezovsky as executive secretary of the CIS and replacing Interior Minister Anatoly Kulikov with former Federal Security Service (FSB) head and justice minister Sergei Stepashin, another member of so-called "war party," the group of Russian officials who initially advocated military intervention in Chechnya.

In retrospect, it is clear that Yeltsin's decision to fire his prime minister of five years was largely spontaneous. This is demonstrated by the Russian president's initial announcement that he himself would temporarily assume the duties of prime minister, followed only hours later by the appointment of the relatively unknown thirty-five-year-old energy minister Sergei Kiriyenko as acting prime minister. Although there have been numerous attempts at postfactum rationalization of the appointment of Kiriyenko, highlighting his youth, competence, commitment to reform, and pragmatic approach to politics, the mechanics of his selection make clear that its principal purpose was to unseat the powerful Chernomyrdin. Kiriyenko, a former Komsomol leader and then business executive in Nizhni Novgorod brought to Moscow by Boris Nemtsov in 1997, had served only three months as a minister and was a virtual unknown to Yeltsin.

Kiriyenko's eventual confirmation by the State Duma was quite predictable. After two strong but nevertheless pro forma rejections of Yeltsin's prime minister–designate, the deputies overwhelmingly approved his candidacy in the face of threats to force new elections with revised rules unfavorable to the opposition and transparent suggestions by the president himself that he would "take care of the deputies' needs" if only they would cooperate.

Ultimately, the Russian Constitution, approved after Yeltsin's 1993 assault on the Supreme Soviet, was the decisive factor. It allowed Kiriyenko to assume office in an acting capacity prior to his confirmation and also ensured that if the parliament rejected Kiriyenko in a third vote, the Duma would face dissolution. The new Duma would still have to vote on Kiriyenko, if not a less palatable presidential appointee. Although the opposition would perhaps have won additional parliamentary seats had it forced new elections, the Duma had so little power that the opposition's strength within it was of little relevance if Boris Yeltsin was unwilling to cooperate with his legislature.

But Russia's circumstances changed radically in the next few months. The country's deepening financial crisis and growing popular discontent emboldened the parliament and limited Yeltsin's options when he decided to replace Kiriyenko and to reappoint Viktor Chernomyrdin as prime minister. Negotiations with the Duma over the appointment eventually collapsed when it became clear that Yeltsin would not share power with the parliament. The failure of Chernomyrdin's candidacy was a setback for Russia's oligarchs, especially Boris Berezovsky, who claimed credit for bringing him back.

Ultimately, Yeltsin appeared unwilling to risk the constitutional crisis that would have been brought about had he nominated Chernomyrdin a third time. The Duma threatened to begin impeachment proceedings against Yeltsin—which would have prevented him from dissolving the parliament constitutionally—and Yeltsin backed down and settled on Yevgeny Primakov as a compromise choice. With no known presidential aspirations, Primakov was seen as a caretaker who would likely prevent collapse—but not as a political powerhouse. Although he is a competent and pragmatic statesman, it is unclear whether he has the political courage to make tough decisions and exercise real leadership while facing domestic turmoil, an assertive parliament, and a president who is down but not out. Should Primakov demonstrate such leadership (to what will be most people's surprise) and should Russia's condition improve, he may well develop greater ambition.

Under these circumstances, Yeltsin might face an even more difficult situation if he seeks a third term as president in 2000. Russia's elected regional governors are much less amenable to guidance from the Kremlin than their appointed predecessors, many of whom orchestrated local support for the Yeltsin campaign in 1996 under threat of dismissal. Regional leaders such as Moscow mayor Yuri Luzhkov and Aleksandr Lebed, recently elected governor of resource-rich Krasnoyarsk, are powerful, ambitious, and charismatic and share Yeltsin's ability to appeal simultaneously to foreign investors, Russian elites, and Russians craving a strong populist leader. On top of the president's deteriorating physical and mental faculties, this new and serious competition persuaded Yeltsin and his entourage that another campaign was not a real option. Newly free of pressure from the president's team, the Constitution Court quickly ruled that a third term for Yeltsin would be unconstitutional.[62] The decision—which would have been highly controversial only several months earlier—was accepted calmly by all of Russia's political parties as an obvious consequence of the country's new political realities.

Whatever may come in Russian politics after Boris Yeltsin, it is important to remember that some 80 percent of the country's citizens reject bringing back communism.[63] The full-scale restoration of communism was very unlikely even during the 1996 elections and is a virtual impossibility today. This does not mean that Russia is out of danger—a host of troubles still face its fractured economy and society, as illustrated by nationwide blockades of rail lines by unpaid miners, teachers, doctors, and students in May 1998.[64]

There is room for cautious optimism regarding Russian democracy. But that optimism is not based on the continuation of present trends; instead, it relies on the expectation that the end of the Yeltsin era may bring an end to self-imposed obstacles to economic growth, a new sensitivity to the importance of public opinion, the destruction of the corrupt system of crony capitalism and its attendant third world–style social inequality, and most immediately, the redistribution of power among Russia's executive, legislative, and judicial branches, leading to the establishment of government by law and legislation in the place of arbitrary rule by decree.

This is not a pipe dream. There were already signs before the 1997–98 financial crisis that Russia's economy was beginning to grow. The combination of Russia's enormous natural resources, its well-educated and still relatively inexpensive labor force, its new entrepreneurial spirit, and its citizens' desire to become masters of their own destiny ensure that Russia need not remain a basket case in the early twenty-first century. But for Russia to live up to its potential, it must have a new, more enlightened government that respects the rule of law. That government need not be perfect, but it must at a minimum stop using Soviet-style techniques in its attempt to develop a market democracy. Such means simply preclude desirable ends.

The real question in Russia is not so much about specific government policies, which, short of an economic meltdown triggering social unrest, are likely to vary across a relatively narrow spectrum. Rather, the question is to what extent those policies will promote—or impede—the introduction of the rule of law, including constitutional changes granting more authority to Russia's weak legislative and judicial branches of government. Because the current political system has been tailored to fit Boris Yeltsin, some change is inevitable in the long term. But it is an open question whether that change will lead to increasingly authoritarian oligarchic rule or the gradual emergence of the rule of law and a true civil society.

There is no doubt that Russia is still in the midst of a historical cataclysm. As the prominent sociologist Boris Grushin observed at the end of 1997, "Of all the questions discussed in Russia today, perhaps the most disturbing is: Where is the country going? It seems to me that we are still almost entirely ignorant on this point." Nevertheless, Grushin wisely concluded that "the best one can hope for is that the government will not impede, will not slow, the real movement that is taking place outside its purview and even against its wishes."[65]

However, the Russian government has already considerably slowed the country's recovery. Russia's financial collapse was a logical result of the policies of the Chernomyrdin and (especially) the Kiriyenko governments, which had relied heavily upon foreign borrowing to sustain federal budget expenditures. When oil prices fell and simultaneously Western investors began to pull money out of Russia to cover their losses in the Asian financial crisis in 1997, the Russian government was forced into greater borrowing at escalating interest rates.

The interest rates on government securities were so high that there was little incentive for Russia's banks, or investors in general, to put money into production. Without that investment, however, there could be no growth in income to allow for the repayment of Russia's mounting debts. At the same time, it became increasingly expensive to support the overvalued ruble. The result was a typical pyramid scheme. When the Kiriyenko government was finally forced to devalue the ruble, it found that it (and Russia's banks) could no longer meet their international obligations.

Key radical reformers, including Anatoly Chubais, have admitted understanding what was happening and the likely consequences.[66] Nevertheless, in the best Russian tradition, they hoped against hope that somehow something would happen to resolve the crisis—or that the Clinton administration and the IMF would again step in to offer a way out. But nothing materialized.

The resulting chaos and collapse of the ruble led quickly to the further decline of Russia's GDP, a new wave of inflation, consumer hoarding and shortages, unemployment, and capital flight. The fact that a reformist government that enjoyed particular confidence in the West had taken the drastic measures compounded the damage to Russia's international credibility. Similarly, Anatoly Chubais's statement that he and the Russian cabinet deliberately deceived the IMF and foreign investors alike about the weakness of the Russian economy delivered a further blow.[67]

Since Primakov came into office as prime minister without a program or a real background in economics, his disjointed cabinet had considerable difficulty developing a coherent economic package while the Russian economy continued to decline. The good news was that since Primakov was appointed through a compromise, he faced no immediate strong opposition. Fearing a further unraveling of the situation, most major political figures, including presidential hopefuls such as Mayor Luzhkov and Governor Lebed, offered the new prime minister their support. At the same time, the Duma's role in Primakov's selection gave the new prime minister greater freedom from Yeltsin's destabilizing meddling than any of his predecessors had enjoyed.

Meanwhile, the Russian people—tired, confused, and preoccupied with their own survival—did not appear to be in a mood to start a new revolutionary uprising. But Russian revolutions have often started in spontaneous and unpredictable revolts. In a nation with a constitutionally powerful but personally weak president and a disaffected, disillusioned population, even a fairly limited protest could start a chain reaction, especially if the fragmented Primakov government does not halt skyrocketing inflation and limit shortages.

In most countries, a crisis of the magnitude of the August–September 1998 events would result in a comprehensive change of leadership. But in Russia, where Yeltsin is a declining tsar rather than a hands-on chief executive, a change of government may suffice if Primakov and his ministers are able to avoid completely alienating foreign investors and cutting off Russia from international assistance. It is also possible if the situation continues to deteriorate that Primakov may be able to reshuffle the government and include responsible reformers in key positions.

If that scenario takes place enough is happening in Russia to allow hope that worst-case scenarios might be avoided. One must at least entertain the possibility that the country may be able to create for itself a new beginning. From the standpoint of social stability, it would probably be best if Boris Yeltsin were to remain in office until the presidential elections scheduled for 2000 while continuing his gradual disengagement from everyday affairs of state. The introduction of the office of vice president— if legally and politically feasible—would contribute to an orderly transition should Yeltsin have to step down before the end of his term, especially if a neutral figure—like Primakov—were appointed. A vice president could serve out the balance of the Russian president's term without being constitutionally obliged to organize a special election within three months (which the prime minister is required to do).

With the exception of Grigory Yavlinsky, head of Yabloko, none of the major contenders for the presidency has strong democratic credentials. Conversely, however, none of them appears to be a dangerous extremist.

Communist Party leader Gennady Zyuganov is the front-runner in every public opinion poll. Despite this, the same polls indicate that he cannot win an absolute majority of the vote—which would ensure his election in the first round of voting—and that he would almost certainly lose to any potential non-Communist candidate in the second round, in which the two candidates with the highest first-round votes would face each other.

Former Prime Minister Viktor Chernomyrdin lost much of his clout after his reappointment was rejected by the Duma. The demise of the oligarchy, even if temporary (and relative), also cuts into his base of support. To have a chance at a comeback, he would need to be rehabilitated—perhaps by being selected as prime minister by President Primakov (which would also require Primakov to become vice president and Yeltsin to step down before 2000). This is highly unlikely, but Russia is a country where miracles do happen.

Yabloko party leader Grigory Yavlinsky is the only candidate other than Zyuganov with a strong constituency and a national party. However, his electoral base is limited to intellectuals and the upper middle class. Also, he has no government experience (beyond brief service during the Soviet era), which is a handicap in Russia's present environment, where voters are looking primarily for someone to get things done rather than an advocate for any particular ideology or philosophy. He may need a successful tenure in the cabinet or an alliance with another major contender to become a credible presidential candidate.

Prime Minister Yevgeny Primakov could become president if Yeltsin leaves office before the end of his term. His position would be strengthened if he became vice president first and, accordingly, did not have to call an election in three months. He has no strong constituency, but few enemies. The fact that he has limited political ambitions—and is not considered presidential material—has helped him to win the support of other key politicians, as have his statements that "Russia will not go down on its knees"[68] and his on-time payment of wages and pensions (particularly to soldiers) for the first time in months. That would change quickly, however, were Primakov to decide to run for office. And few expect he will be able to develop the kind of record which will propel him into the presidency.

The two strongest contenders at this point are Moscow mayor Yuri Luzhkov and Krasnoyarsk governor Aleksandr Lebed. They are roughly even in public opinion polls. Both are ethnic Russians with "common man" backgrounds, charismatic personalities, and populist styles. At present, Luzhkov portrays himself as somewhat left of center—opposed to the oligarchs, supportive of social welfare spending, and committed to protecting Russian interests abroad, especially in the territory of the former Soviet Union. Lebed, in contrast, appears right of center—on good terms with some of the oligarchs (particularly Boris Berezovsky), preoccupied with foreign investment, and a peacemaker (based on his role in ending the violence in Moldova and negotiating Russia's peace agreement with Chechnya).

To what extent the apparent differences between Luzhkov and Lebed are questions of conviction or of expediency is difficult to know. Their positions have evolved over time, neither has as yet presented a well-defined program, and each has a fairly eclectic team of advisors. It is fair to say that for Luzhkov—who was linked to the banker Vladimir Gusinsky in the past and has been accused of building his own system of crony capitalism in Moscow—being a fighter against the oligarchs and an advocate of the needy common person is politically advantageous. Similarly, for a tough former general like Lebed, a new image as a peacemaker will appeal to an electorate wary of new international adventures.

Nevertheless, the fact that Luzhkov and Lebed to some degree resemble mirror images does reflect the current state of Russian politics. Despite enormous hardship, Russia's new voters still prefer pragmatic, result-oriented leaders. An authoritarian streak softened by pledges to maintain democracy is not a liability in a nation eager for a strong hand. At the same time—absent a collapse of the system—Russians are too cynical after repeated disillusionment to be easily attracted to dangerous demagogues.

That the Russian president elected in 2000—almost ten years after the collapse of the USSR—is likely to be a former Communist with ties to the old regime and uncertain democratic credentials is a sad commentary on Russia's evolution under Yeltsin's rule. But because his authoritarianism lacked a systematic approach, was ineffective outside Moscow's beltway, and was practiced with only occasional brutality, Russia's democratic experiment was damaged but not destroyed. All of the likely presidential candidates are serious, flexible people with records of accomplishment and all profess a commitment to democracy and market-oriented reform. And should the transition from the Yeltsin regime lead to a diffusion of authority, increased power-sharing, and stronger checks and balances, the next Russian president may have less ability to act on his authoritarian temptations.

Mayor Luzhkov and Governor Lebed are strong personalities, but each seems to be wise enough not to attempt to swim against the tide of public opinion to create a new authoritarianism in Russia. It will be the Russian political environment rather than either leader's personal predilections that will determine whether Lebed, for example, might become a Pinochet or a de Gaulle. A rough winter, increased political passions, contemptuous American disengagement, and humiliation abroad (perhaps through NATO air strikes against Yugoslavia over Kosovo)—some combination of these could sufficiently alter the political climate to give extremists a new chance or even to cause today's pragmatists to become extremists. The Duma's failure to condemn crude, anti-Semitic remarks by radical Communist ex-general Albert Makashov is an ominous reminder of this possibility.[69]

Fortunately, extremism is not inevitable. Russians are learning to operate in a post-Communist environment, to take charge of their own destinies, and to display entrepreneurial skills. The destruction of Soviet controls has unleashed powerful social forces which—even without the assistance or encouragement of the Russian government—have wrought substantial change in the six years of Russian independence. The fact that Russia's eighty-nine (eighty-eight excluding Chechnya) regions are now led by elected governors rather than appointed presidential representatives is also encouraging; it helps both to mitigate central control and to insulate the rest of the country from twists and turns in Moscow.

What Russia really needs to realize the optimistic assessments of its potential is a government that will accept its own limitations. Such a government would not attempt to be an omnipotent overseer but rather a regulator and a facilitator. Building on a foundation as flawed as today's Russia, the best guidance comes from Thomas Jefferson and his cautious attitude toward creating a government with "tyrannical" powers.

Chapter Nine

•

The New Russian Foreign Policy:
Seeking a Place in the Sun

The opposition victory in the December 1995 Duma elections affected not only Russia's domestic policy but its foreign policy as well, although its international policy had in fact been slowly and quietly evolving for quite some time.

After the collapse of the Soviet Union, Russia was left without a clear conception of its national interests. The end of the Cold War represented a much more complex problem for Russia in defining its interests than for the United States, which had seen its policy goals vindicated. As a result, Russia was forced to create what was almost an entirely new foreign policy.

As Russia gradually learned to identify its new foreign policy interests, Boris Yeltsin became increasingly uncomfortable with the emphasis his foreign minister, Andrei Kozyrev, continued to place on "universal human values," originally a key part of Mikhail Gorbachev's "new thinking" in foreign policy. Yeltsin was also distressed by Kozyrev's willingness to accept guidance from the West, particularly the United States; however, as Kozyrev was among the principal targets of the Communists and nationalists (in addition to Gaidar and Chubais), the proud and defiant Russian president was reluctant to dismiss him under pressure.

Simultaneously, Kozyrev (again, like Gaidar and Chubais) was a symbol of Russian democracy and reform to some of Moscow's most important foreign friends. Thus, many in the West feared that Kozyrev's departure would signify Russia's abandonment of a benign foreign policy and even an end to its willingness to see developments in the world from the Western perspective, which Kozyrev accepted as strategically and morally superior to Moscow's own. The fact that Kozyrev was prepared to absorb a lot of criticism—sometimes bordering on open humiliation—from Yeltsin and that he constantly emphasized his loyalty to the president also did not hurt his case; although the Russian leader is a highly intuitive politician, he has always been a sucker for sycophants.

But the sound defeat of the pro-government parties in the Duma election sent Yeltsin a powerful message. Only six months remained before Russia's 1996 presidential vote, and Yeltsin would have to adjust his policies significantly if he hoped to stay in power. The desire to preserve his own power, always an overriding concern for Boris Yeltsin, quickly led him to oust both Chubais and Kozyrev.

Russia's new foreign minister was Yevgeny Primakov, a Soviet-era politician like Yeltsin himself. Remarkably, Primakov was a member of Gorbachev's inner circle and served as a key international troubleshooter for the Soviet president, particularly during the 1991 war in the Persian Gulf. Although such service would have disqualified most candidates from occupying any key position under Yeltsin—whose government was filled with the second echelon of the *nomenklatura* and almost totally excluded senior Soviet officials, who were by definition too close to Gorbachev— Primakov was particularly skilled in the art of political maneuvering and managed fairly quickly to ingratiate himself with the new regime.

In September 1991, Mikhail Gorbachev appointed Primakov to lead the USSR's foreign intelligence operations and gave him the rank of deputy chairman of the KGB. The appointment, which Gorbachev made in consultation with Boris Yeltsin, was in part to reward Primakov for his refusal to join in the August coup against the Soviet leader. When the Soviet Union ceased to exist at the end of 1991, Yeltsin retained Primakov in the same position with a new title: head of Russia's new Foreign Intelligence Service. Explaining his decision to keep Primakov, Yeltsin said: "Many people from my entourage have advised me to replace Primakov, but . . . they were not correct. I should also say that when I was in disfavor and subject to all kinds of public dishonor, Yevgeny Maksimovich [Primakov] was one of the few state figures who treated me humanely and was not afraid to give me his hand. So let it be!"[1] Primakov was similarly civil in his relations with most other key political figures and, as a result, was able to maintain at least cordial ties with all sides of Moscow's constant infighting.

Primakov carefully treated his new post as nonpolitical and did not join any of the Kremlin's competing factions. He also worked hard to demonstrate that the Russian president could count on him while simultaneously he kept his distance and did not seek to become a part of Yeltsin's entourage. Primakov's management of Russia's foreign intelligence agency during a difficult transition period enhanced his credibility and his reputation as a professional. And his Soviet-era credentials were helpful in placating the Communists and thereby isolating Russian foreign policy from domestic political games as much as possible.

So impressive were Primakov's political talents—particularly his ability to avoid alienating anyone—that his appointment as foreign minister was greeted with almost universal acclaim across Russia's political spectrum. Communist leader Gennady Zyuganov told me that he considered Primakov to be a patriot and a top-notch professional; Grigory Yavlinsky's key associate Vladimir Lukin—chairman of the Duma's International Relations Committee and former ambassador to Washington—said, "We need to put a real man on the seventh floor of the Foreign Ministry instead of a boy who looks to the Kremlin in Moscow and to the White House in Washington before opening his mouth to make sure that he did not misunderstand his latest instructions."

Lukin feuded bitterly with Kozyrev during his posting as ambassador to the United States from 1992 to 1995 and had good reason to be pleased with a change of command at the Russian Foreign Ministry. He also knew Primakov well—both came out of the Russian academic community—and enjoyed a good relationship with him. I was less comfortable with the new foreign minister because of his deep Soviet-era roots, but could well understand why, from the Russian standpoint, it was natural to replace Kozyrev with someone like him.

My last encounter with Kozyrev occurred two years before his dismissal. I had accompanied President Nixon to the Foreign Ministry's mansion on Alexei Tolstoy Street in downtown Moscow during a visit in February 1993. Kozyrev surprised Nixon when he began their conversation by complaining to him about an article I had written in the *Washington Post* in which I argued that Russian foreign policy was driven by a combination of confusion and nostalgia. Although Nixon had actually discussed the

article with me in detail after its publication and seemed to be in general
agreement with me, he was pleased by Kozyrev's complaints: on one hand,
he enjoyed seeing me put a bit on the defensive in his presence; on the
other, he liked the idea that his advisor was someone whose opinions would
matter enough to distress the foreign minister of a great nation.

When he finished with me, Kozyrev switched to Vladimir Lukin, then
still ambassador to Washington, and hinted that Lukin was neither particularly competent nor a true friend of the United States. Nixon knew and respected Lukin, whose brand of nonaggressive "enlightened Russian
patriotism" (as Lukin called it) the former president believed was likely the
best that the United States could hope for from Russian foreign-policy-
makers over the long term. Regardless of who was right in the dispute between Kozyrev and Lukin, however, Nixon was put off by the idea that any
foreign minister would discredit one of his nation's ambassadors in such a
fashion. His indignation sounded a bit disingenuous—a number of career
diplomats complained about being undercut by Kissinger and Nixon himself during his presidency—but it was genuine nonetheless. Kozyrev's con-
frontational attitude to the Congress of Peoples' Deputies also rubbed
Nixon the wrong way; while the former president certainly preferred Yeltsin
over the parliament, he thought that dialogue would contribute more significantly to democracy and stability in Russia than conflict.

I had known Primakov for a long time. Several years after I emi-
grated to the United States and began to develop a reputation as a young
Sovietologist, I learned that Primakov was speaking quite unkindly about
me to his American contacts. He told some, suggestively, that he could
never fully understand my emigration because my conduct in the Komsomol committee at the Institute for World Economy and International
Relations (IMEMO) did not in his view demonstrate any opposition to
the system on my part. With others, he took a different tack and portrayed
me as an extremely junior employee of the institute, someone of no consequence—almost a member of the cleaning staff—who had had no access to anything and was only misleading American specialists by
pretending to be a man of substance.

I was aware that precisely because Primakov was considered to be my
supporter of sorts at IMEMO it was important for him to demonstrate that
there was never any real connection between us; otherwise, he could become vulnerable—particularly given his own Jewish ancestry. Nevertheless,

I felt that he was going a bit too far by attempting to discredit me. Once, after yet another report of Primakov's badmouthing, I decided to send him a letter. Rather than complaining, which would have had no effect, I thanked him for everything he had done for me in the past and said that I was particularly grateful to hear that he still remembered me on so many occasions. I assumed that the letter would make Primakov, then director of the prestigious Institute of Oriental Studies, quite uncomfortable—particularly since he would probably be expected to share it with the KGB representative at the institute, a common practice at the time. I did not expect to get him into any real trouble, but I thought that a gentle reminder that two could play at his game might be constructive. I have no idea whether Primakov received the letter, or whether it had any impact on him, but the stories about him attacking me did finally stop.

During the 1980s, I saw Primakov several times at various U.S.–Soviet summits, including at the December 1987 White House dinner for Mikhail Gorbachev. I also encountered him during my first visit to the Soviet Union with Nixon in March 1991. Primakov and I were both perfectly cordial with one another, but we never had an informal conversation. I did not know much about him beyond what I heard from others and read in the press, but his conduct during the Gulf War—which raised suspicions that he was trying to save Saddam Hussein—did not help him in the eyes of most of my friends in the American foreign policy establishment.

Still, I was not terribly disturbed by allegations that Primakov was a KGB agent. Even if he worked for the old KGB, he would have been employed in a foreign intelligence capacity—not as a political policeman. Given that Russia's president was a former Party apparatchik and its then prime minister had spent six years in the Party bureaucracy before becoming a senior government bureaucrat and a Central Committee member, it would have been hypocritical to become exercised over the foreign minister's old KGB contacts. More to the point, while I never doubted that a person with Primakov's illustrious career had to have close ties to the KGB, it seemed very unlikely that he had ever been a staff officer. If there were any firm institutional rules in the post-Stalin Soviet Union, one such rule was that the Party was above the security services and, therefore, that Party personnel were not allowed to work for the KGB. As a correspondent for *Pravda,* the official party newspaper, in Cairo in the 1960s, Primakov was a part of the Central Committee *nomenklatura.* Because he was directly supervised by the International Department of the Central Committee, it would have been highly unusual for him to simultaneously take orders from the KGB. Lieutenant General Vadim Kirpichenko, a retired first deputy chief of foreign intelligence for the KGB, confirms this in a recent book, where he writes that *Pravda* correspondents such as Primakov maintained "close professional contacts" with KGB station chiefs but "could not be engaged for cooperation."[2]

I knew that Primakov was a pragmatist. For example, his problem with me did not lead him to discourage IMEMO from sponsoring Nixon's first visit to the Soviet Union. As an influential former director turned Kremlin patron of the Institute, Primakov could easily have done so. It seemed to me that Primakov knew how to control his personal likes and dislikes and also how to keep them from influencing his important decisions.

•   •   •

In the two years following Primakov's appointment as foreign minister, Russian foreign policy changed considerably. It lost the emphasis on "universal human values" and the desire to walk in lockstep with the United States, combined with pitifully unrealistic yet bombastic pronouncements of Russia's continuing superpower greatness that were Kozyrev's hallmarks. Because Russia was in the midst of a major transformation, Primakov did not attempt to develop a new conceptual blueprint for a lasting foreign policy. Instead, as a competent statesman with a keen sense of Russia's peculiar international circumstances and changing domestic mood, he adjusted Russian diplomacy in a fairly low-key but still distinct fashion.

There are five elements to this continuing shift in Russia's international behavior. First, it is now clear that Russia has its own unique national interests, that it is prepared to define them on its own—without much help from the West—and that it will pursue them assertively. Second, Russia has accepted that it is no longer a superpower, except in terms of nuclear capability, and that nostalgia cannot serve as a guide for an effective foreign policy. Third, Russia understands that because it is not a superpower, it can play a major role in international affairs only in a "multipolar" world. Consequently, Russia must oppose firmly the premise that the United States should be allowed a special role as the world's only global superpower. Fourth, Russia should pursue its interests without confrontation—particularly during its current period of weakness and continuing dependence on the West. Finally, Russia's new foreign policy—in contrast to Soviet policy—is based not on global ideology but on domestic needs. Accordingly, Russia gives priority to geoeconomics over geopolitics and to defending the interests of the new Russian business elite over abstract theoretical notions with little impact on life at home, such as fighting the first stage of NATO enlargement or opposing U.S.–sponsored nation-building in Bosnia, even when it finds these initiatives disagreeable.

When the Soviet Union collapsed, Russia had no defined national interests. Although Gaidar and his associates at least attempted to explain why it was in Russia's interest to pursue economic reform independently from the rest of the Soviet Union, virtually no thought was given to the foreign policy consequences of Russia's "splendid isolation" from the other former Soviet republics. Boris Nemtsov, who discussed these issues with Yeltsin repeatedly at the time, wrote: "There was a naïve idea that having proclaimed Russian sovereignty, it was possible to be delivered from the indecisive Gorbachev and his policies while saving the Soviet Union. I think it even moved Yeltsin at that time. But in fact they threw out the baby with the bathwater. The battle with Gorbachev ended with the destruction of the USSR. For Yeltsin this was undoubtedly a personal tragedy."[3] This lack of appreciation of the momentous consequences of Russian independence for the Union as a whole was almost inexplicable if one realizes that some of the other Union republics had been integral components of the empire for many centuries and a few—particularly those populated by fellow Slavs— were as close to Russia as the southern states were to the rest of the Union in mid-nineteenth-century America or, for that matter, as Texas and California are to the rest of the United States today despite their previous affiliation with Mexico and their growing Spanish-speaking populations. In the eyes of many, some former Soviet republics were separated from Russia only by arbitrarily established administrative borders that contradicted history, demographics, and economics.

The dilemma of how to respond to separatist tendencies among ethnic minorities was not a new one for Russia. In the nineteenth and early twentieth centuries, many Russian reformers—and especially Russian revolutionaries—had considerable sympathy for non-Russian groups seeking greater autonomy from the empire's extensive and often humiliating central controls. Even among Russia's imperial elites, one influential view called for greater freedoms for ethnic minority regions, to the extent that such freedom could be granted without threatening the disintegration of the empire. Yet there was a prevalent belief, as Sergei Witte graphically wrote, that despite all its faults "Great Russia was created by a glorious thousand-year history (if it had not been glorious then there would be no Great Russia) and accordingly it is necessary to perfect it, but it is not necessary to give it over to the curses and mockery of anyone, the Poles included. Liberation from the arbitrary rule of the bureaucrats and the cretinism of the court cliques is one thing, but the liberation of Russia from itself, from all of its history, from the results of all its historical achievements, from the sum of its thousand-year existence, from memories of the rivers of blood which we Russians spilled creating in ourselves the Great Russian empire—that is another matter."[4] Although Witte's qualified but firm loyalty to an imperfect empire obviously was unpersuasive among Russia's captive peoples, it did represent a widespread view among Russians both before and after the Revolution. In fact, the sense of imperial patriotism he expressed ultimately motivated many originally opposed to the Bolsheviks to contribute to the development of the Soviet state in the 1920s and 1930s. For the Russian ruling class under Yeltsin, however, which had been bitterly disillusioned by the cynicism and corruption of the late Brezhnev era, that enlightened imperial patriotism did not come naturally.

At first, the post-Soviet Russian Foreign Ministry gave little consideration to Moscow's place in the world. For centuries, Russia had played the role of a great power because of its military might—and its perceived willingness to use it. With the empire gone and the Soviet Union replaced with a community of newly independent states in a manner which precluded the establishment of minimally reliable rules for an orderly transition, Moscow lost a major part of its armed forces almost overnight. Since the best-equipped, -staffed, and -trained units—the so-called "first category" divisions—were primarily stationed outside the Soviet Union or in border military districts, the loss of the other fourteen republics, particularly Ukraine, had a disproportionately devastating impact on Russia's military potential.

How would the outside world treat this new and much weaker Russia? Would several years of fairly benign conduct by Gorbachev and particularly Yeltsin be sufficient to persuade Russia's neighbors—both old and new—to overcome centuries of intimidation and mistreatment? I tried on a number of occasions to discuss these questions with Kozyrev and his associates and came to the conclusion that they not only did not have the answers, but had little interest even in raising these kinds of issues. Driven by their desire to help Yeltsin to wrest power from Gorbachev, they accepted on the basis of blind faith that, once the Soviet Union was gone, the other former republics would both thank Russia for its pioneering role in destroying the USSR and recognize that they could not yet stand on their feet without the helping hand of their elder brother.

At the same time, they had romantic expectations of the West. These expectations were not totally without foundation, taking into account the enormity of Soviet and then Russian strategic concessions, but they were quite unrealistic partly because of domestic constraints in the Western democracies and partly because in international politics unilateral gifts from adversaries rarely lead to major payoffs, especially when delivered from a position of weakness and without a quid pro quo. Real payoffs are usually reserved for carefully negotiated deals. Germany and Japan benefited enormously from American generosity during their postwar reconstruction and seem to contradict this rule; however, they are in a different category because each surrendered unconditionally and was occupied by U.S. troops. In contrast, Russia maintained its sovereignty, kept much of its Communist *nomenklatura,* and professed its desire to remain a great power. There was no "clean break" with the past in the Russian case.

Nevertheless, Russian leaders thought that what had been called the evil empire should now be embraced as a republic of good that had no reason to quarrel with its former adversaries and could count on their generous support. Of course, Russia did eventually receive considerable assistance from the West, up to $100 billion (total for all types, including credits) by some estimates,[5] and bears significant responsibility for wasting much of that sum. But according to the conventional wisdom at the time, Russians expected more than money: they expected salvation at home and continued great-power status abroad, all delivered into their deserving hands on a silver platter. These excessively optimistic assumptions were quickly proven false. In the words of Aleksandr Bovin, a leading Russian liberal journalist and former ambassador to Israel, "A new world order has not materialized. Russia has found itself embroiled in a new world disorder. The giveaway play has not worked out. We were surrounded by a world where the egoistic interests and political and economic rivalry were much stronger than the proclaimed sympathy towards 'Russian democracy.' "[6]

•   •   •

Like Russia, the other former Soviet republics were economically devastated. But the radical economic reforms undertaken in Russia were unappealing to most of the other newly independent states. Without Russia's vast natural and human resources—and its ties to the West—the other republics were profoundly ill equipped to follow the Gaidar-Chubais path to capitalism.

At the same time, with the exception of the Baltic states, Georgia, Armenia, and to a lesser extent Ukraine, most of their elites were based on the old *nomenklatura,* which originally desired only greater autonomy. They began to press for independence from Russia only after the central government began to lose its authority. Nevertheless, once independence was a fact, their primary claim to legitimacy lay in raising the nationalist banner. However, the fourteen new states had no armed forces of their own—only the equipment left behind by the dissolution of the Union and units which, while among the best in the USSR, included a large proportion of suddenly foreign Russian officers, particularly in key positions. Even in Ukraine, the loyalty of many ethnic Russian officers could not be taken for granted by the country's new government. Most non-Slavic newly independent states faced a more dire predicament: their officer corps were predominantly Russian and were considered a potential fifth column, not without reason.

Many of the new states found themselves caught up in fratricidal ethnic and political conflicts that made them extremely vulnerable to Russia. Since Russia was not shy about involving itself in the problems of its neighbors, these disputes were a destabilizing factor. In Ukraine, the overwhelmingly Russian population of Crimea demanded autonomous status and showed some interest in either unification with Russia or outright independence. The country's eastern provinces also had large ethnic Russian populations, too—the Russian language was heard more commonly than Ukrainian—and Kiev feared that economic difficulties could encourage separatist tendencies that could easily be exploited by Moscow and might even lead to a civil war and possibly Russian intervention.

In Kazakhstan, where ethnic relations were fairly harmonious, the primarily Slavic population of the country's northern provinces nevertheless showed growing uneasiness at the prospect of minority status among the Muslim Kazakhs. In Moldova, the ethnic Russian population of Transdniester responded to local nationalist tendencies by proclaiming a separate republic. They were protected by Russia's 14th Army under the command of Lieutenant General Aleksandr Lebed. In Georgia, Abkhazia—where ethnic Abkhaz comprised less than 20 percent of the population—proclaimed its independence from Georgia and similarly relied on assistance from Russian troops and the local ethnic Russian population. Another Georgian province, South Ossetia, sought to reunite with North Ossetia, an autonomous republic within Russia, and to join the Russian Federation. In Tajikistan, Russian troops became involved in a civil war between neo-Communists and their Muslim opponents. Russian units in Tajikistan (in which most of the conscripts were Tajiks) were viewed as a key military instrument of the post-Communist regime. With this record, it was predictable that the leaders of the other newly independent states, even those like Kazakhstan's Nursultan Nazarbayev, who regretted the disintegration of the Soviet Union, should consider their principal foreign policy priorities to be establishing their countries' new identities and protecting themselves against Russian meddling.

There was much greater enthusiasm for Yeltsin's Russia outside the former Soviet Union. Russian forces had been withdrawn from Central Europe, Moscow suddenly had no major global role, and the West owed a great debt to Russia for the tremendous international changes brought about by its destruction of the USSR. Japan, however, was an important exception: encouraged by Gorbachev's concessions in Europe, Tokyo felt that in comparison Russia had failed to deliver by refusing to acknowledge Japan's sovereignty over the so-called Northern Territories, known as the Kuril Islands to their Russian residents. Nevertheless, the United States, Western Europe, and Japan were united in their unwillingness to proceed with a program on the scale of the Marshall Plan to rebuild the Russian economy or to accept the Yeltsin government's argument that helping the new, democratic Russia should have the same priority for the capitalist democracies as fighting the Cold War against the Soviet Union.

•   •   •

At first, Russia did not respond systematically to its discovery of these unpleasant realities. With regard to the newly independent states, it chose a combination of nostalgic rhetoric, muscle-flexing in troubled areas, and quiet reconciliation with the new facts of life where it lacked better alternatives. Russia's attitude toward the West at the time was summarized well by Lukin: "Just name us a 'great power,' for God's sake—then you can do whatever you like."[7]

Yeltsin and Kozyrev talked bravely about establishing a new "strategic partnership" with the West. Although Western leaders paid enthusiastic lip service to Russia's status as a great power, they did not treat it as such on a practical level. In Primakov's words, "Instead of strategic relations, 'leader and led' relations have begun to take shape in which we have, of course, been assigned the secondary role."[8]

As was the case with shock therapy, the Yeltsin-Kozyrev foreign policy quickly started to lose domestic support. When I visited the Soviet Union during Gorbachev's last years and then the new independent Russia in 1991–92, fascination with the West, and especially with the United States, was almost universal. The fascination was not limited to Kozyrev asking Nixon for help in defining Russian national interests or to Gaidar and Chubais inviting foreign experts and particularly international financial institutions to guide Russian reform; it was widespread in society (especially among big-city intellectuals). The West and, indeed, individual Westerners were supposed to have all the answers.

I was often embarrassed during my frequent visits to Russia with Nixon and also as chairman of the Carnegie Endowment's Center for Russian and Eurasian Programs when well-educated and intelligent people who had much more experience in Russia than I would ask me how to do things that were totally outside of my area of expertise, such as restructuring the country's armed forces, converting defense plants to civilian production, rejuvenating the Russian Academy of Sciences, or even bringing moral values to the Russian people. My expressions of humility and ignorance were often dismissed as false modesty at best, or as the arrogant reluctance of a former compatriot to share his newly acquired wisdom at worst. Unfortunately, thousands of Western advisors, consultants, foundation executives, and self-important visitors had little inhibition in volunteering their guidance on every topic without much appreciation of local circumstances or any real sense of responsibility for the consequences of their suggestions, should they prove counterproductive.

Nixon shared my growing apprehension with Russia's unrealistic expectations and my concern that they were likely to lead to disappointment

and disillusionment. He benefited from discussions with two equally concerned Russian officials: Yeltsin advisor Sergei Stankevich and Russian ambassador to Washington Vladimir Lukin. At an early 1993 luncheon at the
Russian embassy, Lukin argued strongly that the only way to prevent a major anti-Western backlash in Russia was to preempt the Communists and
extreme nationalists—who were already increasingly vocal in his country—
by developing an enlightened patriotic alternative to Kozyrev's foreign policy. Lukin's approach was based no less than Kozyrev's romanticism on an
appreciation of the pivotal importance of partnership with the West, first
and foremost with the United States. However, it departed from Kozyrev's
policy in that it recognized that Russia had its own distinct interests, that it
was bound to take different approaches to a variety of international issues,
and that relations between Moscow and Washington should look less like
the relations between an enthusiastic teenager and his adult guardian and
more like the traditional ties between major powers, even if one of the powers enjoyed clear superiority at the moment. He mentioned America's troubled partnership with Charles de Gaulle's France as an example.

In 1993, I began to discover growing anti-Western—and especially
anti-American—sentiment in my conversations with Russians. Fortunately,
the demise of the irreconcilable opposition in October 1993 undercut the
most extreme xenophobic tendencies in Russia. But there were growing
signs of anti-Americanism among Russians who only yesterday had been
extremely pro-American, including quite a few senior Russian officials. Although most of them understood that Russia was too weak and too dependent upon Washington to engage in open defiance, their emotional
predisposition was clear and disturbing. They increasingly saw the United
States as a paternalistic and insensitive hegemonic power which—although
it was providing Russia with (what they viewed as token) assistance—ultimately aimed to keep Moscow on its knees.

Nevertheless, by 1995 and particularly 1996, the fiasco in Chechnya
had significantly weakened aggressive impulses in Moscow. Russia was involved in the disastrous war in the Caucasus for almost two years—from
December 1994 to September 1996—after promises from then defense
minister Pavel Grachev that the conflict would be little more than a brief
punitive expedition. Despite frequent optimistic statements from Russian
politicians predicting imminent victory, Russian forces suffered a series of
humiliating defeats at the hands of the Chechen rebels. Eventually, when

the Chechens recaptured their capital, Grozny, in August 1996—in the aftermath of his reelection—Boris Yeltsin realized that a favorable military solution of the problem was increasingly unlikely and let his Security Council secretary, General Lebed, sign a peace agreement leading to the withdrawal of Russian forces from the independence-minded republic. Over 30,000 people—mostly civilians—were killed during the conflict.[9] Lebed was immediately criticized for surrendering to the enemy, just as Sergei Witte had been attacked for making peace with Japan after its 1905 victory over Russia. Then interior minister Anatoly Kulikov—at the time in an alliance with Chubais against the maverick Lebed and an original member of the so-called party of war that initiated the conflict—was particularly vehement in attacking the peace agreement.

Despite the loud criticism, however, the truth was that, as in Witte's case, Russia could not expect to be given at the negotiating table what it had failed to win in two years on the battlefield. And as Lebed told me in February 1998, he had come to the conclusion that at a certain point Russia's "indiscriminate bombardment totally alienated almost everyone in Chechnya and made the war—which had become a war against the entire population—unwinnable." Moreover, the Russian people were exposed on a daily basis to reports of the incompetence, corruption, and atrocities of the military and paramilitary forces—including Kulikov's Interior Ministry troops—deployed in Chechnya. Igor Malashenko's NTV, then still critical of the Yeltsin government, played a prominent role in the public campaign against the war. Ultimately, it was clear that Russian society simply could not stomach the embarrassingly unsuccessful but brutal war, in which Yeltsin's military committed abuses comparable to those for which the West insisted on punishment in Bosnia, including massive bombing and shelling of cities, summary executions of civilians, and torture. Nevertheless, the Chechnya debacle was a blessing in disguise in one respect: it had a profoundly sobering impact upon those who still harbored nostalgic and aggressive impulses. If Russian mothers were unwilling to send their sons to die for Grozny, they would be unlikely to be any more enthusiastic about sacrificing them for Kiev or, for that matter, Sevastopol.

Influenced by the unexpected success of the Communists and extreme nationalists in the December 1993 elections—and by the wise counsel of the new U.S. ambassador in Moscow, Thomas Pickering—the Clinton ad-

ministration began to accept that it was contrary to American interests to ignore most of the Russian political spectrum and work only with the radical
reformers. Kozyrev himself also had to accept that his previously unquali-
fied pro-Western orientation was damaging to his political health. His public statements began to include new references to the need to protect
Russian interests. Even as early as December 1992, Kozyrev managed to
shock a group of Western dignitaries assembled in Stockholm by delivering
a threatening speech, which, at the urging of James Baker, he almost immediately clarified by explaining that his heavy-handed rhetoric reflected neither Russian official policy nor his own opinions. It was, he claimed, a
theatrical performance intended to demonstrate to the West what would
happen if the hard-liners were to come to power in Russia. Still, both outside and inside Russia, commentators began to talk about a new tougher
and more nationalistic Kozyrev. Lukin even commented to me that the
Russian foreign minister was trying to atone for his previous pro-Western
"sins" by moving from one extreme to the other. This zigzagging prolonged
Kozyrev's tenure in office until January 1996, but it came at the cost of further delay in Russia's development of a new foreign policy concept.

·   ·   ·

The first component of the new policy concept is that Russia should define
its national interests on its own without significant guidance from Washington or anywhere else. Primakov emphasized that the "structure [created under Kozyrev] in which one country led the other" was no longer acceptable.
"This is not for Russia," he said. "We want equitable cooperation. Even so,
we realize that we are now weaker than the United States, I think we have
obtained this [equality in U.S.–Russian relations]."[10]

Whether or not U.S.–Russian cooperation may be described as "equitable" given the great disparities in power between the two nations, Moscow
has not hesitated to distance itself from Washington on a wide variety of foreign policy issues in recent years. The current list of disagreements includes
such important matters as American attempts to isolate Iran, Iraq, and Cuba,
sanctions against India, policies toward the Bosnia and Kosovo conflicts, the
Arab-Israeli dispute in the Middle East, Russian arms and nuclear technology sales, the use of economic sanctions as an instrument of foreign policy,

and the right of the outside world to promote democracy in sovereign states. The list is comprehensive and reflects far-reaching discrepancies in American and Russian approaches to the world.

Nevertheless, while defining its own agenda, Moscow has been reluctant to enter into confrontation with the West, and particularly with the United States. Foreign Minister Primakov took particular pride in pursuing Russia's interests without triggering conflict with the West. Russian decision-makers appreciate both the current limits of Russia's financial and other resources and their country's continuing dependence on international monetary institutions and foreign investors. Accordingly, it was not Primakov's style to rock the boat over relatively peripheral issues. After grandstanding from a position of weakness after the Soviet collapse, the Russian political class has developed sufficient self-confidence to be comfortable admitting that now is not the time for Russia to pursue great global designs. Rather, according to Lukin, what Russia needs today is what Lenin (in very different historical circumstances) called a *peredyshka,* or a "breather," in which to rebuild. "Now is the period during which we must gather up strength and carry out a modest, inexpensive foreign policy," Lukin explained.[11] Similarly, Primakov drew attention to Tsar Aleksandr II's foreign minister Aleksandr Gorchakov as a role model for Russian foreign-policy-makers because of his decision to choose temporary tactical restraint over a strategic retreat in international affairs after Russia's defeat in the Crimean War in 1856. For a while, Gorchakov opted to pursue a more modest but still vigorous foreign policy which recognized that until Russia was able to recover from the war, priority should be given, as he wrote the tsar, to its "internal development." But as Primakov approvingly observes, "the pause, as one should have expected, did not last long."[12] While no one in the Russian government dares to predict just how long Russia's current circumstances will endure, it is universally assumed that sooner or later— and perhaps sooner—Russia will recover from its economic and political slide and will reestablish itself as a truly great power, if not quite a superpower.

Meanwhile, while Moscow is forced to accept that the United States is the world's only remaining superpower, it is opposed to the Clinton administration proudly pronouncing America to be an "indispensable nation" destined to shape world politics in accordance with its interests and values. In contrast, Russian politicians emphasize the need to create a "multipolar" world in which no state is allowed to exercise hegemony, no matter how benign. This is a regular theme for both Yeltsin and Primakov. In fact, "strengthening trends toward the formation of a multipolar world" is now also a key Russian foreign policy priority defined in the very first sentence of Russia's new official National Security Blueprint signed by Boris Yeltsin on December 17, 1997.[13] Primakov is quite explicit in claiming that Russia has a special opportunity to exploit "the unquestionable unwillingness of the vast number of states to agree with a world order determined by one power" in order to enable itself once again "to play the part of a leading state on the international scene."[14]

As a practical matter, with its economy weak and declining, Russia may often be prepared to subordinate its own policy preferences to those of the United States. Few international issues would mean enough to the Russian government or, for that matter, to the Russian people (who are preoccupied with their own everyday ordeal) to justify risking a loss of favor with the U.S.—particularly when America has the support of other major industrial democracies. Thus in the case of Bosnia, faced with a choice between entering into a conflict with NATO, staying on the sidelines, or playing second fiddle to the West in a country in which Russia does not have important foreign policy interests, Moscow has opted for the last option. On Kosovo, while Russian foreign minister Igor Ivanov strongly objected to the use of force against Serbia, his country supported a September 23, 1998, U.N. Security Council ultimatum directed at Serbian leader Slobodan Milošević. The resolution included a reference to Chapter VII of the U.N. Charter, which as Moscow undoubtedly knew, Washington has interpreted as authorizing military action against Belgrade without a further United Nations vote.[15]

Similarly, Moscow has sought to avoid provoking a confrontation with Washington over the two countries' differing perspectives on Iraq. Neither Yeltsin nor Primakov is an admirer of Saddam Hussein. In fact, no major Russian politician is supportive of Hussein except Vladimir Zhirinovsky, who, as Zyuganov told me in February 1998, "is too much of a clown to be taken literally on anything." While claiming that the United States had no rights to punish Iraq unilaterally, Zyuganov himself was careful to add with clear disapproval that "we all know who Saddam Hussein is." More important, Moscow has no interest in Baghdad's developing weapons of mass destruction or threatening its neighbors, some of which are quite friendly with Russia, such as Iran, Syria, and lately even Turkey.

Primakov argues, however, that the United States exaggerates the threat from Iraq; he also does not agree with Washington that Iraq will remain a menace so long as Saddam Hussein is in power. "I do not see it so straight-forwardly," he has said. In Moscow's view, Saddam Hussein has been suffi-ciently cut down to size by the Gulf War and the United Nations sanctions. Thus, Primakov argues that the best way to encourage Iraq's continuing compliance with U.N. resolutions is not through further threats but rather through showing "a light at the end of the tunnel." Nor does Primakov deny that Saddam Hussein may be lying to the international arms inspectors; the foreign minister simply emphasizes negotiation rather than force as the best way to achieve results. Russia's reluctance to allow the United States to run the show single-handedly was clearly an important consideration. Com-plaining that Moscow's perspective has not adequately been taken into ac-count on this and other international issues, Primakov said, "Today, one can really think that there is only one superpower in the world—the United States."[16]

The trick for Russian diplomacy has been to dispel the impression of American predominance without alienating the Clinton administration. Primakov more or less achieved that goal through his highly visible diplomacy during the November 1997 Iraq crisis, including his summons to Secretary of State Madeleine Albright and other foreign ministers of the permanent members of the U.N. Security Council to a 2 A.M. meet-ing in Geneva in order to accommodate his travel schedule (Primakov was en route to Latin America). He brokered an informal deal which re-quired that Iraq readmit U.N. weapons inspectors—including the Ameri-cans, whom Baghdad had accused of spying—but also provided Iraq with vague assurances that its compliance would be properly rewarded.

Primakov's handling of the Iraqi crisis—particularly his ability simulta-neously to defend Saddam Hussein from those seeking harsh measures against Iraq and to play the friendly mediator for the Clinton administra-tion—won him universally high marks in Russia. But America's behavior during the crisis and its similar attempts to isolate Iran have triggered in-dignation across the Russian political spectrum. "American foreign policy was never known for being particularly delicate. Lately, Washington's impertinence has gone overboard. The time has come to state this firmly and directly," writes Aleksandr Bovin, an influential columnist and former ambassador to Israel who is widely considered to be among Russia's enlightened and generally pro-Western foreign policy experts.[17]

Despite this frustration, Russian policy-makers can see the difference between an irritant and a real problem. And they also know how to make the best of the inevitable, as illustrated by Russia's response to NATO enlargement. Of course, the Russian government has itself to blame for the fact that NATO expansion became an issue in the first place. It was none other than President Boris Yeltsin who, in Warsaw in September 1993—after having one drink too many with Polish president Lech Walesa—announced that he had no objection to NATO membership for Poland and other Central European nations. Because Yeltsin's statement was an impromptu remark under the influence of alcohol rather than a carefully crafted official Russian position, the Foreign Ministry immediately backtracked and Moscow launched a full-scale peace offensive reminiscent of the Brezhnev era (mixed with occasional bullying). This only heightened the Central Europeans' eagerness to seek protection through NATO and complicated any efforts by Washington, Bonn, or other European capitals to reject their aspirations without appearing to surrender to Russian blackmail.

From the very beginning, I was convinced that there was more smoke than fire to Russia's anti-NATO campaign. Russian officials admitted that with proper safeguards—which were promised to Moscow right away—NATO expansion would not threaten their country's legitimate national security interests, particularly as the prospective alliance members had no common borders with Russia, except for Poland's border with the tiny Russian enclave of Kaliningrad.

Nevertheless, Andrei Kozyrev and others argued that NATO expansion would compromise Russian democrats by demonstrating Western hostility to Russia. This, they added, would lead to a backlash against the Yeltsin government and could even threaten Russia's stability. Despite the suggestion by Anatoly Chubais that ninety-nine out of every hundred Russians oppose NATO enlargement,[18] public opinion polls have consistently demonstrated that the Russian public never really became exercised over the NATO enlargement issue.[19] And after leaving the Foreign Ministry, Kozyrev changed his tune and began to argue that giving in to Russian opposition to NATO enlargement would "play into the hands of the enemies of democracy" and advocated a NATO–Russia agreement.[20] Russia faced too many other urgent problems for an essentially geopolitical abstraction like Central European membership in NATO to have a serious impact on Russian domestic politics.

In fact, Russian officials would acknowledge in private conversations that their anti-NATO crusade served two objectives—neither of which was to prevent enlargement. At home, the fight against NATO was an opportunity for the Russian government to burnish its patriotic credentials on the cheap. Abroad, it was a tactic to extract the best deal possible in return for Moscow's tacit acceptance of a larger NATO. Russia had never opposed the expansion of NATO per se; it simply objected to the growth of the old, un-reconstructed NATO into an arbiter of European security (as illustrated in Bosnia) without Russian participation.[21] Accordingly, Russia's diplomats suggested that perhaps as a part of the expansion process NATO should change its name and its mission as well to become a collective security body along the lines of the Organization for Security and Cooperation in Europe. Curiously, the Clinton administration eventually rejected Russia's symbolic suggestion to change NATO's name but ceded ground on the more substantive issue of NATO's organization and role through the May 1997 Founding Act on Mutual Relations between NATO and Russia. The final judgment on the impact of this decision is not yet in.

Having accomplished its basic mission vis-à-vis NATO enlargement, Russia now seems to be fairly relaxed toward the process—at least as long as there is no serious discussion of a second wave of expansion to include the Baltic states. *Izvestiya* commentator Stanislav Kondrashov was quite struck during his December 1997 interview with Yevgeny Primakov to discover that "NATO expansion plans were not uppermost in his mind."[22]

What was uppermost on Primakov's mind were two major and interrelated objectives of Russian foreign policy: consolidating Moscow's role in the former Soviet territory and harnessing its foreign policy to serve Russia's economic interests. Russia's attitude to the other newly independent states was shaped by two trends which, while they appeared mutually exclusive on the surface, were not truly contradictory. On one hand, an increasing share of Russia's people regret the breakup of the Soviet Union. Thus, in December 1997, 61 percent of Russian citizens were sorry that the USSR collapsed—up from 33 percent in December 1992. Nevertheless, despite this widespread belief that the end of the Soviet Union was a mistake,

Moscow also increasingly realizes that there is no way back and that nostalgia alone cannot guide an effective foreign policy. In Primakov's words, "the present reality is such that sovereignty of the ex-USSR republics should not be subject to whatever doubt."[23] This does not mean that Russia wants to forgo a leading role in the former Soviet region. In fact, to the contrary, Moscow has clear ambitions to establish its own "sphere of influence" there.[24] Primakov calls it more deliberately "the policy aimed at bringing closer together the states formed on the territory of the former Soviet Union."[25] But the meaning is much the same.

However, Moscow has learned the hard way that coercion and intimidation—particularly when they often amount to little more than empty threats—are a poor way to preserve even limited dominance among the Soviet successor states. Paradoxically, and contrary to predictions of a tough Russian response to NATO expansion, Moscow has learned that heavy-handedness in the former Soviet republics can be counterproductive—and that it could even speed up entry into NATO for the Baltic states or Ukraine. As a result, the Kremlin has begun to demonstrate a new flexibility in its relations with its neighbors, both by reducing somewhat its pressure on them and offering security guarantees to the Baltic states. Although the proposed guarantees have been insufficient to reassure the Balts, Russia's new, more cooperative approach has normalized the situation on the Russian periphery to a certain extent (despite major exceptions such as the March 1998 campaign to intimidate Latvia following real but grossly exaggerated mistreatment of Russian-speaking demonstrators by Riga's police force).

Russia still has its disagreements with Ukraine, but the disputes are no longer over potentially explosive issues such as Crimean sovereignty or the division of the Black Sea Fleet; today they have more to do with mutual economic complaints, particularly the problem of Ukraine's nonpayment for Russian energy. Ukraine's new foreign minister, Boris Tarasyuk, considered to be pro-Western, said that he and Primakov had reached "complete understanding" on all major issues during a meeting in Kiev on May 26, 1998. Such a comment would have been unthinkable two years earlier.[26] (Russia and Ukraine also attempted to develop a cooperative effort to mitigate the effects of the economic crisis of fall 1998.) Similar, albeit less conclusive, progress has been made in Russian relations with Moldova, where the new government is pleased with Moscow's new attitude, and with

Azerbaijan, which acknowledges that Russia has recently taken a more even-handed approach (in place of its previous pro-Armenian bias) in dealing with the contentious issue of Nagorno-Karabakh.

This is not to suggest that Russia's neighbors are eager to embrace Russia's new, benign diplomacy. The November 1997 CIS Summit in Chisinau (Kishinev) demonstrated that most post-Soviet states remain uninterested in creating any supranational bodies that could restrict their political and economic sovereignty. Moreover, four of the post-Soviet states—Georgia, Ukraine, Azerbaijan, and Moldova—have created a new group to counterbalance Russian influence. While for obvious reasons the members of the group, known as GUAM, claim that their organization is not directed against any other state, least of all Russia, few commentators doubt that the members are united by quarrels with Moscow and seek to maximize their leverage vis-à-vis Russia.

Nonetheless, in comparison with the situation six years ago, even these mixed results can be considered improvement. At a minimum, the new environment in Russia's neighborhood allows Moscow to focus on pressing domestic problems without worrying so much about instability on its frontiers. Russia makes clear, however, that the current tranquility will not last should the United States attempt to play a greater role in the region. Primakov has sternly warned that the admission of the Baltic countries to NATO could have severe consequences: although it would not mean that "we will move our tanks in reply . . . we will have to revise all our relations with NATO in the event of their admission." In contrast to Russia's campaign against the first wave of NATO expansion, there seems, at the moment, at least, to be true resolve in Moscow not to allow it to happen.

Russia's resolve is at least equally strong that it will become a major player in the development of the Caspian Basin's vast energy resources. Unlike NATO expansion, development of Caspian energy is not an abstract security issue of interest only among military and foreign policy specialists. The exploitation of the Caspian region's energy resources is among Russia's key economic priorities and has immediate impact upon important interests of the oligarchy. That impact is not limited to such key companies as Gazprom and Lukoil, although they have the most obvious stake, but extends as well to many leading bankers, including both Berezovsky and Oneksimbank head Vladimir Potanin, who control other oil companies,

Sibneft and Sidanko, respectively. Where questions of Russian access to the Caspian Basin and pipeline routes are raised, even Boris Nemtsov began to sound like an anti-American hard-liner by promising to fight the United States resolutely for a share of the wealth.

Russia is similarly committed to developing energy and other economic cooperation with Iran. Responding to the American threats of economic sanctions, then deputy prime minister Nemtsov said, "We reject all attempts to influence Russia's Gazprom, and we will protect it."[27] Although normally reluctant to challenge Washington openly, President Yeltsin went even further: "Thank God, Russia, France, and Iran are independent, freedom-loving states, and interference from any state is not to be tolerated."[28]

•   •   •

Such differences between Russia and the United States are of course profoundly less threatening than the ideological and geopolitical conflicts of the Cold War period. They do not entail the risk of war, and they are unlikely even to reach an intensity that would preclude cooperation in other areas where the interests of the two states overlap, ranging from controlling the threat of loose nuclear weapons to protecting the environment and combating international terrorism and drug trafficking.

However, despite President Clinton's assurances that there are no fundamental contradictions between Russia and America, the differences evident today—when the United States is a superpower and Russia is at its weakest point in decades—should serve as a warning that much more serious disputes are likely in the future once Russia manages to improve its economic situation. During the Cold War, when the world was still bipolar, Raymond Aron described the United States and the Soviet Union as "enemies by position." While this description is no longer appropriate—and is likely never to be valid again—it is fair to say that America and Russia are still positioned by the logic of their international interests and values to have substantially different perspectives on world events. In contrast to the Cold War, geoeconomics rather than geopolitics will be the driving force behind the competition. And how Russia is ruled, whether it develops checks and balances or the oligarchy drives Russian foreign policy, will have a considerable bearing on U.S.–Russian relations. As a senior Russian official once said to me, "I worry about our bankers. They are far too pushy. If they dictate our foreign policy, and operate abroad as assertively and ruthlessly as at home, it may be a prescription for trouble."

Conversely, on the American side, if the United States continues to insist on its right, indeed, its responsibility, to determine not only what is important for our national interests but what is good for other nations as well, its relationship with Russia will likely become only more difficult. Alone, Russia no longer has the potential to challenge America's global role. But it will have more and more opportunities through interaction with others—including China, India, Iran, Iraq, and France—to contribute to a world environment in which American unilateralism will be harder and harder to sustain and multilateral approaches on U.S. terms will be increasingly difficult to develop.

It may be difficult to focus on Russia's long-term potential to play a major role in the international system when the country seems trapped in an almost catastrophic economic crisis. Russia today is in a uniquely weak international position; its economic ordeal reduces Moscow's options in foreign policy significantly, and the Russians recognize this. A Russian proverb describes their understanding of the current situation: *"ne do zhiru, byt'by zhivu"*—"do not worry about getting fat [i.e., doing well] when you are struggling to stay alive."

But it would be a mistake for the United States to interpret Russia's current international complacency as endorsement of America's effort to shape a new Washington-based international system. Russia is biding its time until it is able not only to express its preferences but also to do something about them. While it may be some time before Russia can significantly constrain American foreign policy, approaching the country strategically requires realism in assessing not only its presently limited resources but also its potentially more significant impact on the world in the future.

Chapter Ten

•

America's Russian Dilemma

The future of Russia's relations with the outside world will not depend solely on Russia. The impact of events outside Russia, including the policies of Russia's new neighbors and the United States, will contribute importantly to the context in which Russia makes its critical choices. In particular, the manner in which the United States, as the only remaining superpower, conducts its foreign affairs (in general and specifically with respect to Russia) will significantly influence relations between the two nations.

However, predicting American foreign policy is also not an easy task, particularly in the radically transformed post–Cold War world. The demise of its Soviet adversary has presented the United States with unprecedented opportunities to affect the course of history worldwide. Yet, the absence of the apocalyptic threat of nuclear holocaust caused by a single well-defined enemy armed with nuclear missiles has also led to the disintegration of what limited foreign policy consensus existed in the United States during the Cold War. When added to the profound evolution of American politics in recent years and the new emphasis on multiculturalism and diversity encouraged by President Clinton, this loss of consensus has left the United States without a clear purpose—essentially a global leader in search of a mission. Moreover, America's international leadership itself is questioned by other nations, as demonstrated by the fractured response to India's and Pakistan's nuclear tests. Even U.S. allies frequently balk at perceptions of American hegemony.

For a variety of reasons, some of which have nothing to do with American actions, the United States has for a while found itself uniquely able to fill the international vacuum created by the self-destruction of the USSR. But this global role cannot be taken for granted; the United States cannot maintain its singular international position without great clarity of purpose, sensitivity to the interests of others, and considerable cost.

The importance of domestic cohesion to America's clarity of purpose cannot be underestimated. Samuel Huntington warns that "if multicultural-ism prevails and if the consensus on liberal democracy disintegrates, the United States could join the Soviet Union on the ash heap of history."[1] Of course, even if the worst should come to pass and, as Huntington suggests, uncontrolled immigration and divisions within American society should threaten to break down the country's domestic unity, we are decades away from such a predicament. Nevertheless, those who would dismiss out of hand the danger to America's social cohesion would do well to remember that the Soviet Union appeared to the rest of the world to be at the height of its power a mere two decades ago.

The Clinton administration has been unable to provide a foreign policy concept beyond the promotion of market economies, democracy, and stability worldwide—goals so unexceptional as to defy operational interpretation. Absent strong presidential leadership, as James Schlesinger observes, "domestic constituencies, most notably ethnic groups, have acquired an excessive influence over our foreign policy. The inevitable consequence is that our policy lacks overall coherence. Rather than reflecting a hammered-out vision of the national interest, America's present policy consists largely of the stapling together of the objectives of these individual constituencies. In terms of traditional standards it can scarcely be said that we have a foreign policy at all."[2]

This problem is exacerbated by the fact that most Americans are losing interest in foreign affairs as something relevant to their lives—illustrated by Senator Connie Mack's observation during the Senate debate over NATO enlargement that "No one is interested in this at home."[3] This further heightens the influence of groups with particular agendas in the foreign policy process. Consequently, the process of determining America's foreign policy increasingly ignores the deliberate discussion of U.S.

national interests as a province of the "outmoded establishment." Instead, it puts a premium on the volatile interplay of competing inputs from ethnic constituencies, single-issue interest groups (from anti-abortionists to environmentalists), and the business community. States and causes with strong domestic interest groups, such as Israel and Armenia, benefit greatly. Conversely, nations that lack such support, such as Serbia and Russia, find themselves at a considerable disadvantage. American foreign policy has always had a strong domestic component, but the current fragmentation of the foreign policy decision-making process is without parallel.

At the same time, there are internal structural constraints on the ability of the United States to provide effective global leadership. The more ambitious we are in defining the American mission in the world—that is, the more it begins to resemble social engineering on a global scale rather than international relations—the more what Huntington calls "the domesticization of foreign policy" will be an obstacle to the U.S. ability to act with even minimal levels of sophistication and consistency. Fortunately, the damage done by such a foreign policy is ultimately self-limiting: just as inadequate resources have circumscribed the possibilities for international mischief by both the Soviet Union and Russia, America's greater but not unlimited wealth (not to mention popular willingness to spend either wealth or blood on peripheral pursuits) would constrain its capacity to sustain ill-considered policies produced by the domesticized decision-making process. But self-correcting mechanisms do not protect the United States against incidents of irresponsible overreach leading to bloody, humiliating defeats, as the Clinton administration learned the hard way in Somalia.

Under such circumstances, Lord Palmerston's classic statements that "we have no eternal allies and no permanent enemies" and that "our interests are eternal, and those interests it is our duty to follow,"[4] are increasingly replaced in foreign policy thinking by the sentiment that our national interests are a fashion of the moment and that whichever cries arise most strongly from the cacophony of domestic voices should determine America's international course. Remarkably, this notion is advanced with the simultaneous but incompatible expectation that other nations should see the inherent righteousness of this approach to foreign affairs and naturally welcome the opportunity to embrace its outcomes. It is unlikely that many will do so.

•   •   •

It is illustrative that thus far the Clinton administration has utterly failed to develop a hierarchy of objectives in dealing with Russia's transformation other than support for Yeltsin when necessary and the radical reformers when possible. Deputy Secretary of State Strobe Talbott outlined the administration's approach to Russia in late 1997: "Our goal, like that of many Russians, is to see Russia become a normal, modern state—democratic in its governance, abiding by its own constitution and by its own laws, market-oriented and prosperous in its economic development, at peace with itself and with the rest of the world."[5]

While these objectives sound so attractive that critiquing them may seem like attacking motherhood or apple pie, they are in fact contradictory and uninformed. First of all, democratic governance has been difficult to achieve under the country's current constitution, which was imposed after the show of force against the Supreme Soviet and—as pro-reform and Communist politicians agree—gives the president almost unlimited powers. Also, as Kissinger observes, "In Russia, democratization and a restrained foreign policy may not necessarily go hand in hand."[6] In fact, the Clinton administration has a propensity to support Yeltsin no matter what precisely because he has tended to subordinate Russian foreign policy interests to Western, particularly American, preferences to a much greater extent than the parliament or Russian public opinion. In a more democratic system, the Russian government would probably face greater public pressure to protect the ethnic Russian majority in Crimea against the Ukrainian government, which has not only denied the separatist yearnings of the local population but also reduced Crimean regional autonomy. Russian public opinion is also more radical than the government with respect to the protection of ethnic Russian minorities in the Baltic states. It is hard to imagine a democratically elected Russian government sending military units to serve under NATO command in Bosnia when NATO, despite strong Russian claims that all of the parties to the conflict had committed excesses, launched airstrikes solely against the Orthodox Serbs.

Thus, the underdevelopment of democracy in Russia has in fact helped the Clinton administration to apply pressure on President Yeltsin to win Russian acquiescence in U.S. foreign policy actions. This is possible in relations with a weak and dependent Russia, but it is not likely to work with a stronger and more confident nation. A resurgent Russia under authoritarian rule would be contrary to American interests.

In dealing with major nations, particularly during periods of historical upheaval, a responsible foreign policy recognizes the necessity of trade-offs and attempts to balance short-term and long-term interests. It also accepts that even with the most sophisticated analysis and the best possible planning, foreign policy must often grapple with the unknown and, accordingly, should not become too ambitious or be based on overly optimistic assumptions. In this sense, the Clinton administration's formulation of American foreign policy toward Russia has hardly been well considered.

Preoccupied with tactical considerations, the Clinton administration has essentially overlooked the long-term strategic consequences of supporting the increasingly unpopular Yeltsin regime. So long as Russia's economy remains weakened—and its government unpopular—Moscow has no alternative to blustering a little but then surrendering to American preferences, at least on those issues that do not affect the regime's survival.

But what will happen when Russia begins to recover economically? It will of course start from a very low base; Russia's economy is now smaller than those of India, Brazil, Indonesia, Mexico, and South Korea,[7] and its GDP is expected to fall as much as 9 percent in the second half of 1998.[8] Whoever comes to power will be forced to accept Russia's limitations. There are two dangers. First, if during its recovery Russian society is again so polarized that rational considerations no longer prevail and that extremism rather than moderation becomes the political fashion, then the country may explode. Under such circumstances, the Clinton administration may discover that its past blind support for a discredited regime in order to prevent a victory by extremist forces has created a self-fulfilling prophecy. Second, the Clinton administration should remember well that welfare recipients are rarely grateful to the state and may even become hostile when no longer on the dole. If wounded pride becomes a factor in our relations with Russia, even sensible and democratic leaders may be inclined to defy Washington, particularly when the IMF credits stop coming.

The dilemma for U.S. foreign policy is whether it is more important to sustain a compliant government in Moscow today or to build lasting ties to Russia based on mutual interests and respect. The Clinton administration has clearly preferred the former.

Quite a few members of the Clinton foreign policy team opposed the

U.S. role in Vietnam, criticized the invasion of Grenada, argued against the
Reagan administration's deployment of intermediate-range missiles in Europe in the early 1980s, considered American support for anti-Communist
guerrilla movements in Nicaragua and Angola to be unnecessary and immoral, and opposed the American-led military assault on Saddam Hussein
in 1991. But now that they are no longer faced by the Soviet superpower,
the risks for American activism have been dramatically reduced, and the
public does not particularly care about foreign policy (unless it becomes too
expensive in blood and treasure), one-time peaceniks have developed great
courage and self-confidence. They have become interventionists with a
sense that they have all the answers for almost any situation around the
world. At the same time, to use Secretary of State Madeleine Albright's favorite expression, the administration likes to deliver "messages" to leaders
of other nations, from Yugoslavia's Milošević to Israel's Netanyahu or Pakistan's Sharif, and seems to expect that these "messages" will be valued.
That the administration's guidance is in many such instances contrary to the
democratically expressed will of the people of friendly nations (as in the
case of Israel) or, in other cases, unrealistic (like the pressure on Yugoslavia
to withdraw special police units from Kosovo while claiming to advocate
only autonomy for the region's firmly pro-independence Albanian majority)
rarely constrains the administration's zeal in aggressively promoting its preferred solutions. Former Ambassador to Moscow Jack F. Matlock, Jr., as-
sailed the latter position, terming it the latest error in "a pattern of strategic
misjudgment" that will once again force the administration to choose between making the situation worse and having its bluff called. Instead, Matlock argued, the United States should require leadership in resolving the
ongoing conflict in the Balkans from Europeans—in whose neighborhood
the conflict has occurred and whose interests are at stake.[9] The fact that Europeans may not be capable of providing such leadership does not reduce
the potentially disastrous consequences of the Clintonites' temptation to
consider every international crisis—or at a minimum every international
crisis covered well on CNN—as something for which the United States is
obliged to offer a quick and attractive resolution.

As convinced as the Clinton administration may be about the correctness of its course in Bosnia and Kosovo, its officials should nonetheless realize that others may have a different perspective. For example, while the
outside world's failure to attempt to prevent the Bosnian Serbs' ethnic

cleansing is at worst a sin of omission, American inaction during the Bosnian Croats' later ethnic cleansing in Krajina—after the Croats were armed by the United States and were given at least a yellow light to attack—is a sin of commission.[10] The Clinton administration bears indirect responsibil-ity for its results, including the creation of 150,000 new refugees.[11] Yet, the president who recently apologized to Africans for slavery has not displayed much moral anguish over the Krajina Serbs' suffering and even said that the offensive represented "a moment of real promise" to end the conflict.[12] This perceived double standard is of course at least equalled by Russia's own pro-Serbian bias. Russia has a history of involvement in the Balkans, tradi-tionally strong sympathy for the Orthodox Serbs, and—in contrast to the United States—relatively little domestic support for the Catholic Croats or the Muslims. However, the administration's belief in its right to assess the Serbs' transgressions and enforce its own vision of justice makes Russia think about what could come next. Will the United States feel entitled to re-spond similarly to violence inside Russia?

The credibility of U.S. positions is undermined by the fact that in con-trast to former Chancellor Kohl of Germany and President Chirac of France, President Clinton did not condemn Estonian and Latvian (before it was addressed by the Latvians themselves) discrimination against the two Baltic countries' ethnic Russian minorities.[13] This weakens the moral au-thority of American policy in Russia and heightens Russian feelings that the United States is hypocritical in its approach to human rights. Washington was remarkably quiet about Russia's atrocities in Chechnya in order to pro-tect Boris Yeltsin. But this kindness to the current Russian president will do little to reassure Russian politicians that the United States may have a dif-ferent approach to Russia once Yeltsin is out of office.

When confronted with arguments of this nature, the administration of-ten retreats behind the cover of international organizations, especially the United Nations, from which it claims to have a mandate for its actions. It is important to remember, however, that this is the same United Nations whose General Assembly routinely denounced American imperialism and international Zionism during the Cold War. Why is the United Nations now so accommodating toward the United States? The reason is not so much due to a change in its composition, although some Central European countries have become genuine democracies. Rather, it is a result of a dra-matic shift in the balance of power that makes going along with American preferences much more attractive to many nations. While it is perfectly appropriate for the United States to rejoice at this new reality and to take advantage of it, it is self-deceptive to believe that the United Nations has suddenly become a voice of enlightenment and justice. It reminds me of a senior Soviet official with whose children I was friendly before emigrating from the USSR. He once argued that his dogmatic anti-Western positions had to be correct because they were advanced in editorials in *Pravda* and *Izvestiya*. What he did not mention and apparently did not even consider relevant was that he had personally instructed the two papers to print the editorials. It is somewhat disingenuous to ignore American influence in the United Nations when using the U.N.'s authority to justify U.S. actions that may or may not be defensible on their own merit.

Ultimately, the administration's tough stands—and its willingness to use force to back them up—do not often correlate with the importance of the U.S. interests at stake. Instead, they correlate primarily with the requirements of American domestic politics and with the size and strength of the foreign opponent, which makes Washington seem to be an international bully: courageous with the weak but rarely with the strong. This is demonstrated by several cases. Rather than being punished for their violations of international agreements and threats to U.S. interests, those who can mount formidable resistance like North Korea and Iraq have been rewarded; the former received significant assistance (beyond humanitarian aid to prevent deaths from starvation), including a deal to provide advanced nuclear reactors, while despite a direct challenge to the sanctions regime the latter saw its oil sales quota through the U.N.'s oil-for-food humanitarian program more than doubled (from $2 billion to $5.2 billion).[14] Although the Clinton administration threatened to go to war with Iraq in the fall of 1997, it ultimately backed down and accepted a U.N.–brokered compromise. The administration was again timid in the face of new Iraqi resistance in the summer and fall of 1998 and even constrained U.N. inspections in order to avoid confrontation with Baghdad. In contrast, the Somalis, Haitians, and Bosnian Serbs—none of whom meant to challenge American interests or threatened to invade neighboring countries—faced military intervention. This does not enhance the image of the United States as a formidable but benign superpower.

In all fairness, the U.S. Congress has offered little counterbalance to the administration's urge for global hegemony on the cheap. To the contrary, the

Congress has alienated key allies by passing a number of laws applying sanctions to foreign firms for their failure to comply with American legislation, such as the Iran and Libya Sanctions Act and the Helms-Burton Act. Sanctions have become the punishment of choice for virtually any transgression. Seventy-five nations, including the two most populous in the world, India and China, are under or threatened with some form of American economic sanctions. Lee Hamilton, a widely respected, recently retired Congressional Democrat and former chairman of the House International Relations Committee, noted in a presentation at The Nixon Center that "nearly every unilateral sanction measure of the past several years has originated in Congress."[15]

The Congress has also consistently supported the administration's prized programs to promote democracy abroad. It is particularly ironic that the Republicans in Congress, who were so offended by the possibility that China may have sought to influence U.S. presidential elections through campaign contributions, have rarely hesitated to approve funding of the National Endowment for Democracy, which prides itself on not only promoting elections in many other nations, but on affecting their outcome through financial support for opposition groups as well. Of course, the NED's efforts may be perfectly legal and entirely constructive in the host countries; nevertheless, the outrage in the United States over alleged Chinese political meddling should sensitize American policymakers to how other nations often view what are frequently much more far-reaching attempts by Washington to have an impact on their domestic governance.

There is no moral equivalency between even the imperfect promotion of democracy abroad and interference in American domestic politics by authoritarian foreign governments. Nevertheless, simple logic suggests that attempts to influence the domestic politics of other nations, particularly when their goal is to weaken the levers of control upon which many governments continue to depend for their survival, come at a price. At a minimum, such attempts will reduce the willingness of the government in question to accommodate the United States on other issues, some of which—such as nuclear proliferation or international terrorism with weapons of mass destruction—may affect vital American interests. To remain true to itself, the United States should continue to combat extreme brutalities such as genocide, should encourage others to enhance liberty, and should serve as a model of democracy. But it must avoid reckless moralistic posturing, which only demeans and damages America.

•   •   •

Clearly, how—and by whom—American interests are defined vis-à-vis Russia will have a major impact on the future of U.S.–Russian relations. If American interests are defined in a deliberate and analytical manner, Russia's reemergence one day as a major power will be much easier to manage. This is not to say that Moscow and Washington will agree on everything—they certainly will not. Nevertheless, with its vastly reduced capabilities, Russia cannot realistically threaten vital American interests for quite some time. And America will retain sufficiently impressive leverage to affect Russian calculations on other issues important—but not vital—to Moscow.

One of the better overall frameworks for assessing American interests was developed in 1996 by the Commission on America's National Interests (on which I served as one of three codirectors), sponsored jointly by Harvard University's Center for Science and International Affairs, RAND, and The Nixon Center. Attempting to counter the overuse of the concept of the "vital national interest" to include every international problem from Bosnia to Somalia and beyond, the commission's final report defined as "vital" only those interests that "are strictly necessary to safeguard and enhance the well-being of Americans in a free and secure nation and to protect which the United States should be prepared to use military force."[16] Of the five vital interests defined by the commission, none can be threatened seriously by Russia today or in the near future. Only three are relevant to Russia—the U.S. desire to:

- "prevent, deter, and reduce the threat of nuclear, biological, and chemical (NBC) weapons attacks on the United States";
- "prevent the emergence of a hostile hegemon in Europe or Asia"; and,
- ensure the survival of U.S. allies."

Russia is not in a position to threaten the United States with nuclear, biological, or chemical attack. Although Russia may have the technical capability to launch such an attack, its vast military inferiority precludes doing so unless the United States initiates large-scale hostilities. Similarly, Russia is far from becoming "a hostile hegemon in Europe or Asia." Even if one were to combine the most optimistic economic scenarios with the most pessimistic political outcomes, Moscow cannot realistically aspire to predominance anywhere beyond its own periphery for decades. As an extension of this point, it is highly unlikely that Russia will threaten the survival of U.S. allies (defined as nations with which the United States has signed formal mutual defense agreements, e.g., NATO countries), despite its nuclear potential—unless the alliance further expands to the Russian border.

Russia can have more impact on American interests which, while not vital, are extremely important. In the commission's typology, "extremely important" interests are those which, "if compromised, would severely prejudice, but not strictly imperil, the ability of the U.S. government to safeguard and enhance the well-being of Americans in a free and secure nation."[17] These include the U.S. desire to:

- "prevent, deter, and reduce the threat of the use of nuclear or biological weapons anywhere";
- "prevent the regional proliferation of NBC weapons and delivery systems";
- "promote the acceptance of international rules of law and mechanisms for resolving disputes peacefully";
- "prevent the emergence of a regional hegemon in important regions, such as the Persian Gulf";
- "prevent the emergence of a reflexively adversarial major power in Europe or Asia"; and,
- "prevent and, if possible at reasonable cost, end major conflicts in important geographic regions."

Moscow's cooperation is obviously quite important in these areas despite (and, to an extent, because of) Russia's present weakness. Russia continues to possess a huge arsenal of weapons of mass destruction, which, while not likely to be used, remain a danger. The issue of so-called "loose nukes"—the risk of accidental or unauthorized use of nuclear weapons of which General Lebed and other Russian politicians like to remind the West—is also a problem. Although the Russian government regularly attempts to reassure concerned foreigners, one cannot exclude the possibility that a few warheads might make their way into the hands of terrorists or a rogue regime. Russia is also home to a highly sophisticated military-industrial complex searching desperately for customers—a major potential source of weapons proliferation. Ambassador Frank Wisner, President

Clinton's former special envoy responsible for investigating the export of Russian missile technology to Iran, has explained that under such circumstances it is virtually impossible for Moscow to block the leakage of technology fully.[18]

As a permanent member of the United Nations Security Council with a long record (during the Soviet and Russian periods) of supporting those regarded by the United States as rogue states, Russia can have a significant impact on the international system, including the creation and maintenance of norms of conduct and the resolution of disputes. Moscow's high-profile opposition to military punishment of Iraq during Saddam Hussein's defiance of the U.N.'s weapons inspectors in late 1997 and early 1998 illustrates its international influence even as a relatively weak regional power. Similarly, despite its present troubles, Russia could create a great deal of mischief in its own very large neighborhood, including the strategically important Caspian Basin region. Supplying missiles and nuclear technology to Iran could fundamentally alter the balance of power in the Middle East. Were Russia to succumb to the neo-imperial temptation, the United States would be forced to devote significant attention and resources to the new challenge and at a minimum to pay a considerable price to overcome Russian defiance in various international forums. The Indian and Pakistani nuclear tests in May 1998 only underscore the importance of Russian cooperation in the U.N. Security Council and elsewhere. Despite Moscow's notable interest in avoiding the emergence of additional nuclear powers close to its borders, Russian cooperation cannot be taken for granted, particularly if the relationship with the Unites States is in disarray.

While less likely today than in the earlier years of Russia's transformation, civil war in Russia remains a danger. Such an occurrence would not only represent a "major conflict in an important geographic region," but would also risk unpredictable but dire consequences for its thousands of nuclear warheads, nuclear power stations, and chemical and biological weapons depots (their use, their proliferation, or even accidents could carry great costs). This threat was among the most important to the United States during the initial years of the post-Soviet period. If anything, the risk of major domestic upheaval increased somewhat in 1998 as a result of the country's economic crisis. Although the risks subsequently diminished, Russia's economic downfall—and Yeltsin's declining authority—have again made the possibility of conflict and chaos in Russia a major concern for the outside world.

The crisis has also undermined U.S. economic interests in Russia's vast new markets. Still, fair access for American investors and a reduction in obstacles to investment, such as Russia's overwhelming corruption problem, should be among U.S. priorities.

As Secretary of State Madeleine Albright observed in her October 2, 1998, speech at the U.S.–Russia Business Council, the good news about the Primakov cabinet was that "Russia now has a government with a mandate from both the parliament and the president."[19] While the inclusion of ministers associated with the Communist and Agrarian factions in the government makes it more difficult for the cabinet to develop a coherent pro-reform program, to the extent that it is possible to do so, the plan may benefit from more support from the Duma than any previous government initiatives. At the same time, because the Duma can no longer excuse its obstructionism by pointing to the contempt with which the executive treats it, the parliament finds itself under pressure to cooperate constructively with the cabinet. This creates an opening for economic change to be implemented through legislation rather than less credible presidential and government decrees—if the Primakov team manages to function effectively.

In the long run, successful cooperation between the branches of government is important to establishing a viable democratic system in Russia. More immediately, it may be essential in avoiding a social explosion. Much is at stake here for both Russia and the world; while new turmoil is possible if unlikely, its consequences could be so profound that trying to avoid—or at least not to facilitate—such upheaval should be a priority for the United States in dealing with a Russia on the brink.

In this context, it was appropriate for Secretary Albright to advise against "taking a census of reformers in the Kremlin." Still, the secretary of state could not resist the temptation to do precisely that by expressing doubts about the Primakov government, saying, "We can only wonder if some members of Primakov's team understand the basic arithmetic of the global economy."[20] She was also unable to conceal her disappointment that America's radical reformer protégés were no longer in government.

Beyond the increased risk of domestic conflict in Russia, there are other fundamental problems. Despite a major—estimated by one source at

$100 billion[21]—American-led Western effort to assist Russia in its transformation, Russia's citizens feel little gratitude to the United States and even increasingly see Washington as the root cause of many of their country's problems. In fact, many Russians across the political spectrum believe that the United States is helping Russia only in order to keep its former adversary on its knees.

According to this widespread view, Washington is unwilling to accept Russia as a major power and eager to discourage Russian integration with other post-Soviet states. Russians who share this perspective also generally believe that the United States wants to deny their country a major role in developing the energy resources of the Caspian Basin, limit its participation in the international arms and high-technology markets, and make its economy chronically dependent upon loans from (as they see them) arrogant and dictatorial international financial institutions.

This resentment of America is tempered by the recognition that the United States is the only remaining superpower and, as such, has a significantly greater impact on Russia than vice versa. Accordingly, it is important to Russia's political and economic recovery for Moscow to stay in America's good graces. Many Russians also have a sense that American civilization has much to offer them; in contrast to radical Islam, it is not the American way of life that troubles Russians, but rather a perceived double standard that is seen to complicate Russia's own efforts to achieve for itself what America already has.

Almost no one in Russia believes that the country has a chance to regain the Soviet Union's superpower status anytime soon. And Russian politicians, even those critical of the United States, do not want to allow disagreements between Moscow and Washington to lead to the isolation of their country—notwithstanding Vladimir Zhirinovsky's theatrics. Instead, to checkmate American hegemony, they count on their own future strength in combination with a variety of possible international coalitions, ranging from Yeltsin's proposed "special relationship" with France and Germany to an interest in building a new strategic understanding with China.

·   ·   ·

The key to a sensible U.S. relationship with Russia is treating it like a serious power. Russia is no longer an adolescent in need of constant encouragement and instruction—if it ever was. Nor is it a reincarnation of the "evil empire." Rather, it is an emerging but troubled major power with a tragic past and an uncertain future, with which the United States is bound to have both overlapping interests and serious disagreements. As with other major powers, we should focus on Russia's international conduct rather than particular personalities or even factions within Russia. It is not, of course, in the American interest to see hard-line Communists or extreme nationalists come to power in Russia, but the chances of that happening are by now negligible in any but the most catastrophic circumstances (unless the U.S. provokes explosive indignation within Russia by continuing to prop up the Yeltsin regime artificially). The United States should be able to do business with any Russian leader who gains office through a democratic process.

There is a rationale for accommodating Yeltsin so long as he remains Russia's president. But he personally is not so central to U.S. interests as to justify needlessly alienating other Russian politicians, and even the Russian people, by siding so visibly and indiscriminately with their unpopular leader. Also, in an effort to help Yeltsin, the Clinton team has made substantive foreign policy concessions to Moscow, including pressuring U.S. allies to support Russia's unwarranted inclusion in the G-7 and leaning on the IMF to make loans unjustified on their merits. Worse, the administration has misled the American people about the nature of the Yeltsin regime. This not only makes it more difficult to develop public support for sensible policy toward Russia but also creates a real danger of backlash when Russia inevitably fails to act in a democratic or unreservedly pro-American fashion. The result is that U.S. policy toward Moscow swings wildly between unnecessarily effusive support and righteous indignation.

The Russians may resent American predominance, but they understand that it is a fact of life. As long as the American government does not attempt to meddle in Russian domestic politics by choosing sides in Moscow's often bewildering intrigues, chances are that almost anyone who should come to power in Russia (short of a disastrous political explosion) will be interested in normal relations with the United States. All major contenders for power, including Lebed, Luzhkov, Yavlinsky, Chernomyrdin, and even Zyuganov pay regular visits to the United States and actively seek American support. Zhirinovsky is an exception, but his chances of taking power in Russia are near zero. Thus, playing favorites in Russian domestic politics is unnecessary and does not help Russia's political stability or U.S.–Russian relations in the long run.

Furthermore, while the United States should be under no illusions that even a fully democratic Russia will act according to American preferences—and our ability to shape Russia's evolution will only decline as Russia's recovery gains momentum—it is clearly against U.S. interests (not to mention principles) to pressure Moscow to pursue policies that will shortcut the democratic process. Of course, there may be critical situations involving extremely important national interests—such as obtaining Russian acquiescence in U.S. military action against an aggressor state in the Persian Gulf—when concern over the potential negative impact on Russian democracy should not be allowed to prevent the United States from doing what is necessary. Short of such extraordinary circumstances, however, Washington should be careful not to squeeze the Kremlin too hard when very important U.S. interests are not at stake. This is especially true with respect to Russia's domestic policies. Intense American pressure on Russia's leaders to maintain a particular inflation rate or budget deficit level (which would be challenging even for the United States), for example, serves only to contribute to the authoritarian temptation and provoke anti-American sentiment.

From this perspective, American support (both directly and through the IMF, as a proxy) for doctrinaire and radical Russian monetarists is a risky policy, particularly when pursued in a high-profile and self-congratulatory fashion, as the Clinton administration has done. The International Monetary Fund has no expertise in, and accepts no responsibility for, the political and social upheavals that may arise as a result of the policies it imposes upon recipient nations. This was highlighted by the IMF's insistence on higher energy prices in Indonesia, which triggered widespread riots and ultimately contributed to the downfall of Suharto in May 1998.[22] Although one may argue that Russia, or any other country, can always refuse IMF assistance should it consider IMF conditions too onerous, in fact, a clean bill of health from the IMF has become virtually an essential precondition for loans from the World Bank and Western commercial banks, to say nothing of foreign investment.

Russia's future is far too important to the United States to be left to unelected international economic bureaucrats and their sponsors in the Clinton administration who, while exercising great influence on IMF de-

cisions, can easily disclaim responsibility for any undesirable consequences. There is already a dangerous vicious cycle of Russian dependence on the IMF, which insists on new government spending cuts as a
condition for further loans. These cuts lead to mass protests against the
Russian government and damage to the economy, which drives Moscow
to seek new loans. This cycle was evident in May 1998, when Russian
miners went on a nationwide strike and blocked key rail lines to protest
mounting wage arrears caused in part by the IMF's strict financial guide-
lines. The strike cost the Russian economy many millions of dollars and
contributed to a sudden loss of confidence in the Russian economy and the
near collapse of the stock market—which, in turn, led to a new round of
IMF lending.[23]

Similarly, while Russia desperately needed better tax collection, the
IMF's insistence on immediate increases in tax revenue gave priority to col-
lecting more taxes at the expense of rationalizing Russia's tax system. But
in an economy in which it was estimated that 60 percent of cash turnover is
taking place in the shadow economy,[24] beyond the reach of tax authorities,
and where 75 percent of transactions took place through barter, a new tax
system was of much greater importance to the Russian economy. This drive
to bring in money by whatever means possible further strained the government's relations with the State Duma—making the necessary tax legislation
less likely—because many deputies, including those committed to reform,
perceived tax collection efforts (including widely publicized raids by
hooded tax inspectors armed with automatic weapons) as either arbitrary or
politically motivated attacks on opponents of the government and it allies.
Pressure to increase tax receipts also stifled the development of Russia's
cash-starved businesses and scared off foreign investors, whom Moscow often saw as an easy source of additional revenue.[25] As in the case of Yegor
Gaidar's government, the Kiriyenko government (which Gaidar advised)
proceeded in a cavalier fashion with hastily conceived radical measures implemented in an authoritarian style instead of developing a systematic approach to a complex problem.

Although, as the Commission on America's National Interests observed, the promotion of democracy abroad for its own sake is "less
important or secondary" in terms of U.S. interests, it should not be undermined casually and unnecessarily. At a minimum, the United States should
avoid encouraging actions that contravene the rule of law and the clearly

expressed will of the people in other nations simply in order to support a favorite leader or to assure the success of a less than essential domestic—or,
for that matter, foreign—policy.

Also, it is not enough to acknowledge rhetorically that Russia is a major power; it is important to accept it genuinely as such. Here the United
States would do well to start by trying to show greater empathy for Russia's
past (even if deeply flawed) greatness to the extent that it remains a psychological phenomenon rather than a framework for a revanchist foreign
policy. Such nostalgia is not unique to Russia—Japan, Britain, Italy, and
particularly France have experienced their share of it as well after the loss
of their empires earlier in the twentieth century. It would be superhuman for
Russians not to feel at least a certain sadness over the loss of the Soviet
Union's superpower status after only a few years. This is particularly true
given that millions of their former compatriots, many of them ethnic Russians, now live in foreign states that most Russians were led to believe were
an integral part of their own country—their attitude was not much different
from that of white Americans who believe that San Antonio and San Diego,
both taken from Mexico through conquest, are an inseparable part of the
United States.

Under such circumstances, nostalgia is a perfectly legitimate sentiment
as long as it does not become a guide for official policy. Forcing Russia's
citizens to confront their country's diminished status gratuitously and
whenever possible may be emotionally satisfying to some (particularly
those Americans also nostalgic for the Cold War or whose homelands suffered from Soviet or earlier Russian abuse), but it is not likely to encourage
cooperative behavior by Russia, particularly in the long run.

This does not mean that the United States should grant Russia a disproportionate role in international affairs simply to ease its wounded pride. On
the contrary, such an approach serves only to develop unrealistic expectations in Moscow. (This will be among the likely consequences of Russia's
inclusion in the G-7.) As former secretary of state James Baker observes in
his memoirs, one of the Bush administration's problems in soliciting
Moscow's cooperation during the 1990–91 Persian Gulf crisis was "Soviet
self-delusion over its declining geopolitical status." With the Soviet Union
no longer prepared to serve as Iraq's protector, "once the 'all necessary
means' resolution had been passed by the United Nations in late November,
Soviet diplomacy had become far less significant in terms of shaping the fi-

nal outcome" of the crisis.[26] The Bush administration was right to disregard the USSR's unjustified and dangerous belief that it was essential to the solution of the crisis.

Nevertheless, while it is not America's responsibility to treat Russia as if it were still a superpower, common sense suggests that unnecessarily pointing out Moscow's second-rate status is unwise. Even those Russians well disposed toward the United States complain increasingly that American officials, members of Congress, and opinion leaders fail to show respect to their country. For example, Alexei Pushkov, a sophisticated Russian commentator with close ties to the United States, wrote in response to editorials in the American press demanding the resignation of then Russian foreign minister Yevgeny Primakov that "ready as they are to applaud James Baker and Henry Kissinger, the Americans cannot bear the thought that an equally tough and flexible diplomat is heading Russia's foreign ministry. What exhilarates them in themselves is hated in others."[27]

However, American empathy should not come at the expense of clarity of purpose, particularly in communications with the Russian government. While showing Russia the respect it deserves, the United States should not hesitate to tell Moscow—tactfully but firmly—when its actions are contrary to American interests and especially when they are incompatible with normal relations with Washington. As Henry Kissinger writes, "Russo-American relations desperately need a serious dialogue on foreign policy issues. It does Russia no favor to be treated as immune from normal considerations of foreign policy, for this will have the practical result of forcing it to pay a heavier price later on if it is lured into courses of action from which there is no retreat."[28]

Drawing the line in relations with another major power must be done carefully and selectively. "Delivering messages"—in Secretary Albright's language—to other serious international players in a capricious and indiscriminate fashion will only irritate their leaders and their people, and undermine U.S. credibility. However, when the United States takes the position that its extremely important interests in the Persian Gulf are at stake and sends a military armada to deal with Saddam Hussein's continuing transgressions, those who want to maintain friendly relations with America and continue to receive preferential treatment should understand that attempts to sabotage U.S. policy will have consequences.

The United States should help create a new security architecture in

Eurasia which, without resembling the openly hostile containment policy of the past, would discipline Russia through constraints on aggressive conduct—regardless of who may come to power in Moscow in the future. The expansion of the NATO alliance is a key component of creating such a security architecture in Europe.[29] The genius (or at least the saving grace, in the eyes of critics) of the first stage of NATO enlargement is that it extends NATO's security umbrella to the former Soviet border and consolidates the historic gains of Central Europe's peaceful revolutions without threatening any legitimate Russian interests. Poland, Hungary, and the Czech Republic have no common borders with Russia (with the exception of the tiny Russian enclave of Kaliningrad). Relations between each of the three states and Russia are cordial, at a minimum, and are free of disputes that could create the impression that the United States and NATO are siding against Moscow.

When discussing the Russian dimension of the process, opponents of NATO expansion usually mention the absence of a Russian threat, without which they see no reason for expansion, and opposition by the Russian government and particularly the Russian parliament, which they see as raising the cost of NATO expansion prohibitively. Both objections miss the point. Unless one is prepared to argue that a future Russian threat is impossible in principle, the best time to address a potential threat is now—preemptively, during a time of relative tranquility, when the cost is minimal both politically and financially. As far as Russian opposition to NATO enlargement is concerned, Russian politicians have been remarkably less vocal than American opponents of NATO enlargement, particularly in the wake of the May 1997 signing of the Founding Act on Mutual Relations, Cooperation, and Security between NATO and the Russian Federation. Moreover, public opinion polls consistently demonstrate that NATO expansion is at the very bottom among the concerns of ordinary Russians. During a March 1998 visit to Washington, moderate nationalist presidential aspirant General Aleksandr Lebed highlighted this lack of interest in NATO by noting that only a small minority of the citizens in Krasnoyarsk, where he was then campaigning for the governorship (which he later won), knew or cared about the alliance's plans. The IMF's shock therapy package has far more potential to generate anti-Western nationalist sentiment.

Opponents of NATO expansion in Russia and the United States claimed that it would complicate the ratification of the START II Treaty by the Russian Duma. This argument has little value. First, in the five years since the START II agreement was signed by George Bush and Boris Yeltsin—most of which predates the Clinton administration's enthusiastic support for NATO expansion—the Yeltsin administration has done very little to ensure the ratification of START II. Second, it is precisely now that the enlargement of NATO has become for all practical purposes imminent that senior Russian officials and Duma leaders alike have begun to discuss the need for START II. As Duma Foreign Affairs Committee chairman Vladimir Lukin observed in an interview, the chances for ratification of the treaty have improved in 1998 as increasing numbers of parliamentarians— including Communist and other opposition deputies—realize that the treaty is in Russia's interest.[30] The Russian military establishment has become aware of the fact that as its strategic nuclear systems grow obsolete, the Duma's failure to approve START II will be detrimental to Russia's military position with respect to the United States. Major General Vladimir Dvorkin, head of the Fourth Central Scientific Research Institute in the Russian Defense Ministry, said in March 1998 that START II ratification has become a "hostage to political ambitions which are not related to its contents" and that Russia will have to withdraw its missiles from service regardless of the treaty.[31] It was not NATO enlargement but rather the dismissal of Viktor Chernomyndin, Russia's financial crisis, and the polarizing impact of the IMF bailout and the dispute over Kosovo that again delayed START II ratification.

Nevertheless, while the admission of Poland, the Czech Republic, and Hungary into NATO will contribute to European security, we should remember that it is possible to have too much of a good thing. Supporters of NATO enlargement should appreciate the difference between alliance membership for these three Central European nations and for Ukraine or the Baltic states. NATO membership for Latvia and Estonia would be especially provocative to Russia because of disputes over discrimination against ethnic Russians (which does exist, although not to the extent that Moscow would have us believe).

This does not rule out eventual Baltic membership; rather, it acknowledges that an effort to normalize Baltic-Russian relations should precede the three states' entrance into NATO. There is no urgency to admitting them to the Alliance. Moreover, as long as NATO enlargement remains open-ended, the United States can make it known that their admission will be accelerated if Moscow misbehaves. In that context, encouraging the Latvians and Estonians to be more generous in granting citizenship and other rights to their Russian minorities—something the Clinton administration has pursued only timidly, apparently out of the fear of alienating Baltic-Americans—is essential to improving both nations' relations with Moscow and their prospects for their eventual membership in NATO without triggering a crisis with Russia.

With respect to Ukraine, advocates of NATO enlargement must remember the difference between responding to the legitimate aspirations of potential members and encouraging such aspirations in states where they are not official policy. In this context, Zbigniew Brzezinski's suggestion that the West "begin pointing to the decade 2005–15 as a reasonable time frame for the initiation of Ukraine's progressive inclusion"[32] in NATO seems premature when set against Kiev's own statements that it does not yet seek membership in the alliance and that it would not join NATO without guarantees that membership would not hurt its relations with Russia.[33]

At present, the southern option is preferable for those who are serious about continuing NATO enlargement while avoiding unnecessary trouble with Russia. Romania, Slovenia, and even Bulgaria are all possibilities; membership for the eager applicant Romania, which borders on both Ukraine and Moldova, could also enhance the security of these two post-Soviet states in the same manner in which common frontiers with the alliance helped neutral states such as Austria and Finland during the Cold War.

More broadly, the United States should continue efforts to promote economic development and political stability in the newly independent states. This effort should be presented not as a new policy of deterrence directed against Russia but rather as the reflection of an appropriate American interest in helping the other post-Soviet states, many of which are especially significant strategically, like Ukraine, or have considerable energy resources, such as Kazakhstan, Turkmenistan, and Azerbaijan. The less Russia's new neighbors are subjected to internal tensions and upheavals, the less Moscow will be tempted to exploit their weaknesses for its own ends.

Again, as in the case of NATO enlargement, it is essential to maintain a sense of perspective. Neoimperial impulses in Russia would likely be strengthened by the perception that the United States is opposed to any political and economic integration whatsoever, including voluntary integration, among post-Soviet states. This would be especially dangerous if there were a simultaneous perception that the United States itself seeks to dominate the Russian periphery. There is no reason for the United States to grant Russia a "sphere of influence"—particularly as most of the other post-Soviet states, with the notable exception of Belarus, are fiercely opposed to such ideas. Nevertheless, care should be exercised to avoid creating the impression that we believe the United States has a universal sphere of influence while Russia is entitled to none. Russia has legitimate interests in its own backyard and attempts to deny it an important role there are likely to make Moscow's conduct less rather than more moderate.

Similarly—and again without creating the impression that the United States is building an anti-Russian coalition—America has an interest in improving its ties with other important regional powers, including Iran and especially China. Normalization of relations with Tehran is essential to the administration's stated policy of building multiple pipelines in the Caspian Basin. As Geoffrey Kemp—a former Reagan NSC official now with The Nixon Center—writes, because pipeline routes through Russia are the principal logical alternative if routes through Iran are excluded, "the United States has a major long-term interest in securing energy routes from the Caspian Basin through Iran."[34] The isolation of Iran forces the United States to choose between allowing the pipelines to go through Russia—and consequently giving Moscow significantly greater leverage over the entire region—or opposing Russian routes, which not only generates a considerable amount of destabilizing ill will but also increases both the costs and the time required to bring the region's energy to world markets. Multiple pipeline routes determined by market forces rather than political pressures from Moscow or Washington appear preferable from the standpoint of U.S. interests.

A normal relationship with China, the emerging superpower of the twenty-first century, is certainly in the U.S. interest on its own merit. And the last thing the United States should want is to alienate Moscow and Beijing simultaneously in a manner likely to encourage Russia and China to attempt to alter the international power equilibrium against the United States. Conversely, by depriving Russia of the China card, the United States objectively contributes to moderate Russian behavior by shaping the environment in which Moscow makes its foreign policy decisions. Challenging America alone—without the support of other major powers—will not be an attractive option even for more assertive Russian leaders.

In building a new international security architecture to encourage moderate Russian conduct (and therefore Russia's lasting acceptance of its reduced geopolitical status), the United States would do well to combine determination, even in the face of Moscow's inevitable objections to some American policies, with care and, indeed, humility in its foreign relations. American global overreach could push Russia toward nationalism, obstructionism, and ultimately even neoimperialism. As President Nixon reminded us on many occasions, there are considerable pitfalls to treating Russia as a defeated power destined to a marginal role. Russian politicians of all stripes expressed indignation (and satisfaction at having their views confirmed) when Zbigniew Brzezinski was quoted calling Russia "a regional third-world power with still substantial nuclear potential," in an interview with the Russian newspaper *Komsomolskaya pravda*.[35] While today's Russian economy may resemble that of a third-world nation, no developing state possesses Russia's combination of size, natural resources, a highly skilled labor force, a strong technological base, leading universities, a demonstrable if often misguided entrepreneurial spirit, and a seat among permanent members of the United Nations Security Council. The only nation which comes close—China—also hardly merits such a description. Moreover, while Russian commentators like the respected journalist Pavel Felgenhauer justifiably criticize the new stagnation under Yeltsin,[36] Russia has shown impressive dynamism in recent years which, when added to its historical sense of mission, suggest that its geopolitical comeback may take less time than its currently pitiful economic condition implies.

American officials of course are too diplomatic to put down Russia openly. Nevertheless, the Clinton team often acts as if Russia's perspective on international affairs can be explained only by Moscow's failure to understand what is right and what is ultimately in its own best interest. In reality, however, Moscow and Washington have genuinely different views on many international issues—from Bosnia to Iran and Iraq, and from the meaning of national sovereignty to the role of international organizations. There is a subtle but important distinction between explaining American positions (and making clear the costs of working against them) and pretending, as Secretary Albright often does, that there is only one sensible approach, developed in Washington, and that it is time for everyone else to get the message. James Schlesinger observed only half-facetiously that this attitude, which is certainly not limited to Ms. Albright or for that matter the Clinton administration, represents "our American version of benign imperialism—which has now culminated in the entire world becoming our protectorate."[37] If this attitude would become a lasting American policy, it is virtually certain that sooner or later—and perhaps sooner—Russia will offer vigorous opposition.

It is not easy for Americans, particularly in our current triumphant mood—only slightly moderated by the impact of the global economic crisis—to appreciate the perception that U.S. conduct may generate in Russia. American actions such as NATO enlargement, resistance to Russian domination of pipeline routes out of the Caspian Basin, efforts to discourage Russia from sharing weapons and high technology with those who do not play by the rules internationally, and the imposition of strict conditions on international economic assistance to Russia make sense individually on their merits. But we should be careful not to overplay our hand. Collectively, these policies could contribute to an impression—not only among xenophobes and conspiracy theorists, but also among mainstream Russian public opinion—that the United States is deliberately exploiting Russia's vulnerability. These steps have been seen by some as the aggressive expansion of a hostile military alliance, an attempt to restrict Russian access to key oil resources and lucrative investments, an effort to monopolize the internatinal arms and technology markets, the hypocritical use of military force against Russia's Serbian friends, and, in the case of economic assistance accompanied by conditions that prevent economic growth in Russia, a policy intended to keep the country weak and dependent upon the West. That this is certainly not a fair picture of U.S. intentions or, for that matter, Clinton administrative policy, is beside the point if Russian public opinion believes that this is the net result of American actions. Also, while the administration cannot be accused of deliberately undermining Russia's progress, it was not above taking advantage of Moscow's continuing weakness (to which it contributed) to marginalize Russia on a variety of international issues. With regard to NATO air strikes against Yugoslavia, for example, Secretary Albright said dismissively, "if force is required, then we will not be deterred by the fact that the Russians do not agree with that."[38] This only contributes to the development of a "Weimar Russia" psychological syndrome, the avoidance of which must also be a priority for U.S. policy-makers.

If a perception of hostile American intentions begins to guide Russian foreign policy, Russian attempts to counteract U.S. policy would likely follow even before Russia regains its economic feet. It is this threat—the threat of consistent and firm resistance to U.S. policy around the globe— which is the challenge most likely to be posed by Russia in the twenty-first century. The dangers of instability in Russia—that is, the risks of civil war, "loose nukes," and similar troubles—will hopefully decline over time unless the IMF and its sponsors in the Clinton administration help to turn them into self-fulfilling prophecies. Similarly, aggression by Russia against its neighbors is also becoming less likely as the post-Soviet region as a whole stabilizes and the new states develop stronger identities and legitimacy. Although this does not exclude Russian mischief, the United States should be able to manage Moscow's transgressions before they become a serious threat if it can organize other leading nations in Europe and Asia to constrain Russian ambitions. However, if the United States seeks a form of benign global hegemony, and particularly if it interprets what is benign through the prism of American domestic politics, Russia will likely take an active role in organizing an opposing coalition that might include some of today's U.S. allies.

After the spectacular triumph of the Cold War, it is tempting for Americans to believe that the United States has brought about the end of history: that from now on, democratic and free-market values will dominate the globe and other nations will be prepared at least to tolerate, if not to welcome, the United States acting as an international facilitator when possible and enforcer when necessary. Commentators William Kristol and Robert Kagan illustrate this attitude in their statement that "American hegemony is the only reliable defense against a breakdown of peace and international order. The appropriate goal of American foreign policy, therefore, is to preserve that hegemony as far into the future is possible."[39] History strongly suggests that this optimism is an illusion. The end of the Cold War is not the end of history but precisely the reverse: it is the end of an unusual period in history and, accordingly, the beginning of a return to historical normalcy. Most of history has been characterized by the interaction of a variety of powers on the international stage, each of which seeks to balance its interests against those of its competitors at an affordable cost. Arrangements created during times of overwhelming and dire danger, such as that presented by the Nazi or Soviet Communist threats, rarely survive intact after the threats disappear. And the leaders of such victorious alliances are even more rarely able to expand their hegemony without facing serious opposition from other states, including their erstwhile allies.

Twenty-five centuries ago, the Athenians were startled to discover after playing a leading role in the Greek victory over Persia that many of their fellow Greek states responded with resentment rather than gratitude to Athenian demands for predominance in the Hellenic world. Like America today, Athens was the most economically developed and the most democratic power of its world. It also had the greatest power projection capabilities. But as Thucydides writes, when the Athenians insisted on obligations being exactly met, they "made themselves unpopular by bringing the severest pressure to bear on allies who were not used to making sacrifices and did not want to make them."[40] This led to the formation of an opposing coalition led by Sparta, the long and devastating Peloponnesian War, and the eventual defeat of Athens, which contributed to the decline of Greek civilization as a whole.

India's and Pakistan's nuclear tests may be a blessing in disguise if they put an end to triumphalism in America's foreign policy debates and demonstrate the need to see the world the way it is rather than the way the United States would like it to be. In that real world, military power still very much matters, nuclear weapons are viewed as both a status symbol and a security asset, national interests have priority over the opinions of the "international community" (whatever that means), and domestic politics is frequently a determining factor in the making of foreign policy. Approaching today's divided, dangerous, and extraordinarily complex world as if the United States is responsible for everything and everyone else should yield to us is a prescription for disaster.

Victory is sometimes no less a test for a great power than defeat. Debate has raged since the origins of the United States between those who sought to promote America's unique virtues abroad and those who believed in the words of John Quincy Adams that "wherever the standard of freedom and independence has been or shall be unfurled, there will her [America's] heart, her benedictions and her prayers be. But she goes not abroad, in search of monsters to destroy. She is the well-wisher to the freedom and independence of all. She is the champion and vindicator only of her own."[41] Until World War I, America's missionary impulses were limited to the Western Hemisphere, where the United States was unquestionably predominant and did not need to fear the emergence of an opposing coalition of states. After the death of the short-lived international initiatives promoted by Woodrow Wilson, the United States did not develop ambitious global designs until confronted with the threats of Hitler and Stalin. Moreover, those designs were based on vital U.S. national interests and supported by a policy-making process relatively free from today's fragmentation. Equally important, many if not most American allies were prepared to defer to American preferences in order to escape incomparably greater danger. Despite this, the softheaded pursuit of idealistic goals without the hardheaded will to do what was necessary to achieve them led the United States to the Vietnam debacle.

In the post–Cold War environment, however, American attempts to make the world safe for our own brand of democracy can easily be transformed in the eyes of others from a necessary price to pay for U.S. protection against the Soviet Union to unnecessary irritation—and in some cases even a direct threat to their own vital interests. Pressure to observe human rights as defined by powerful U.S. domestic constituencies may similarly be viewed by some governments as a demand to surrender power or even to sacrifice the territorial integrity of a state. Few authoritarian leaders will share Mikhail Gorbachev's commitment to relaxing controls rather than cracking down on dissent when their survival is at stake—particularly after witnessing Gorbachev's outcome. And if the United States decides to use its superior power to force governments or factions to act against what they perceive as their own vital interests, it should not be surprised when the strong band together for protection against America and the weak resort to terror. Using cruise missiles and stealth bombers to rap the knuckles of uncooperative pupils may teach them an unintended lesson—that America is their enemy. This is particularly dangerous when it is in the grasp of numerous others to develop the capability to deliver weapons of mass destruction—with or without Russian help—to American soil.

The alternative to the self-righteous attempt to remake the world in the image of the United States is not isolationism or timidity in promoting genuine American interests. Commentators such as Lawrence Kaplan, a fellow at Washington's Paul H. Nitze School of Advanced International Studies, miss the point when they criticize "prominent conservatives . . . prescribing nonintervention in the affairs of others as a means to ensure the United States does no harm to the world" and suggest that "their quarrel often seems to be less with the promotion of democracy than with democracy itself."[42] It is concern for not doing harm to U.S. interests rather than to the world as a whole that is the principal motive for conservatives from the realist school, who are not known for excessive sentimentalism. A U.S. campaign to impose American-style democracy around the world is almost certain to breed resentment and, ultimately, to contribute to the formation of a coalition of hostile states determined to limit American interventionism. Kaplan also ignores one of the most fundamental elements of the foreign policy of a democratic state: respect for the sovereignty of other nations. No effort to promote American values abroad can succeed if it is viewed as hypocritical.

Realists like Henry Kissinger, James Schlesinger, and Samuel Huntington have no inhibitions against using American power and influence robustly to enhance U.S. interests. Rather, they oppose the pursuit of overly ambitious, capricious policies that bring the United States little gain and reflect more the preferences of various domestic constituencies than fundamental American values. As Huntington writes, America needs "a policy of restraint and reconstitution aimed at limiting the diversion of American resources to the service of particularistic subnational, transnational, and nonnational interests. The national interest is national restraint, and that appears to be the only interest the American people are willing to support at this time in their history."[43] Appreciating one's own limitations and acting with respect for the rights and opinions of other nations—especially when no important interests are at stake—helps a great nation to have its way in international affairs.

National restraint is a precondition for a successful policy of national strength. Such restraint is essential for the United States if it seeks to persuade other nations to accept American leadership in multilateral responses to international problems today and in the future. And it is no less a prerequisite to America's ability to conduct unilateral military action (when important U.S. interest are at stake) without unduly alarming other governments.

Should the United States manage to pursue a less ambitious foreign policy more effectively, with more direction and consistency as well as domestic support, most foreign nations will be strongly disinclined to challenge American interests. In such a geopolitical context, Russia would have powerful incentives to maintain favorable ties with the United States and could be disciplined if it chose to work against fundamental American objectives. America has very strong cards to play in its relations with Russia—but they will mean little if they are not played right.

Notes

Introduction

1. Deputy Prime Minister and Minister of Economics Yakov Urinson, Moscow Interfax (in English), 1048 GMT, January 14, 1998.
2. Richard Nixon, *Beyond Peace* (New York: Random House, 1994), p. 57.
3. Richard Nixon, *Six Crises* (Garden City, N.Y.: Doubleday, 1962), p. 19.
4. Dimitri K. Simes, "Richard Nixon: A Reappraisal," *Christian Science Monitor,* August 8, 1984.

Chapter One: The Beginning of the End

1. Stephen Sestanovich, speech on Russian-American relations at the Heritage Foundation, January 15, 1998, from *USIS Washington File.*
2. George F. Kennan, "The Sources of Soviet Conduct," *Foreign Affairs,* vol. 25, no. 4 (July 1947), pp. 580–82.
3. V. Medvedev, *Chelovek za spinoi* (Moscow: Russlit, 1994), pp. 101, 115.
4. A. M. Aleksandrov-Agentov, *Ot Kollontai do Gorbacheva* (Moscow: Mezhdunarodniye Otnosheniya, 1994), p. 273.
5. Yegor K. Ligachev, *Zagadka Gorbacheva* (Novosibirsk: Interbuk, 1992), p. 92.
6. I encountered Ligachev at a small meeting at Washington's Kennan Institute for Advanced Russian Studies on November 14, 1991.
7. Raisa M. Gorbacheva, *Ya nadeyus,* cited in Valery I. Boldin, *Krusheniye pedestala: shtirikhi k portretu M.S. Gorbacheva* (Moscow: Respublika, 1995).
8. Vladimir Kryuchkov, *Lichnoye delo,* vol. 7 (Moscow: Olimp, 1996), pp. 294–99.

Chapter Two: The Unmaking of the Soviet State

1. Mikhail Gorbachev, *Memoirs* (New York: Doubleday, 1996), p. 334.
2. *Ibid.,* p. 336.
3. *Ibid.,* p. 576.

4. Conversation with the author, July 13, 1998.

5. F. I. Tyutchev, "To Prince Suvorov," in *Poems and Political Letters of F. I. Tyutchev,* trans. Jesse Zeldin (Knoxville: University of Tennessee Press, 1973), p. 144.

6. Boris Yeltsin, *Against the Grain: An Autobiography,* trans. Michael Glenny (New York: Summit Books, 1990), p. 55.

7. *Ibid.,* p. 75.

8. *Ibid.,* p. 70.

9. *Ibid.,* p. 185.

10. *Ibid.,* p. 199.

11. Ligachev, *op. cit.,* p. 76.

12. Vasily Klyuchevsky, *Kurs Russkoi istorii,* vol. 3 (Moscow: Izdatelstvo Mysl, 1988), pp. 48–49.

Chapter Three: The Yeltsin Challenge

1. Klyuchevsky, op. cit., p. 8.

2. S. F. Platonov, *Lektsii po Russkoi istorii* (Petrozavodsk: AO Folium, 1996), p. 195.

3. Nikolai Berdyayev, *Istoki i smysl russkogo kommunisma* (Paris: YMCA Press, 1969), p. 9.

4. Richard Pipes, *U.S.–Soviet Relations in the Era of Detente* (Boulder: Westview Press, 1981), p. 197.

5. *Nash Sovremennik,* no. 2 (1990), p. 4.

6. *Izvestiya,* August 13, 1990.

7. S. Yu. Witte, *Vospominaniya,* vol. 2 (Moscow: Izdatelstvo Sotsialno-Ekonomieheskay Literatury, 1960), p. 129.

8. "Yavlinsky Announces Resignation 17 October," Moscow Television Service (in Russian), in *Foreign Broadcast Information Service Daily Report* (hereafter, *FBIS Daily Report*), FBIS-SOV-90-203, October 19, 1990.

9. In 1989, 1.76 million Tatars resided in the Tatar ASSR, compared to some 963,000 Estonians in the Estonian SSR. In the USSR as a whole, there were over 6 million Tatars—scattered by Stalin—and slightly more than 1 million Estonians. Donald D. Barry and Carol Barner-Barry, *Contemporary Soviet Politics* (Englewood Cliffs, N.J.: Prentice-Hall, 1991), pp. 241–47, and *First Book of Demographics for the Republics of the Former Soviet Union 1951–1990* (Shadyside, Md.: New World Demographics, 1992).

10. Witte, *op. cit.,* p. 380.

11. Shakhrai Opposes Decree Powers," Moscow Domestic Service (radio; in Russian), in *FBIS Daily Report,* FBIS-SOV-90-189, September 28, 1990, p. 47.

12. Nikolai Ryzhkov, *Perestroika: Istoriya predatelstv* (Moscow: Novosti, 1992), p. 24.

13. Boris Yeltsin, *Against the Grain,* Trans. Michael Glenny (New York: Summit, 1990), p. 263.

14. "B. Yeltsin Explains His Position," *Pravda,* September 27, 1990.

15. Bill Keller, "Lithuanian Dead Buried as 'Martyrs,' " *New York Times,* January 17, 1991.

16. David Remnick, "Gorbachev Heartens Baltic Chiefs," *Washington Post,* June 13, 1990.

17. Boris Yeltsin, *The Struggle for Russia* (New York: Random House, 1994), p. 36.

18. *Ibid.,* p. 36.

19. *Ibid.,* p. 37.

20. Dimitri K. Simes, "Specter of Soviet Civil War," *Washington Post,* October 25, 1990.

21. Private correspondence from Richard Nixon to the author, November 16, 1990.

22. Richard Nixon, "Hard-Headed Detente," *New York Times,* August 18, 1982. Reprinted September 30, 1990.

23. Richard Nixon, "We're Not Cold War Victors—Yet," *Los Angeles Times,* April 15, 1990.

Chapter Four: Russia Is Reborn

1. Interestingly, Alexander II also supported his father's idea that Russia had a historic duty to protect friendly regimes in Europe—a principle later reinvented, in a different context, by Soviet leader Leonid Brezhnev.
2. A. A. Kornilov, *Kurs istorii Rossii XIX veka* (Moscow: Vyshaya Shkola, 1993), p. 202.
3. During the attacks on Yakovlev, Kryuchkov went so far as to charge that Yakovlev had been recruited by the CIA during his study at Columbia University in 1959. In his own memoirs, however, Kryuchkov later admitted that the KGB had no evidence other than vague denunciations dating from the 1960s and Yakovlev's suspiciously pro-Western views. Typically, the Soviet president neither defended Yakovlev nor punished him. Rather, he instructed Kryuchkov to have a heart-to-heart talk with the alleged spy. When Yakovlev predictably did not volunteer a confession, Kryuchkov asked for permission to launch an investigation. Gorbachev suggested that another informal conversation might be more appropriate. Vladimir Kryuchkov, *Lichnoye delo,* vol. 1 (Moscow: Olimp, 1996), pp. 282–99.
4. Mikhail Gorbachev, *Memoirs* (New York: Doubleday, 1996), p. 579.
5. Kenneth T. Walsh, "Nixon's the One for Bush," *U.S. News & World Report,* March 4, 1991, p. 31.
6. These comments were printed in the *Washington Post*'s "Personalities" column, by Chuck Conconi, on March 19, 1991.
7. The story of how Nixon's meeting with Gorbachev finally came about amusingly illustrates the extent to which some aspects of life in the Soviet Union remained unchanged. Just days before the former president was scheduled to return to the United States, no meeting had yet been scheduled with the Soviet leader. In a last-ditch attempt to pressure Gorbachev into seeing Nixon, the former president and I had a long conversation in his hotel room—which we knew to be bugged by the KGB—in which Nixon said that he had essentially given up on the meeting with Gorbachev and that it would not be a problem for him to meet only with Yeltsin early the next day and then to fly home ready to dismiss the Soviet leader as an increasingly irrelevant force who was not enough of a man to save his country. No meeting had yet been scheduled with Yeltsin, but we decided to use the KGB and its eavesdropping equipment to give Gorbachev's staff a little scare.

   Four hours later, the telephone rang: the general secretary would be pleased to see Nixon the following morning. The decisive influence of our disinformation was proven the next day when, after the meeting with Gorbachev, the Soviet press agency Tass issued a wire story about the Nixon-Gorbachev meeting which mentioned that Nixon had already met with Yeltsin. The Yeltsin meeting in fact took place later that day—it was scheduled only after we could tell Yeltsin's staff that a meeting with Gorbachev had been arranged.
8. The quotations are based on an April 3 Tass report of the meeting and were subsequently verified to me by President Nixon.
9. The greatest exception being ethnic Russians residing outside the Russian Republic.
10. Curiously, Kryuchkov was reportedly something of an admirer of Nixon, whom he considered a tough law-and-order man—an image the KGB head tried to cultivate himself. He also apparently believed that Nixon had fallen victim to a Jewish liberal conspiracy, something with which Kryuchkov also seemed to identify personally.
11. Dimitri K. Simes, "Behind Kremlin Doors: What Nixon Discovered," *Washington Post,* April 14, 1991.
12. Although he owned a car, Yeltsin generally used public transportation in Moscow to bolster his populist credentials. Once he was elected president, however, the Russian leader took to riding around the city in a black ZIL stretch limousine surrounded by security cars. Often, his secu-

rity staff would stop traffic as far as a mile ahead of the presidential vehicle. All of this happened while Gorbachev was still in office.

13. Dimitri K. Simes, "Russia Reborn," *Foreign Policy,* no. 85 (Winter 1991–92), p. 62.
14. Gorbachev, *op. cit.,* p. 643.
15. Such has certainly been the case with the charter of the Commonwealth of Independent States, which effectively replaced the Union Treaty. Signed in December 1991 and intended to regulate the relations among the former Soviet states, the agreement has been followed only loosely.
16. Gorbachev, *op. cit.,* p. 647.
17. *Ibid.,* p. 659.
18. Dimitri K. Simes, *op. cit.,* p. 62.

Chapter Five: The Face of the New Russia

1. Jonathan Aitken, *Nixon: A Life* (Washington, D.C.: Regnery, 1993), p. 337. Nixon also greatly admired Theodore Roosevelt, Charles de Gaulle, and Winston Churchill.
2. Henry Kissinger, *Diplomacy* (New York: Simon & Schuster, 1994), p. 706.
3. *Ibid.,* p. 816.
4. *Ibid.,* p. 817.
5. Address by Richard Nixon at Moscow's Institute for the World Economy and International Affairs, March 19, 1991.
6. Richard Nixon, "The Real World," a presentation at the Moscow Center of the Carnegie Endowment for International Peace, February 17, 1993.
7. "Excerpts from Clinton's Remarks: 'You Have to Play by the Rules,' " *New York Times,* September 2, 1998.
8. Thomas L. Friedman, "Nixon Scoffs at Level of Support for Russian Democracy by Bush," *New York Times,* March 10, 1992.
9. Marvin Kalb, *The Nixon Memo: Political Respectability, Russia, and the Press* (Chicago: University of Chicago Press, 1994), p. 74.
10. Dimitri K. Simes, "How Not to Lose Russia," *Washington Post,* January 31, 1993.
11. Strobe Talbott, "U.S. Must Lead a Strategic Alliance with Post-Soviet Reform," statement before the Subcommittee on Foreign Operations of the House Appropriations Committee, Washington, D.C., April 19, 1993, cited from U.S. Department of State's *Dispatch,* vol. 4, no. 17 (April 26, 1993).
12. Richard Nixon, "Moscow, March '94: Chaos and Hope," *New York Times,* March 25, 1994.
13. "Excerpts of President Clinton's News Conference," *Washington Post,* June 23, 1997.
14. *Ibid.*
15. The USSR occupied the islands in 1945, after the historic American atomic bomb attacks on Hiroshima and Nagasaki and in violation of its neutrality agreement with Japan. The islands had been under Japanese control since 1875, when Russia ceded its interest in them in exchange for the Japanese withdrawal from Sakhalin.
16. Steven Erlanger, "Russia Sits with 'Big 8,' Party Crasher No More," *New York Times,* June 22, 1997.
17. Liliya Shevtsova, *Politicheskiye zigzagi postkommunisticheskoi Rossii* (Moscow: Carnegie Endowment for International Peace, 1997), p. 19.
18. David Hoffman, "Despite Yeltsin's Promises, Workers Remain Unpaid," *Washington Post,* March 6, 1997.

19. "Poll Indicates Communists Would Do Best in Early Parliamentary Elections," Radio Free Europe/Radio Liberty (RFE/RL) *Newsline,* June 23, 1997.
20. Steven Erlanger, "Russia Sits with 'Big 8,' Party Crasher No More," *New York Times,* June 22, 1997.
21. Aleksandr Korzhakov, *Boris Yeltsin: C rassveta do zakata* (Moscow: Interbuk, 1997), p. 205.
22. Paul Quinn-Judge, "The Perils of Catching Cold," *Time,* December 22, 1997.
23. Bill Powell, "Just How Sick Is Boris?" *Newsweek,* December 22, 1997.
24. State Department Deputy Spokesman James Foley, State Department Noon Briefing, December 10, 1997, transcript from USIA Washington File, Internet, http://www.usia.gov.
25. "Inokhodets," an interview with Luzhkov by Gennady Bocharov, *Izvestiya,* May 28, 1997.
26. Grigory Yavlinsky, "Shortsighted," *New York Times Magazine,* June 8, 1997, p. 66.
27. Thomas Graham, "The New Russian Regime," *Nesavisimaya gazeta,* November 23, 1995.
28. "How Russia Is Ruled: The Political and Economic Lobbies," a confidential cable dated March 17, 1995. As noted in the text, the cable is over the signature of then ambassador to Russia Thomas Pickering and is addressed to Secretary of State Warren Christopher.
29. From an April 1, 1993, speech by President Clinton to the American Society of Newspaper Editors in Annapolis, Md. Quoted by Gwen Ifill in "President Urges America to Back Help for Moscow," *New York Times,* April 2, 1993.
30. President Bill Clinton, "American Leadership and Global Change," a speech delivered at American University in Washington, D.C., on February 26, 1993. Cited from *U.S. Foreign Affairs* on CD-ROM, January 1990–June 1995, vol. 3, no. 3, released September 1995 by the U.S. Department of State, Bureau of Public Affairs.

Chapter Six: Russia's Founding Father

1. Aleksandr Korzhakov, *Boris Yeltsin: C rassveta do zakata* (Moscow: Interbuk, 1997), p. 94.
2. Moscow NTV (in Russian), 1200 GMT, September 18, 1997, in "Russia: TV Reports on 5,000 Students to Have Job Training," *FBIS Daily Report,* FBIS-SOV-97-261, September 18, 1997.
3. Liliya Kuznetsova, ITAR-TASS (in English), 1717 GMT, December 16, 1997, in "Russia: Nemtsov: 'Court' Influence on Yeltsin Highly Exaggerated," *FBIS Daily Report,* FBIS-SOV-97-350, December 16, 1997.
4. Igor Klyamkin and Andranik Migranyan, interviewed by Georgii Tselms, "Nuzhna 'Zheleznaya Ruka'?," *Literaturnaya gazeta,* October 16, 1989, p. 10.
5. Liliya Shevtsova, *Politicheskiye zigzagi postkommunisticheskoi Rossii* (Moscow: Carnegie Endowment for International Peace, 1997), p. 21.
6. Korzhakov, pp. 253–54.
7. Yegor Gaidar, *Dni porazheniy i pobed* (Moscow: Vagrius, 1997), p. 107.
8. Korzhakov, *op. cit.,* p. 287.
9. Vyacheslav Kostikov, *Roman s prezidentom* (Moscow: Vagrius, 1997), pp. 311–12.
10. Such suspicions in Moscow were in part based on the gap between the public support Nixon received from the Clinton White House and private communications from Washington delivered by then ambassador Thomas Pickering. While the administration confirmed publicly that President Clinton was fully aware of Nixon's plans to meet with opposition leaders and also favored Nixon's seeing Yeltsin, the private communication asked only that Yeltsin arrange "meetings with officials of the presidential administration and the government"—a diplomatic statement that pointedly excluded a session with Yeltsin himself. The message conveyed by Pickering put further distance between the White House and Nixon with the language "the

President realizes that this has not been an easy situation for President Yeltsin, and will respect any decision he makes." This was interpreted in Moscow as a clear statement that the White House did not care whether Yeltsin saw Nixon or not.

11. S. F. Platonov, *Lektsii po Russikoi istorii* (Petrozavodsk: AO Folium, 1996), p. 725.
12. Kostikov, *op. cit.,* p. 84.
13. Michael Specter, "My Boris," *New York Times Magazine,* July 26, 1998, p. 27.
14. Boris Yeltsin, *The Struggle for Russia* (New York: Random House, 1994), p. 149.
15. *Ibid.,* p. 205.
16. Oleg Poptsov, *Khronika vremen "Tsarya Borisa"* (Berlin: Edition Q Verlags Gmbh, 1996), p. 81.
17. *Ibid.,* p. 433.
18. David Hoffman, "The Kremlin Drifts as Yeltsin Dithers," *Washington Post,* October 5, 1998.
19. Peter Rutland, "Yeltsin: Problem, Not Solution," *National Interest,* no. 49 (Fall 1997), pp. 33–34.
20. Yeltsin himself admitted that his desire to oust Gorbachev drove many of his decisions: "Why hide it—the motivations for many of my actions were embedded in our conflict." Yeltsin, *op. cit.,* p. 16.
21. *Ibid.,* p. 151.
22. *Ibid.,* p. 142.
23. Poptsov, *op. cit.,* p. 80.
24. Quoted in Steven Erlanger, "Reform School," *New York Times Magazine,* November 29, 1992, p. 78.
25. Yeltsin, *op. cit.,* p. 157.
26. Korzhakov, *op. cit.,* p. 121.
27. *Ibid.,* p. 122.
28. Aleksandr Rutskoi, *O nas i o sebe* (Moscow: AOZT Izdatelskaya Kompaniya "Nauchnaya Kniga," 1995), pp. 148–49.
29. Gaidar, *op. cit.,* p. 160.
30. Korzhakov, *op. cit.,* pp. 158–60.
31. Kostikov, *op. cit.,* p. 147.
32. Gaidar, *op. cit.,* p. 276.
33. Kostikov, *op. cit.,* pp. 19–20.
34. Kostikov, *op. cit.,* p. 43.
35. ITAR-TASS, September 1, 1997.
36. Aleksandr Gamov, "Is It True That Yeltsin Will Go?" *Komsomolskaya pravda,* September 3, 1997, p. 2. Cited in "Russia: Yeltsin Merely 'Testing the Water' on Reelection," *FBIS Daily Report,* FBIS-SOV-97-246, September 3, 1997.
37. Korzhakov, *op. cit.,* p. 308.
38. *Ibid.,* pp. 315–16.

Chapter Seven: The New Oligarchy

1. Anatoly Chubais, interviewed on *Meet the Press,* June 22, 1997.
2. Chyrstia Freeland and John Thornhill, "Russia's Cowboy Capitalists," *Financial Times,* September 26, 1997, p. 17.
3. Interview with Boris Nemtsov by Aleksandr Bushev and Nikolay Dolgolopov, "Boris Nemtsov: Enough of Building Gangster-Style Capitalism," *Komsomolskaya pravda,* July 29, 1997, in *FBIS*

Daily Report, "Nemtsov Defends Svyazinvest Deal," document number FBIS-SOV-97-210.

4. Gaidar, *Dni porazheniy i pobed* (Moscow: Interbuk, 1997), p. 88

5. Avi Shama, "Notes from Underground: Russia's Economy Booms," *Wall Street Journal,* December 24, 1997.

6. *Library of Congress Information Bulletin,* vol. 56, no. 16 (November, 1997).

7. Gaidar, *op cit.,* p. 92.

8. ITAR-TASS World Service (in English) 2136 GMT, February 6, 1992, in BBC Summary of World Broadcasts, February 8, 1992. See also Yeltsin's October 28, 1991, speech to the Congress of People's Deputies of the Russian Federation.

9. Bruce Clark, *An Empire's New Clothes: The End of Russia's Liberal Dream* (London: Vintage, 1995), p. 54.

10. Joseph R. Blasi, Maya Kroumova, and Douglas Kruse, *Kremlin Capitalism: Privatizing the Russian Economy* (Ithaca, N.Y.: Cornell University Press, 1997), p. 31.

11. Elaine Sciolino, "U.S. Is Abandoning 'Shock Therapy' for the Russians," *New York Times,* December 21, 1993.

12. "The Road to Ruin," *The Economist,* January 24, 1997, p. 25.

13. *Kommersant-Daily,* December 9, 1997.

14. *Izvestiya,* November 13, 1997.

15. *Izvestiya,* November 11, 1997.

16. Interfax (in English), 1501 GMT, September 21, 1997, in "Yavlinsky on Russian Economic Data, Political Corruption," *FBIS Daily Report,* FBIS-SOV-97-264, September 21, 1997.

17. Gaidar, *op. cit.,* p. 127.

18. James Morton Smith, ed., *The Republic of Letters: The Correspondence Between Thomas Jefferson and James Madison, 1776–1826* (New York: Norton, 1995), p. 588.

19. *Segodnya,* December 23, 1993.

20. *Izvestiya,* December 18, 1993.

21. David Hoffman, "Pre-Election Pause in Privatization," *Washington Post,* March 30, 1996.

22. Fred Hiatt, "Russia Auctions Off State-Owned Firms," *Washington Post,* April 4, 1993.

23. Press Conference at the Kremlin, June 10, 1994, in "Kremlin: Press Conference with RF President Boris Yeltsin," transcript by Federal News Service.

24. "Profile of Boris Nemtsov," *Open Media Research Institute Russian Regional Report,* vol. 2, no. 11, March 20, 1997. Nemtsov won the governorship in December 1995 with 60 percent of the vote. He was appointed Yeltsin's representative to Nizhni Novgorod in September 1991 and elected governor by the regional legislature (not in a popular election) in November 1991. Also, Aleksandr Sadchikov, "From Moscow to the Very Outskirts: Yuri Luzhkov as the Gatherer of Russian Lands," *Kuranty,* no. 47 (November 26–December 2, 1997), in "Russia: Luzhkov vs. Regional Centrifugal Forces," *FBIS Daily Report,* FBIS-SOV-97-346, December 12, 1997.

25. Michael Specter, "Russia's most Hated Official Is Given Control of the Economy," *New York Times,* March 8, 1997.

Chapter Eight: Whither Russian Democracy ?

1. Liliya Shevtsova, *Politicheskiye zigzagi postkommunisticheskoi Rossii* (Moscow: Carnegie Endowment for International Peace, 1997), p. 65.

2. Aleksandr Korzhakov, *Boris Yeltsin: C rassveta do zakata* (Moscow: Interbuk, 1997), p. 294.

3. Grigory Yavlinsky, "Russia's Phony Capitalism," *Foreign Affairs,* vol. 77, no. 3 (May–June 1998), p. 72.

4. Shevtsova, *op. cit.,* p. 64.

5. *Izvestiya,* January 11, 1996.

6. *Washington Post,* December 24, 1995.

7. *Kommersant,* February 6, 1996.

8. See Alessandra Stanley, "The Burning of a Russian Crusader," *New York Times,* November 30, 1997. David Hoffman of the *Washington Post* has used similar language.

9. Yavlinsky, *op. cit.,* p. 73.

10. *Izvestiya,* February 17, 1996.

11. Korzhakov, *op. cit.,* p. 322; *Pravda,* February 6, 1995.

12. *Izvestiya,* April 27, 1997.

13. *Nezavisimaya gazeta,* May 18, 1996.

14. *Kommersant,* June 7, 1996.

15. *Segodnya,* June 18, 1996.

16. *Sovetskaya Rossiya,* June 27, 1996.

17. Valery Streletsky, *Mrakobesiye* (Moscow: Detektiv-Press 1998), p. 251. Yeltsin's chief aide Viktor Ilyushin gave this instruction to Procurator General Yuri Skuratov.

18. *Sovetskaya Rossiya,* June 27, 1996.

19. Korzhakov, *op. cit.,* pp. 10–11.

20. "*Izvestiya* Chronicles Events of 19–20 June," *OMRI Russian Presidential Election Survey,* no. 10 (June 21, 1997).

21. Streletsky, p. 250. Streletsky was a senior official in the Presidential Security Service at the time. His reporting of this conversation is based on transcripts of a discussion between Anatoly Chubais and Viktor Ilyushin captured by a wiretap set up by Russia's security services. The credibility of the transcript is widely accepted in Russia and has not been challenged directly by any of the parties to the conversation.

22. *Nezavisimaya gazeta,* June 21, 1996.

23. *Izvestiya,* July 11, 1996.

24. *Nezavisimaya gazeta,* October 19, 1996.

25. Leonid Krutakov, *Moskovsky komsomolets,* December 17, 1997.

26. *Washington Post,* December 28, 1997.

27. Interview with Grigory Yavlinsky, *Moscow News,* September 25, 1997.

28. Mikhail Berger, "Chertova dyuzhina bankovskogo schastya," *Izvestiya,* January 17, 1997. A former long-term supporter of Chubais, Berger eventually broke with the first deputy prime minister over his economic policies.

29. David Hoffman, "Weakened Yeltsin Seems Unable to Take Command of Second Term," *Washington Post,* February 9, 1997.

30. Andranik Migranyan, "Kto kovo na etot raz ubedit?" *Rossiiskaya gazeta,* January 14, 1997, p. 2.

31. "Moscow Meetings Underscore Importance of Russian Bankers," *Jamestown Foundation Monitor,* March 7, 1997

32. Peter Rutland, "Nemtsov's Agenda," *OMRI Daily Digest,* no. 55, pt. 1, March 19, 1997.

33. Boris Nemtsov, "Budushchee Rossii: Oligarchiya ili demokratiya?" on Nemtsov's World Wide Web home page: www.nemtsov.ru.

34. David Hoffman, "Russia's Clans Go to War," *Washington Post,* October 26, 1997.

35. Ulyan Kerzonov, "Anatoly Chubais Striving for Complete Control over Russia. To Realize His Intentions He Is Strengthening Oligarchical, Not Democratic Trends in Country's Development," *Nezavisimaya gazeta,* September 13, 1997.

36. Address by Boris Yeltsin to the Federation Council, Moscow ORT television network (in Russian), 0600 GMT, September 24, 1997, translated by Foreign Broadcast Information Service.

37. Lidiya Timofeyeva, "Russia's Would-Be President Has Three Faces for Now," *Passport*, no. 4, 1997, pp. 18–19. See also Michael Specter, "Russian Media, Free of One Master, Greet Another," *New York Times*, March 16, 1997.

38. Interview with Grigory Yavlinsky, "What Do We Do with a Boeing," *Moskovskiye novosti*, no. 38 (September 21–28, 1997), in "Russia: Yavlinsky on Year 2000 Elections," *FBIS Daily Report*, FBIS-SOV-97-267, September 24, 1997.

39. David Hoffman, "Russia's 'People's Capitalism' Benefitting Only the Elite," *Washington Post*, December 28, 1997.

40. "Chubais is to blame that only ten percent of the electorate voted for the Our Home Is Russia movement. Had it not been for the mistakes he made in economic policy, the turnout could have been at least twenty percent." Press Conference by Boris Yeltsin, January 19, 1996, Moscow, ITAR-TASS (in Russian), 1309 GMT, in "Yeltsin Blames Chubais for NDR's Failure in Duma Election," *FBIS Daily Report*, FBIS-SOV-96-013, January 19, 1996.

41. Interview with Jeffrey Sachs, "In the Years of Reforms, $100B in Wesern Aid Was Taken out of Russia," *Novoye izvestiya*, October 7, 1998.

42. Anders Aslund, "Why the Doomsayers Are Wrong About Russia," *The Weekly Standard*, December 29, 1997–January 5, 1998, pp. 24–26; and Michael S. Lelyveld and John Helmer, "Once Bullish Economist Sees Collapse for Russia," *Journal of Commerce*, October 8, 1998.

43. *Ot Yeltsina k Yeltsinu: prezidentskaya gonka-96* (Moscow: Terra, 1997), p. 90.

44. "Text: World Bank Announces Loans to Aid Russian Economic Reform," *USIS Washington File*, December 19, 1997.

45. "Russian Economist Says Russian, World Crises Unrelated," *Interfax*, June 24, 1998.

46. NTV Moscow (in Russian), 2015 GMT, July 19, 1998.

47. Fedorov is under investigation for his role in the disappearance of $178 million in diamonds and precious metals from Russia's state treasury during his tenure as finance minister. See Vasiliy Ustyuzhanin, "Boris Fedorov Has Turned Out to Be 'Involved' in the 'Diamond Affair,'" *Komsomolskaya pravda*, January 21, 1997, in "Former High Officials Investigated in Diamonds Scam," *FBIS Daily Report*, FBIS-TDD-97-003-L, January 21, 1997. See also David E. Kaplan and Christian Caryl, "The Looting of Russia," *U.S. News & World Report*, August 3, 1998, pp. 29–30.

48. Aleksandr Bekker, "S veroy v chudo," *Moskovskiye novosti*, no. 27, July 12–19, 1998.

49. "Sem let prezidenta v otsenkakh Rossiyan," *Interfaks-AiF*, June 6–12, 1998.

50. Leonid Krutakov and Ivan Kadulin, "Kredituy ili proigrayesh: Istoriya o tom, kak Anatoly Chubais okazalsya dolzhnikom Aleksandra Smolenskogo," *Izvestiya*, July 1, 1997.

51. Laura Belin, "Duma Accuses Chubais of Breaking Laws," *OMRI Daily Digest*, February 6, 1997.

52. Peter Reddaway, "Questions About Russia's 'Dream Team,'" *CSIS Post-Soviet Prospects*, vol. 5, no. 5.

53. Alessandra Stanley, "Russia Aide Cuts Ties to Harvard Center That Ousted Advisors," *New York Times*, May 31, 1997.

54. David Hoffman, "Yeltsin Asserts Full Support for Chubais," *Washington Post*, November 26, 1997.

55. Kirill Viktorov, "Shadow Empire. 'Anatoly Chubais and Co.' Individual Private Enterprises Successfully Operating in the Country," *Moskovsky komsomolets*, December 10, 1997, in "Russia: Chubais' Business 'Empire' Exposed," *FBIS Daily Report*, FBIS-SOV-97-350, December 16, 1997.

56. "Chubais Provokes More Controversy," *Jamestown Foundation Monitor,* December 17, 1997.

57. Interview with Boris Nemtsov by Yuri Shchekochikhin, " 'Nastoyashchaya demokratiya—eto garantiya ot podlosti,' " *Novaya gazeta,* no. 48 (December 1, 1997).

58. Aleksandr Gamov, "Five Years of Viktor Chernomyrdin," *Komsomolskaya pravda,* December 11, 1997, in "Russia: Chernomyrdin-Yeltsin Relations Assessed," *FBIS Daily Report,* FBIS-SOV-97-358, December 24, 1997.

59. "Chubais Just One of Many in Corrupt Oligarchy," *St. Petersburg Times,* November 24–30, 1997.

60. "Yeltsin Hints at Government Reshuffle," *Jamestown Foundation Monitor,* vol. 4, no. 1 (January 5, 1998).

61. "Yeltsin Echoes Berezovsky," *Jamestown Foundation Monitor,* vol. 4, no. 1 (January 5, 1998).

62. Nataliya Panshina, Mosow ITAR-TASS in English, 0900 GMT, November 5, 1998, in "Constitutional Court Rules Yeltsin 'May Not Run' in 2000," *FBIS Daily Report,* FBIS-SOV-98-309, November 5, 1998.

63. Galina Baryshnikova, "As Public Opinion Polls Show, 80% of Russian Citizens Reject a Return to the Communist Past, Academician Gennady Osipov Says," RIA Novosti, December 30, 1997.

64. Celestine Bohlen, "Yeltsin, Facing Impeachment Vote, Tries to Keep Investors Calm," *New York Times,* May 21, 1998.

65. Boris Grushin, "The 'Social Earthquake' Continues: The New Russia Is Still Undefined," *Prism,* vol. 3, no. 21, pt. 3 (December19, 1997).

66. Interview with Anatoly Chubais by Yevgeniya Albats, "Anatoly Chubais: nas zhdut ochen' tyazhelye poltora-dva goda," *Kommersant-daily,* September 8, 1998.

67. *Ibid.*

68. Daniel Williams, "Russia's Plan Focuses on Tax Cuts, More Rubles," *Washington Post,* November 1, 1998.

69. Albert Makashov, "Userers of Russia," *Zavtra,* October 20, 1998, in "Makashov Blames Crisis on Jews," *FBIS Daily Report,* FBIS-SOV-98-307, November 3, 1998. Only 107 Duma members (of 450) voted to support a statement deploring Makashov's remarks. (See "State Duma Rejects Draft Against Makashov's Statements," *FBIS Daily Report,* FBIS-SOV-98-308, November 4, 1998.)

Chapter Nine: The New Russian Foreign Policy: Seeking a Place in the Sun

1. Ed. Sergey Maslov, "Lieutenant General Vadim Kirpichenko Says in His Book: Primakov Is Not at All Characterized by an Idiotic Standing on Principle," *Komsomolskaya pravda,* September 12, 1998, in "Kirpichenko Airs Views on Primakov's Career," FBIS-SOV-98-267, September 24, 1998.

2. *Ibid.*

3. Boris Nemtsov, *Provintsial* (Moscow: Vagrius, 1997), p. 82.

4. S. Yu. Witte, *Vospominaniya,* vol. 3 (Moscow: Izdatelstvo Sotsialno-Ekonomicheskoy Literatury, 1960), p. 162.

5. William V. Roth, Jr., and Richard G. Lugar, "NATO's Open Door," *Washington Times,* March 18, 1998. See also Benjamin A. Gilman, "Stop Coddling Yeltsin," *Washington Post,* June 19, 1998.

6. Aleksandr Bovin, "Russia Returns to Realm of World Politics," *Izvestiya,* December 26, 1997, from RIA Novosti.

7. Interview with Vladimir Lukin, "V. Lukin: 'In Those Areas Where Our National Interests Are

Directly Affected—There We Will Be Reckoned With and Our Words Will Carry Weight," *Mezhdunarodnaya zhizn,* October 1997.

8. Yevgeny Umerenkov, "Russia Is Not Picking on Anyone, But Will Not Allow Itself to Be Pushed Around," *Komsomolskaya pravda,* December 24, 1997, in "Russia: Primakov Sums Up Diplomacy in Past Year," *FBIS Daily Report,* FBIS-SOV-97-358, December 24, 1997.

9. David Hoffman, "Chechen, Lebed Sign Peace Deal," *Washington Post,* August 31, 1996. Aleksandr Lebed and Russian interior minister Anatoly Kulikov presented widely differing figures for the civilian casualties; Lebed argued that 80,000 had died, while Kulikov insisted that civilian deaths were limited to 18,500. See Penny Morvant, "Interior Minister Renews Attacks on Lebed," *OMRI Daily Digest,* no. 195, pt. I (October 8, 1996).

10. Interview with Yevgeny Primakov by Stanislav Kondrashov, "We Have Our Distinct Identity and We Never Sought Confrontation," *Izvestiya,* December 23, 1997, from RIA Novosti.

11. *Mezhdunarodnaya zhizn,* October 1997.

12. Yevgeny Primakov, "Russia in World Politics: A Lecture in Honor of Chancellor Gorchakov," *International Affairs,* Summer 1998, p. 8.

13. "Russian Federation National Security Blueprint," Russian Federation Presidential Edict no. 1300, dated December 17, 1997.

14. Primakov, p. 10.

15. Barbara Crossette, "U.N. Debates a Demand for Kosovo Cease-Fire; Resolution Called a Warning to Milošević," *International Herald Tribune,* September 24, 1998.

16. *Nezavisimaya gazeta,* December 30, 1997.

17. Aleksandr Bovin, "13-y punkt Kodeksa," *Izvestiya,* November 5, 1997.

18. I. Sedykh, "The Arguments of Anatoly Chubais Against the NATO Expansion Plans Which He Aired at Davos," *Rossiiskiye vesti,* February 5, 1997.

19. See, for example, David Hoffman, "Few Russians Worry About Bigger NATO," *Washington Post,* February 6, 1997.

20. Andrei Kozyrev, "NATO Is Not Our Enemy," *Newsweek,* February 10, 1997, p. 31.

21. *Ibid.*

22. *Izvestiya,* December 23, 1997.

23. Yevgeny Primakov, "Russia in World Politics: A Lecture in Honor of Chancellor Gorchakov," *International Affairs,* vol. 44, no. 3 (1998): p. 11

24. Dmitri Yevstafyev, "Trip Without a Compass; Moscow's Foreign Policy Held Hostage by Economy," *Interfax-AIF,* no. 48 (December 1–7, 1997).

25. Primakov, *op. cit.,* p. 11.

26. ITAR-TASS, May 26, 1998.

27. Interfax, October 29, 1997.

28. ITAR-TASS, October 1, 1997.

Chapter Ten: America's Russian Dilemma

1. Samuel P. Huntington, "The Erosion of American National Interests," *Foreign Affairs,* vol. 76, no. 5 (September–October 1997), p. 35.

2. James Schlesinger, "Fragmentation and Hubris: A Shaky Basis for American Leadership," *National Interest,* Fall 1997, p. 4.

3. Quoted in David S. Broder, "Deciding NATO's Future Without Debate," *Washington Post,* March 18, 1998.

4. Quoted in Henry Kissinger, *Diplomacy* (New York: Simon & Schuster, 1994), p. 96.

5. Strobe Talbott, "The End of the Beginning: The Emergence of a New Russia," address at Stanford University, Palo Alto, Calif., September 19. 1997.

6. Kissinger, *op. cit.,* p. 817.

7. Aleksey Arbatov, "The National Idea and National Security," *Mirovaya ekonomika i mezhdunarodnaya otnosheniya,* no. 5, in "Arbatov on New National Security Approach," *FBIS Daily Report,* FBIS-SOV-98-208, July 27, 1998.

8. "Ruble Rallies Slightly, Economy Contracts," *Radio Free Europe/Radio Liberty Newsline,* September 9, 1998.

9. Jack F. Matlock, Jr., "Too Many Arms to Twist," *Washington Post,* March 22, 1998.

10. Richard Holbrooke, *To End a War* (New York: Random House, 1998), pp. 72–73.

11. John Pomfret and Christine Spolar, "Croats Gain Key Ground Against Serbs, on and off the Battlefield," *International Herald Tribune,* August 23, 1995.

12. *Ibid.*

13. "Wide Range of Issues Discussed at 'Troika' Meeting," *RFE/RL Newsline,* vol. 2, no. 56, March 27, 1998.

14. State Department Briefing, Federal News Service, August 11, 1998.

15. Lee H. Hamilton, "Sanctions, Congress, and the National Interest," *Nixon Center Perspectives,* vol. 3, no. 3 (July 20, 1998): p. 1. The seventy-five nation figure is also drawn from these remarks.

16. *America's National Interests* (Washington, D.C.: Commission on America's National Interests, 1996), pp. 4, 14–17.

17. *Ibid.,* p. 5.

18. Frank Wisner, "Addressing Nuclear Proliferation," a presentation at The Nixon Center on May 27, 1998.

19. Address by Secretary of State Madeleine K. Albright to the U.S.–Russian Business Council," October 2, 1998, in *USIS Washington File,* www.usia.gov, accessed October 5, 1998.

20. *Ibid.*

21. William V. Roth, Jr., and Richard G. Lugar, "NATO's Open Door," *Washington Times,* March 18, 1998.

22. Seth Mydans, "Indonesia-IMF Talks Show Flexibility on Ending Impasse," *New York Times,* March 20, 1998.

23. Michael R. Gordon, "IMF Giving Russia $670 Million Loan," *New York Times,* May 29, 1998.

24. "Expertise: Tax-Evading Shadow Business Accounts for 60 Percent of Cash Turnover," RIA Novosti, August 13, 1998.

25. "Russia Bails," *The Wall Street Journal,* August 12, 1998.

26. James A. Baker III, with Thomas M. DeFrank, *The Politics of Diplomacy: Revolution, War, and Peace, 1989–1992* (New York: Putnam, 1995), p. 402.

27. Alexei Pushkov, "Who Wants Primakov Out?" *Nezavisimaya gazeta,* March 20, 1998.

28. Kissinger, *op. cit.,* p. 817.

29. For further detail on the points elaborated below, please see my testimony before the Senate Foreign Relations Committee on October 30, 1997. *The Debate on NATO Enlargement* (Washington: U.S. Government Printing Office, 1998).

30. Moscow Interfax (in English), 0752 GMT, March 14, 1998, in "State Duma Becoming More Positive on START II Ratification," FBIS-SOV-98-073, March 14, 1998.

31. Moscow Interfax (in English), 1600 GMT, March 19, 1998, in "Russian General—START II 'Hostage to Political Ambitions,' " FBIS-SOV-98-078, March 19, 1998.

32. Zbigniew Brzezinski, *The Grand Chessboard: American Primacy and Its Geostrategic Imperatives* (New York: Basic Books, 1997), p. 121.

33. "Ukraine Clarifies Position on Joining NATO," *RFE/RL Newsline,* vol. 2, no. 56 (March 27, 1998).

34. Geoffrey Kemp, *Energy Superbowl: Strategic Politics and the Persian Gulf and Caspian Basin* (Washington, D.C.: Nixon Center, 1997), p. viii.

35. Interview with Zbigniew Brzezinski by special correspondent Andrei Kabannikov, "You Could Be a Rich and Happy Country: The Legendary 'Anti-Soviet and USSR Enemy No. 1' Granted Andrei Kabannikov, Our Correspondent in Washington, an Exclusive Interview," *Komsomolskaya pravda,* January 6, 1998.

36. Pavel Felgenhauer, "Defense Dossier: Yeltsin's Stagnation Politics," *Moscow Times,* March 26, 1998.

37. Remarks by James Schlesinger on the centennial of the sinking of the *Maine,* February 15, 1998.

38. Roger Cohen, "Americans Rebuke Yugoslav Leader," *New York Times,* October 9, 1998.

39. William Kristol and Robert Kagan, "Toward a Neo-Reaganite Foreign Policy," *Foreign Affairs,* vol. 75, no. 4, July–August 1996, p. 23.

40. Thucydides, *History of the Peloponnesian War,* trans. Rex Warner (New York: Penguin, 1986), p. 93.

41. Kissinger, *op. cit.,* p. 35.

42. Lawrence F. Kaplan, "Leftism on the Right: Conservatives Learn to Blame America First," *Weekly Standard,* February 9, 1998, p. 27.

43. Huntington, *op. cit.,* p. 49

Index

272

Index

28 1/4 DAYS